A savage song

Manchester University Press

Racism, Resistance and Social Change

FORTHCOMING BOOKS IN THIS SERIES

The Red and the Black: The Russian Revolution and the Black Atlantic: David Featherstone and Christian Høgsbjerg (eds)

Revolutionary lives of the Red and Black Atlantic after 1917: David Featherstone, Christian Høgsbjerg and Alan Rice (eds)

Citizenship and belonging: Ben Gidley

Transnational solidarity: Decentring the radical sixties: Zeina Maasri, Cathy Bergin and Francesca Burke (eds)

Spaces of Black solidarity: Anti-black racism and urban activism in Paris: Vanessa Eileen Thompson

PREVIOUSLY PUBLISHED IN THIS SERIES

Race talk: Languages of racism and resistance in Neapolitan street markets: Antonia Lucia Dawes

Black resistance to British policing: Adam Elliott-Cooper

Global white nationalism: From apartheid to Trump: Daniel Geary, Camilla Schofield and Jennifer Sutton (eds)

In the shadow of Enoch Powell: Shirin Hirsch

Black middle-class Britannia: Identities, repertoires, cultural consumption: Ali Meghji

Race and riots in Thatcher's Britain: Simon Peplow

A savage song

Racist violence and armed resistance in the early twentieth-century U.S.–Mexico borderlands

Margarita Aragon

MANCHESTER UNIVERSITY PRESS

Copyright © Margarita Aragon 2021

The right of Margarita Aragon to be identified as the author of this work has been asserted by them in accordance with the Copyright, Designs and Patents Act 1988.

Published by Manchester University Press
Oxford Road, Manchester M13 9PL

www.manchesteruniversitypress.co.uk

British Library Cataloguing-in-Publication Data
A catalogue record for this book is available from the British Library

ISBN 978 1 5261 2167 7 hardback
ISBN 978 1 5261 7874 9 paperback

First published 2021

The publisher has no responsibility for the persistence or accuracy of URLs for any external or third-party internet websites referred to in this book, and does not guarantee that any content on such websites is, or will remain, accurate or appropriate.

Typeset
by New Best-set Typesetters Ltd

For my mom, my dad, and my sister

Contents

Series editors' foreword	viii
Acknowledgments	ix
Introduction: The twentieth century dawns in blood	1
1 Imagining slaves and sovereigns	25
2 This land of barbarians	56
3 The Mexican has a country	87
4 Without a tremor	118
5 War to the knife	151
Epilogue	183
Bibliography	196
Index	211

Series editors' foreword

John Solomos, Satnam Virdee, Aaron Winter

The study of race, racism and ethnicity has expanded greatly since the end of the twentieth century. This expansion has coincided with a growing awareness of the continuing role that these issues play in contemporary societies all over the globe. *Racism, Resistance and Social Change* is a new series of books that seeks to make a substantial contribution to this flourishing field of scholarship and research. We are committed to providing a forum for the publication of the highest quality scholarship on race, racism, anti-racism and ethnic relations. As editors of this series we would like to publish both theoretically driven books and texts with an empirical frame that seek to further develop our understanding of the origins, development and contemporary forms of racisms, racial inequalities and racial and ethnic relations. We welcome work from a range of theoretical and political perspectives, and as the series develops we ideally want to encourage a conversation that goes beyond specific national or geopolitical environments. While we are aware that there are important differences between national and regional research traditions, we hope that scholars from a variety of disciplines and multidisciplinary frames will take the opportunity to include their research work in the series.

As the title of the series highlights, we also welcome texts that can address issues about resistance and anti-racism as well as the role of political and policy interventions in this rapidly evolving discipline. The changing forms of racist mobilisation and expression that have come to the fore in recent years have highlighted the need for more reflection and research on the role of political and civil society mobilisations in this field.

We are committed to building on theoretical advances by providing an arena for new and challenging theoretical and empirical studies on the changing morphology of race and racism in contemporary societies.

Acknowledgments

I would like to thank John Solomos, Satnam Virdee, and Aaron Winter for giving me the opportunity to contribute to this important series. Over the past few years, Aaron has frequently offered a sounding board for my ideas and generously shared his expertise on far-right racism in the U.S. Satnam's initial encouragement and subsequent comments on the manuscript have been invaluable. Kiran Grewal, Katherine Robinson, and Miranda Iossifidis have read various drafts of some of the chapters herein and provided much-needed feedback. As well as reading draft chapters, over the years Brett St Louis and Ben Gidley have given intellectual guidance without which I wouldn't have started, much less finished, this book. Daniel HoSang Martinez, whose nuanced understanding of U.S. racism has been formative to my thinking for many years, provided insightful advice on the manuscript that undoubtedly helped me to improve it. I am grateful for the camaraderie of my colleagues in the Sociology Department at Goldsmiths. Katherine Robinson and Vik Loveday in particular have provided constant encouragement and commiseration. I am grateful to those at Manchester University Press, and especially Tom Dark, for their help in preparing the manuscript, as well as Jessica Cuthbert-Smith for her skillful editing. My research is indebted to E.R. Bills and Constance Hollie-Jawaid, who have worked to bring the history of the Slocum Massacre to public light. I hope that my chapter will contribute in some small way to the ongoing struggle for recognition and justice. Kelly Francis-Love, archivist at the Museum of South Texas History, was exceptionally helpful in enabling me to access documents related to the Plan de San Diego uprising. Madeline Moya undertook proxy research assistance in several Texas archives that has been essential to the project. My friend Betty Marín has graciously provided her excellent translation skills whenever I've messaged her at odd hours with random questions about early twentieth-century Spanish-language texts. My mom, Laurie, proofread every chapter without complaint. My partner, Peter, and children, Aella, Gabriel, and Peter Rafel, have endured many weekends and evenings of me sitting in front of a computer or away in the library. Whether or not they ever read this book, their presence and support have sustained me through the long and arduous process of writing it.

Introduction: The twentieth century dawns in blood

In the late summer and autumn of 1910, talk of war emanated from Texas. At the end of July, a "race war," Americans were told, had erupted in a rural community called Slocum outside of the small town of Palestine. In the various versions of the story printed in newspapers across the country on July 31, it was reported that the black men in the area had armed themselves and were preparing to "rise up" to kill the local white people. The white women and children were placed under armed guard in the schoolhouse for several nights while white men from around the county rushed to help quell the uprising. Although the county sheriff and his deputies quickly ascertained that there had been no insurrection to speak of, accounting for the number of black people shot down by the white posse who rode through Slocum on horseback was more difficult. The *New York Sun* noted that while "twenty dead bodies of victims have been found scattered along the roads and over the country," the total number of murders "may never be definitely known."[1] Just months later, in November, some 400 miles southwest of Slocum, rumors of another armed threat to the white denizens of Texas emerged. A band of armed Mexicans, it was said, was preparing to march upon the town of Rock Springs, whose inhabitants had recently burned a Mexican national at the stake. The victim, Antonio Rodriguez, had allegedly murdered the wife of a white rancher. As in Palestine in July, white Texan men from the surrounding area "poured into" Rock Springs, with their revolvers and rifles, anxious to meet the invaders, who never materialized. The rumors were given force, however, by fervent demonstrations taking place against the lynching in Mexico itself, where protestors desecrated American flags and attacked residents of local American enclaves.[2]

This book examines the use of violence by police and white citizens against African Americans and ethnic Mexicans in the early twentieth century and the ways in which black and Mexican writers, political thinkers, and armed men resisted this violence and the racial order it worked to enforce.[3] In particular, it examines how killing and dying became symbolic sites for the racially infused production – and negation – of manhood and nationhood. In addition to the massacre in Slocum and the lynching of Rodriguez, I consider two remarkable instances of armed resistance against state violence. In 1915 ethnic Mexicans in the Rio Grande Valley launched an uprising, denouncing the brutality of the Texas Rangers, a paramilitary border police force. Between 1907 and 1912, Rangers and other "peace officers" had killed sixteen Mexicans who had "resisted" arrest in Hidalgo and Cameron counties, both areas of low population density.[4] In a document titled the "Plan de San Diego," the visionaries of the rebellion proposed to establish a new republic in the lands annexed from Mexico by the United States. As part of this process, they proposed to liberate the black race and to return to the "Redskins of the territory" the land that had been stolen from them.[5] In response, the Rangers and civilian militias unleashed a devastating convulsion of repression against all Mexicans in the valley, whether they supported the rebellion or not. "The bodies are lying along the roads and in the brush. Whether they were killed in a fight or were shot down on sight cannot be learned," the *Washington Post* observed sanguinely of the "30 Dead Mexicans" found along the Texas side of the border.[6]

Two years after the rebellion was initiated and several hundred miles to the northeast, approximately a hundred black soldiers of the Twenty-Fourth Infantry, a segregated regiment of the U.S. Army, marched on the city of Houston to look for the white police officers who had recently brutalized two of their comrades. Over the course of several hours on the night of August 23, they killed four white police officers and two white national guardsmen. Nine civilians – eight white men and a Mexican American man – were also killed in the latter case by a stray bullet.[7] The men had been subject to abuse by the police and white citizens since they had been stationed at nearby Camp Logan. Their march also took place in the shadow of the massacre of possibly hundreds of black civilians in East St. Louis, Illinois, by mobs of white people less than two months before. The pogrom had been preceded by rumors of black uprising and complaints of black "insolence."[8] As with the victims in Slocum and the Mexicans killed in the Rio Grande Valley (and unlike the white victims killed in Houston, whose names, accomplishments, and funeral details were widely circulated), the nation's press did not burden itself with the task of counting or naming the dead of East St. Louis: "Negroes are lying in the gutters every few feet in some places." As a result of three separate courts-martial, the army hanged a total of nineteen soldiers of the Twenty-Fourth, in what some black observers judged acts of "military lynching."[9] In the chapters to come, I will ask how a range of actors made sense of these violent encounters as part of ongoing historical struggles for freedom, sovereignty, and racial destiny in the Americas or as flashes of futures to be realized.

In the period's eugenic-tinged evolutionary narratives of global and local violence, the death and degeneracy of racial others often formed the definitive contrast to white Americans' racial vigor and national coherence. Arguing that the "subjugation of life to the power of death" has been the defining expression of modern political sovereignty, Achille Mbembe highlights the profound conceptual intimacy of death and race in those spaces constructed as sites of perpetual war, always outside the sanctified realm of law and order – the colony, the plantation, the camp, the ghetto, the border. As a schema for imagining incommensurable divisions between supposed types of human beings, marking some as incapable of history and civilization, racism provided a ready logic for articulating who must live and who must die. As Michel Foucault described the eugenic-infused racism of twentieth-century fascists, the death of the other becomes the means of life – "the death ... of the inferior race (or the degenerate, of the abnormal) is something that will make life in general healthier: healthier and purer."[10] As I will argue in the following chapters, in U.S. cultural and political discourses, the racial degeneracy of black and Mexican men was not only delineated in the acts of savagery they supposedly committed or threatened to commit – the raping or killing of innocent white people – but also in the profuse, public, and abject manner in which they died. Indeed, narratives of white vulnerability to black or Mexican violence in media print and cultural memory were very frequently intertwined with those of white mastery and ruthless punishment.

Alongside racial assertions of degeneration and danger, death has also been an essential ingredient in modern discourses of manhood, in which the willingness to die has been idealized, as Veena Das notes, as the necessary means of securing "gendered belonging in the nation-state."[11] Mexicans and African Americans resisting U.S. violence also sometimes deployed masculinist discourses of living and dying that, like hegemonic nationalisms, sanctified death and sacrifice as an expression of manhood, and that, implicitly or explicitly, equated survival with submission. While such rhetoric could subvert white Americans' claims to domination, it could also sometimes work to restrict the lens through which historical actors might be recognized, as well as naturalizing the subordination of femaleness, queerness, and, in some cases, blackness.

The violence of the 1910s emerged from overlapping and ongoing struggles. The massacre in Slocum constituted an aftershock of the counter-revolution in which the unfreedom of Jim Crow was consolidated by extensive state apparatus as well as ravaging extra-legal violence in the form of lynching, massacres, and expulsions. The protests at the lynching of Antonio Rodriguez in Mexico became the foreshocks of the first successful revolution of the twentieth century.[12] The period which historians have called the nadir of anti-black racism in the United States coincided with a period of intensified U.S. imperialism within Mexico, as well as increased Anglo settlement in south Texas. Imperialism and domestic racism were mutually invigorating. U.S. projects of empire in the new century in the Caribbean and Asia drew upon and in turn gave national validation and new resonance to doctrines of the white supremacy that Southerners had developed to re-subjugate African Americans after the end of Reconstruction.[13] Imperialist exhortations of Americans' "right" in Mexico, as bankers, capitalists, and colonists came to own nearly 30 percent of Mexico's land, as well as justifications of anti-Mexican violence in the U.S., further fomented toxic national discourses of white civilization, Anglo-Saxon might, and global destiny.[14]

As I will examine in the chapters to come, the Mexican Revolution and World War I, the larger cataclysms within which these local moments unfolded, gave new significance to Mexican and black men's killing and dying. However, I will also trace the ways in which broader histories of domination and dispossession reverberate through these encounters. In their work on political violence in late twentieth-century Venezuela, anthropologists Fernando Coronil and Julie Skursi emphasize the role of historical memory in shaping the means through which violence is both implemented and interpreted. "Violence," they write, "is wielded and resisted in the idiom of a society's distinctive history," shaped by particular myths of collective identity and the corresponding imaginaries of danger and threat which necessarily inhere in such myths. The meaning of violence, "as a set of practices and cultural forms, can only be deciphered by understanding the historical memory and the social relations of the society within which it arises, takes form, and achieves effects."[15] As we will see in the following chapters, the manner in which participants and observers justified or denounced contemporary violence frequently employed the multivalent themes of savagery and civilization emanating from centuries of enslavement and conquest.

Traversing history and borders

Building on the ground-breaking research that has begun to illuminate the dimensions of anti-Mexican mob violence in the Southwest, I have attempted to bring a nuanced scrutiny to the construction of racialized masculinities, forms given meaning through their imagined relation to and distance from each other.[16] As scholars have long explored, the U.S.–Mexico borderlands have been shaped by complex interactions of violence as well as interdependence between states, empires, and indigenous polities, creating boundaries that have been both rigid and porous.[17] Through the nineteenth and twentieth centuries, Mexican migrants and radicals, U.S. capitalists, white and African American travelers and colonists, fugitive slaves and stateless indigenous peoples, Texas Rangers, and soldiers and raiders from both nations traversed the U.S.–Mexico border. Just as these crossings germinated ideas and practices of race and gender, my study is not always contained within the U.S. nation state. Drawing on newspapers and magazines from across the United States, and to a lesser extent, Mexico, as well as state documents and texts produced by black and Mexican intellectuals, activists, and armed rebels, I examine the ways in which these finite moments of violence in Texas bear the traces of global processes of expropriation and dispossession.

Twentieth-century cultures of violence in Texas were a palimpsest of the earlier forms of community and state violence used to maintain slavery and to secure projects of settler expansion, each of which produced ideologies of white manhood that legitimated the exercise of brutality over civilizational enemies.[18] The genocidal violence waged against Native Americans, and their responses to it, are outside the scope of this book. Yet in various ways this violence lingers in the instances of mass killing examined in the chapters to come. In delineating the practical and symbolic importance of "Indian killing" to the formation of lynching culture in Texas, William Carrigan notes that as Native Americans were not incorporated as American citizens until 1924 and were thus outside the bounds of the legal system, white men who killed them were usually seen as "Indian fighters" rather than vigilantes or lynch mobs. Nevertheless, "Indian fighting," "both in its daily operation and in its mythic justifications," deeply shaped practices of mob violence. White men who killed native people were lionized as "he-men who fought the battles of the wilderness," normalizing the use of terror by private citizens and agents of the state.[19] White Americans wove mythologies of a fierce and supposedly vanishing Indianness to facilitate their own claims to native status and manhood, as well as to attenuate others. As such, the imagined figure of "the Indian" and nationalist fantasies of Indian "extinction" form a contouring focus of some of the chapters to come.

The history of racist state and collective violence in the U.S. is wider than the particular forms of anti-black terror that emerged from racial slavery and its ravaging afterlife.[20] Yet the national scope, intensity, and duration of this violence, and the proliferation of popular and scientific discourses that rooted it in the supposed racial abnormality of black people themselves, have had profound and far-reaching consequences. The astonishing scale and demographic diversity of the protest that exploded after the police murder of George Floyd and Breonna Taylor in the spring of 2020 demonstrates the weight of this history, even as it sought to upend it. The newfound public deliberation on state violence and the willingness of unprecedented numbers of non-black Americans to take to the street against the killing of black people have undoubtedly been fomented by conditions of intense political instability.[21] The COVID-19 pandemic and global quarantine, as well as the fascistic tremors of a presidential administration contemptuous of the comforting decorum of democracy undoubtedly prompted a new urgency in considerations of state violence and power. Within this moment of upheaval, the profoundly disruptive nature of the seemingly simple insistence that "Black lives matter" reveals the extent to which black people's premature deaths have been a normative feature of national life since the nation's inception.

The ambivalent manner in which the massacre in Slocum and the execution of the black soldiers of the Twenty-Fourth Infantry was responded to by journalists, authorities, and political commentators offers us insight into the popular and scholarly modes of thought and action through which the killing of black people was made to seem expected, inevitable, and, if regrettable, nevertheless comprehensible within the needs and workings of civilization. The practice of U.S. anti-black violence, and the transnational permutations of anti-black racism, as I will examine in the following chapters, also shaped discourses of anti-Mexican racism, and Mexican resistance to U.S. racism, on both sides of the border.

Reading histories of racism relationally

In juxtaposing these instances of mob terror and armed resistance to violent U.S. racism, I do not wish to overemphasize their similarities. Stuart Hall long ago warned of the dangers of treating different racisms as if they were merely variants of the same universal phenomenon, a tendency which slides into naturalizing historically specific relations of power as the inevitable outcome of a timeless and irresistible "racial itch."[22] However, even as particular racisms arise within their own historical locations and social relations, they do not arise in exclusion or isolation from each other. Emphasizing the need for scholars to eschew comparative models which imagine each set of racial conditions to be discrete and bound, David Theo Goldberg suggests we must trace the "inter-coursing connectivities" of racisms across time and space. As instruments of racial ordering and control have proliferated and circulated globally, local and historically specific arrangements of race are shored up and given meaning, he argues, to varying degrees, through the elaboration of other arrangements elsewhere and across time: "histories, logics of oppression and exploitation are linked, whether causally or symbolically, ideationally or semantically."[23] While Goldberg is interested in connections across national contexts, relational analysis is also necessary for the examination of the multiple racisms that are seemingly contained within nation states but which have been forged and reformed in global processes.

A number of scholars have highlighted the need for theory and history that elucidate the interdependence of enslavement and settler colonialism and its uneven consequences. Patrick Wolfe has examined how these distinct but dependent regimes produced complementary but antithetical racisms. Settler narratives imagined Indian race as "vanishing" and assimilable, while black race was constructed as permanently and unalterably separate, each ideology serving the "unitary end in increasing white settler property in the form of land and an enslaved labor force."[24] American imperial endeavors in the borderlands and Mexico itself, as well as the racialized subjugation of Mexicans in the United States, were materially tied to and ideologically informed by both settler colonial dispossession of Native Americans and the enslavement of African Americans. After the U.S. waged a war of conquest to take lands claimed by Mexico, itself a colonial power in the borderlands, anti-war commentator Abiel Abbot Livermore likened the "dismemberment" of Mexico to the United States' ongoing projects of domination: "Our treatment of both the red man and the black man, has habituated us to 'feel our power, and forget right.'"[25] From their geopolitical relations with the Mexican nation and their localized relations with Mexicans as an internal population, Americans produced variegated constructions of Mexican race that often employed both "the Indian" and "the Negro" as reference points. Looking at the encounters of violence and conflict examined in this book together allows some insight into the tangle of gendered racisms that emerged from the expansion of racialized capitalism in the Americas and the enduring material and cultural legacies of slavery, conquest, and settler colonialism.[26] Of particular importance for this book is tracing the multiple points of connection between these racisms across time, examining how the race-making of earlier struggles sediments, contouring the grounds of possibility for new configurations of social relations.

These interconnections are not always the grounds for easy solidarity. In its investigation of the Houston Mutiny, black radical magazine the *Messenger* set out the context for the confrontation by suggesting that the ongoing history of anti-Mexican police violence in the state shaped the social landscape in which the men of the Twenty-Fourth found themselves. As they arrived in Texas, they felt the "terrible ring of brutality encircling them," perhaps remembering "the cruel treatment meted out to Mexicans by Texas 'Rangers' and other 'peace' officers." The author also noted, however, that the frustration the men experienced in the city was aggravated by a system of public subordination that placed them beneath other marginalized men. One soldier reported, "We had to walk lots of times on account of street cars being filed up behind the 'Jim Crow' signs, yet Mexicans and other workmen were allowed to sit any place."[27] As Daniel HoSang Martinez and Natalia Molina observe, the point of relational analysis is not simply to chart commonalities or differences, but to "examine the intersections and mutually constitutive forces" between distinct and historically specific regimes of racism.[28] In the chapters that follow, I am particularly concerned with how the legacies of transatlantic slavery have shaped understandings and experiences of race, nation, and masculinity in the Americas, for Americans as well as Mexicans.

Goldberg's observation that racialized orders in one context provide symbolic and technical resources for the imposition of racialized order elsewhere is also true, of course, for strategies and ideologies of resistance among those subject to such powers. These real and potential links are made apparent both in the activities of the African American and Mexican actors, as well as in the corresponding fears of enslavers, Anglo settlers, and federal agents. However, the mutually constitutive relationship between modes of racial order and resistance has often left troubling imprints upon the latter. If Mexicans often contemplated opportunities for resistance and common cause in the oppression of black people in the United States, such visions were sometimes tinged with a logic and imagery that took black subjection at its racist face-value. Furthermore (and relatedly), both black and Mexican resistive politics in the period were articulated through an idiom of male power that often worked to reinforce the abjection of the less powerful as unmanly and abnormal.

A savage song: U.S. narratives of race and violence

For the remainder of this introductory chapter, I will begin to outline some of the social and historical context from which the particular moments of violence examined in the book emerged and were given meaning. In her seminal work on the complex and multivalent discourses of race and gender in the early twentieth century, Gail Bederman makes an important differentiation between masculinity – treated as the primal qualities of being male, attributes that all men had – and manliness, a state of self-restraint, morality, and authority that only civilized men could attain. "Manliness," she writes, "was the achievement of a perfect man, just as civilization was the achievement of a perfect race." Though white civilization had long been linked with manliness, characterized by self-restraint and control, rather than masculinity, in the early twentieth century masculine virility and white men's imagined drive to dominate were increasingly invoked, by politicians, scientists, and cultural commentators, to explain the white race's domination of subjugated races, domestically and globally. Violent conflict, for which virile, primal masculinity was the conduit, "allowed the fittest species and races to survive, ultimately moving evolution forward towards its ultimate, civilized perfection."[29] Preoccupied with the potentially devitalizing effects of civilization and observing the voracious imperialism spreading across the globe, Americans increasingly subscribed to the idea that "the capacity for 'primitive' racial violence was an inherent part of masculinity." The influential psychologist G. Stanley Hall, for example, asserted that a "genocidal urge" was the engine of the species' evolution. "Man early became the wanderer and destroyer par excellence," Hall wrote in 1904.[30]

This evolutionary frame for understanding violence from genocide to lynching was explored in more bellicose terms by the journalist and novelist Jack London in an essay on the global domination of the so-called Anglo-Saxon race. "The twentieth century dawns in blood," he declared, observing that over the course of the closing hundred years, "millions of human beings were destroyed through contact with superior civilization." The brutal facts of evolution as a trajectory of extermination could be observed domestically as well as globally. "We are not unaccustomed to a community burning one of its members at the stake," he noted of his home country, adding that such rituals might include such "communities" taking home pieces of their victim's torn body. The mass killings of modernity differed from previous centuries only in their scale: "We no longer think in feudatories and provinces, but in continents."[31]

Whereas Hall suggested that the masculine racial passion to destroy lower life forms was immoral and ideally benevolently restrained by white men in their dealings with primitives, London reflected without sorrow or apology on the mass death of the primitive races, fitted neither for "organization, government, and the exploitation of nature," slain by the world's dominant races. London's essay captures the multivalent uses of the concept of savagery in the period's discourses of race-gender. "Savagery" features as the source of stagnation, degeneration, and/or death of those feeble "decadent people" incapable of adapting to civilization. On the other hand, the savagery of the white race was masculine, a primal force of deadly progress. Evoking Rudyard Kipling's paean to the white man's global duty to wage "savage wars of peace," London wrote: "When Kipling sings his savage song of sweat and toil and blood-welter, the race as savagely responds."[32] As we will see in the chapters to come, within U.S. discourses of racist violence, the primal savagery of white men is constructed, in different veins, as an essential quality of the virile white manhood, as well as a force necessary for the policing and extension of civilization, whether within the nation or at its borders. While London's vision of global race struggle swept the world's decadent peoples into the same unfortunate category, distinct imageries of violence and racial degeneracy were produced in the particular struggles I consider in this book, grounded in their own social relations.

Counter-revolution and terror

The demise of slavery and the subsequent struggles of black people to build a new world was met with a firestorm of bodily and ideological violence. During Reconstruction, the period after the Civil War during which the U.S. government attempted to incorporate the freedpeople of the South into the national polity, the Fourteenth and Fifteenth Amendments enshrined the citizenship of the formerly enslaved and the voting rights of formerly enslaved men in the Constitution. In his seminal 1935 work *Black Reconstruction*, W.E.B. Du Bois cataloged the terror waged across the Southern states by armed paramilitaries – murder, whippings, and massacres – which federal authorities failed to halt, describing this reactionary movement as a new civil war unleashed upon freedpeople, a war that had yet to end. As the national government abandoned its efforts to enforce black citizenship and political participation in the South, a "dictatorship of property" took hold in the South, uniting the interests of Southern planters and Northern capitalists. It replaced "equality with caste" and built "inordinate wealth on a foundation of abject poverty."[33] Popular opinion in the North rationalized the nation's relinquishment of its efforts to protect black people's social, political, and human rights as the failure of black people themselves to measure up to the demands of free citizenship. The *New York Tribune* asserted, "after ample opportunity to develop their own latent capacities," Negroes had proven themselves lazy and unworthy.[34] Heather Cox Richardson argues that judgments on black incapacity were rooted in freedpeople's demands for land, social services, and civil rights, which were deemed to "subvert the American way." This perceived rejection of Northerners' free labor ideals of private property and self-improvement fed wider anxieties about labor unrest and expanding government.[35]

The rejection of black people's demands and these dissimulating claims about black incapacity were heavily bolstered by American social and medical sciences, which continually found new evidence to demonstrate, in the words of the U.S. Surgeon General, black people's racial "proclivity to death and disease." After the publication of the 1890 census, economist and statistician Francis Amasa Walker published an article confidently asserting that post-emancipation fears of an accelerated black birth rate and the prospect "Negro Supremacy" were unfounded; to the contrary, their accelerated rate of mortality suggested that they were moving toward the brink of "extinction," particularly in the industrialized cities of the North. Walker explicitly linked high mortality with abnormal morality: "Indeed in the case of an untrained and ill-developed race, any cause, whether diminution of marriages or persistence in the criminal practices, which diminishes the birth rate is more than likely to accelerate the death rate."[36] At the turn of the twentieth century, scientific common sense asserted that while the protective care of slavery had allowed the abnormal and unfit black race to thrive in white civilization, now thrown into open competition, the laws of nature determined its doom. Capturing the violent intent of such discourse beneath its detached scientific veneer, one doctor in Chicago suggested that perhaps white society ought to "help along the process of extinction."[37] Like the medical discourses that "discovered" the debilitating impacts of emancipation on black people, political and social science discourses rationalizing anti-black violence were predicated on claims of black people's unfitness for freedom.

As the terrorist convulsions of Reconstruction subsided, lynching was recast as a necessary regulatory mechanism to punish and control "black rape" rather than a means of enforcing political and civic subordination. The framework of criminality did not so much replace that of political threat as infuse it, as black political demands were continually equated with rape and sexual transgression.[38] In 1929, Walter White, soon to be executive secretary of the National Association for the Advancement of Colored People (NAACP), observed that lynching had become "an almost integral part of our national folkways": "An uncomfortably large percentage of American citizens can read in their newspapers of the slow roasting alive of a human being in Mississippi," he wrote, "and turn, promptly and with little thought, to the comic strip or sporting page."[39] The stock account of anti-black lynching that steadily coursed through U.S. print recreated the victim's agony, terror, and helplessness before his captors. In the mythology of lynching, Robyn Weigman argues, the graphic depiction of his terrible vulnerability to violence and bodily suffering ritually re-enacted the black man's excision from the ideal of the disembodied, universal citizen.[40]

As the perfected male body was imagined to be impenetrable and contained, the imagery of black susceptibility to the debilitating transgressions of white violence produced in these widely circulating representations of lynching ascribed both a racial and gender abnormality to mob victims. As we will see, this mass mediated imagery of black dying shaped the discursive terrain from which Mexicans rejected the racist violence directed against them in the United States. In various ways, the imagery and narratives of anti-black violence, with their figures of primal white savagery and infirm, violated blackness, also appeared in the responses of the state, white newspapers, and African American writers to the massacre in Slocum and the hanging of the black soldiers of the Twenty-Fourth Infantry, as well as the lynching of Antonio Rodriguez.

Conquest, expansion, and outside enemies

The violent relations between Mexicans and Anglos in Texas were inseparable from wider projects of U.S. military aggression and imperialism.[41] This is made clear in the history of the Texas Rangers. In 1836 the newly independent Texas government formed the Texas Rangers from an ad hoc collection of "Indian fighters" to provide protection against "those savage hordes that infest our borders." A decade later, a regiment of Rangers joined American forces invading Mexico in the U.S war of expansion. Giving a celebratory account of the Rangers' bloody sojourn in Mexico City, early twentieth-century Texas historian Walter Webb mused that Americans had previously been killed in the city but now "men had come who took eye for eye, tooth for tooth." The civilians receiving this talionic justice included a man shot down by a Ranger for attempting to steal his handkerchief and another who threw a stone.[42]

In the twentieth century, Nicolas Villanueva notes that Antonio Rodriguez's lynching in 1910, the year the Mexican Revolution erupted, marks the beginning of an escalation in mob violence against Mexicans in Texas. Over the next decade, against the large-scale context of revolutionaries violently seizing and attacking the property of U.S. capitalists in Mexico, and the local attacks on Anglo property and authority in south Texas, more Mexicans would be lynched than in the previous thirty years combined.[43] Both trajectories of conflict – the relations between the U.S. and Mexico internationally and the local war between Anglos and Tejanos in the Rio Grande Valley – were imagined in idioms of savagery and civilization, degeneration and renewal that drew upon earlier discourses of American expansion. As I will examine in the following chapters, the outbreak of the revolution in Mexico, the first direct challenge to U.S. hegemony in Latin America in the new century, saw a proliferation of U.S. discourses constructing Mexicans as self-destructive semi-savage agents of chaos.

For those Americans who wanted to intervene aggressively in the Mexican Revolution to protect American property, historical memories of nineteenth-century U.S. expansion into Indian and Mexican lands offered a useful range of images and justifications, as I will explore in Chapter 3. The denigration of Mexico as a nation also worked to justify, implicitly or explicitly, the violent repression of ethnic Mexicans in the United States. In his history of the Rangers, Webb admitted that many innocent Mexicans were killed by American civilians and state agents along the border in a conflict that constituted an "orgy of bloodshed." Explaining this unfortunate situation, under the subheading "Dead Men on the Rio Grande," he wrote, "the Mexican Revolution tended to overrun the border and to produce in southern Texas ... conditions similar to those that existed in Mexico itself." The "reign of terror" initiated at the hands of Rangers, peace officers, and local posses against Mexicans, then, was not an expression of U.S. national civilization in the borderlands, but rather its as yet incomplete consolidation.[44]

As I will examine in the next chapter, Americans often racially differentiated "semi-savage" Mexicans from the masculine and fierce "wild tribes" of North America to explain the degeneration of Mexico and the failure of Mexicans to settle the annexed territory. Just as Mexicans had lacked the ingenuity to exploit and develop natural resources, they could not wield the nation-building violence to discipline and remove natural peoples. While Walter Webb distinguished Mexicans, whose Indian ancestors' blood was like "ditchwater" in comparison to that of the Plains Indians, he casts both Mexicans and Native Americans as "outside enemies" in the racial struggle for supremacy in Texas in his history of the Rangers. Explaining the role of the Ranger, Webb writes that when he had to deal with "enemies from his own society – outlaws, train robbers, highwaymen and thieves," the Ranger acted as a policeman. However, when "he was going to meet an outside enemy – Indians or Mexicans – he was pretty close to being a soldier."[45] As we will see in narratives of the anti-Mexican repression in 1915–1916, the conceptual framework of "outside enemies," employing a varied imagery of savagery and semi-savagery, was used to morally launder the killing of ethnic Mexicans.

The Texas Revolution also provided a generative mythical encounter for anti-Mexican violence and a particular strain of white Texan nationalism. The noble struggle against a supposedly tyrannical government provided an emotionally evocative, allegedly historical means of morally cleansing anti-Mexican violence. As Américo Paredes put it, "had the Alamo, Goliad and Mier [sites of Mexican atrocities against Texan soldiers] not existed, they would have been invented."[46] In his memoirs published in 1959, Texas rancher William Hale wrote that "Killing a Mexican is like killing an enemy in the independence war."[47] Nationalist Texan accounts of these experiences operate through gendered representations of death. The massacre of the Alamo's defenders was presented as an act of revolutionary martyrdom, with apocryphal descriptions of mass Mexican death helping to solidify the heroism of the defenders – Jim Bowie killed Mexican soldiers from his deathbed; Davey Crockett died surrounded by piles of Mexican bodies; 1,000 Mexican soldiers were killed in all.[48] A virulent settler masculinity was reproduced in twentieth-century narratives of the Rangers' anti-Mexican violence, casting a nostalgic innocence around the repression in national press.

White Americans' exercise of the "power of death," in the state-sanctioned form of execution, in the "pacification" of the border, in the excesses of killing mobs, marked African Americans and Mexicans as outside the bounds of civilization and the sanctified realm of gendered citizenship. However, these powers were exercised within distinct social relations and mobilized distinct sets of imagery and historical memories. Along the border, as outside enemies and "semi-savage" marauders, the bodies of "dead Mexicans" could be examined through the historical lens of Texas's glorious revolution against Mexican tyranny and invigorating frontier warfare. In his 1890 *Indian Depredations in Texas*, John Wesley Wilbarger recorded eye-witness accounts of "battles, forays, adventures, murders, massacres, etc, etc" to ensure the sacrificial feats of early colonists would be remembered into the twentieth century. The men who pacified the frontier, he writes, valiantly defended the "advance guard of civilization from the tomahawk and the scalping knife."[49] In the narratives considered here, the warfare of the border and the lynching of Mexicans was cast by many white Americans within the discursive framing of expansion and white frontier settlement and thus as part of the nation's global destiny.

On the other hand, in the early twentieth century, in U.S. cultural and political discourse slavery might be nostalgically longed for as a lost past or lamented as a national tragedy, but in either case the black people of the present were deemed a problem for American civilization. Capturing the eugenic discourse that presented slavery as a terrible mistake because of the racially disruptive population it had permanently lodged in the national body, Lothrop Stoddard, whose work will be examined more closely in the next chapter, described the nation's "large resident negro element" as "a tragic anomaly from our earliest times."[50] Discourses of black death and extinction figured African Americans as a body of corruption and social disintegration. This was put in nauseating imagery by Edgar Gardner Murphy, of the Southern Education Board, who urged support for Booker T. Washington's program of segregation and industrial education by asserting that the decay of the black race had implications for the entire nation, as "the rotting body of its dissolution is polluting the atmosphere we breathe."[51] In contrast to narratives of frontier violence, in which civilization is extended, white people condemning anti-black violence, as well as those justifying it, perceived white violence to be induced by proximity to a troubling and abnormal population whose permanent presence drove white men to acts of savagery and thus continually threatened to erode American civilization.

The day will come: discourses of manhood and resistance

African Americans and Mexicans challenging U.S. racial violence and the order it enforced articulated resistance through notions of masculine power and destiny. In a context in which suffrage was legally restricted to men, the restriction of citizenship rights of black men under Jim Crow was equivalent to an exclusion from manhood. The rejection of racism and its often violent social and civic exclusions from normative gender was frequently framed as a struggle for manhood. In such a framework, the term manhood signified the ability to exercise political rights and economic independence, and to protect dependents. Rather than simply the status of individual men, it was invoked to refer to the moral and political status of race as a whole. As Patricia Schechter notes it had evolutionary connotations, as fully evolved races were understood to have passed from the infancy of barbarism to the full manhood of civilization. The term also described a "'people's peoplehood,' the full humanity and prestige of a group." As such, black activist women such as Ida B. Wells and Ana Julia Cooper championed an invigorated black manhood, as well as asserting the rights of black women to politically represent the race. Likewise, as Adriane Lentz-Smith has shown, black women protesting the execution of the black soldiers of the Twenty-Fourth Infantry who had killed white policemen in a conflict sparked by a policeman's abuse of a black woman, articulated a "cooperative notion of manhood that fused the aspirations of African American men and women."[52]

However, even if not always a matter of explicit emphasis, the ideal of manhood requires socially legitimated authority over gendered and classed others, whose own autonomy and independence must necessarily be circumscribed. Capturing the social restrictions that inhered in the realization of manhood as a social status, when the early twentieth-century black sociologist E. Franklin Frazier lamented slavery's supposed deterioration of black families, he observed that "neither economic necessity nor tradition had instilled [in the black woman] the spirit of subordination to masculine authority."[53] As I will explore further in the next chapter, the ideal of manhood was defined not only through its relation to women and children but through its contrast from unmanly men. In contemplating the effects of oppression in *Black Reconstruction*, Du Bois, for example, observed the "disastrous" effects of oppression on many black people in distinctly masculinist terms, describing their "servility and fawning ... failure to achieve dignity and self-respect and moral self-assertion, personal cowardliness and submission to insult and aggression; exaggerated and despicable humility."[54]

As in hegemonic discourses of nation and gender, the legitimate use of violence was an essential ingredient in many black discourses of manhood. The militant black journalist John Edward Bruce, for example, advocated that black men must take "[their] lives in [their] hands" and practice forceful self-defense as the only salvation for black people in a barbaric civilization. "If they burn your houses, burn theirs. If they kill your wives and children, kill theirs. Purse them relentlessly." While some white race theorists and polemicists predicted the ultimate doom of black men in the United States,

Bruce and other African Americans had dark predictions of their own for a civilization built on terror. Invoking Thomas Jefferson's gloomy rumination on the possibility of a wrathful God intervening on behalf of enslaved people seeking justice, Bruce commented, "[T]his modern barbarism practiced upon the Negro in Christian America by white men who boast of high civilization makes *me* 'tremble for this country when I remember that God is just.'"[55] As black men were trained and armed as soldiers during World War I, assertions of willingness to die, and to kill, in self-defense were given electrifying new significance, as we will see in the fraught struggles over the meaning of the black soldiers' killing and their execution after the Houston Mutiny. As I will explore further in the next chapter, however, the masculinist framing of violence and resistance often found many actual black men wanting.

In the Texas borderlands, Mexican fury at Anglo aggression and Ranger violence was articulated in similarly belligerent tones. In Mexico itself, in the first four years of the revolution, miners, workers, and citizens attacked American estates and armed insurgents of various revolutionary factions sought to expel Americans and redistribute their property. In one instance in 1912, women in southern Mexico marched onto an American sugar plantation and burned the cane.[56] As the energy of the revolution suffused the borderlands, such dramatic encounters surely inspired those envisioning a reckoning north of the border. In 1914, an unattributed article appeared in *Regeneración*, contemplating the case of an unarmed Mexican man assassinated by the police in Texas; armed revolt it reasoned, was the only viable option left for Mexicans in that savage land. The answer to Americans' "armed crime," it asserted, was "armed justice." It offered a dark vision of the future, in which the tides would be reversed and it would no longer be the bodies of Mexican men hung from trees and found along roadsides:

> The day will come when the bodies of the "white" bandits will hang from the state's mesquite trees, when the groves will shake with the death rattle of so many Texan assassins who have denied the Mexican the right to life in the savage southern state.[57]

Mexican men on both sides of the border envisioned their struggles against U.S. racism, capitalism, and dictatorship in Mexico in deeply gendered terms. After detailing the violence inflicted upon Mexicans in Texas by "the miserable Rangers," a circular issued in 1915 by Ancieto Pizaña and Luis de la Rosa, the leaders of the rebellion in the Rio Grande Valley, asked: "Enough of tolerance, enough of suffering insults and contempt ... It is necessary for all good Mexicans, the patriots, all those in whom there remains a sense of shame and pride, it is necessary I repeat, for us to repair to arms."[58] The clear implication of this call to arms is that oppression is a matter of shame, not only for its authors but also for its recipients.

Such themes were portrayed more explicitly in political discourse of Mexico's revolutionary culture, which often drew a stark division between virility and effeminacy. A visceral imagery of virility and progress, and their antitheses of submission and betrayal, is readily apparent in the work of Mexican anarchist revolutionaries, the Partido Liberal Mexicano (PLM). The PLM's paper, *Regeneración*, found an enthusiastic borderlands readership in the early decades of the twentieth century, including Pizaña and de la Rosa.[59] Akin to African American women's use of the language of manhood, the Mexican women active in the PLM claimed a stake in the struggle and the necessary development of a revolutionary virility among their men. Party activists Teresa and Andrea Villareal, for example, penned an editorial that asserted, "We have the right to demand strength from those who hesitate to fight."[60] The party ideology emphasized women's liberation and their shared oppression under capitalism, and even condemned the bourgeois institution of marriage. However, it also often emphasized the "natural" qualities of the sexes and envisioned women's role in the struggle as auxiliary – to cajole men to fight and to "be there when he suffers."[61] Furthermore, the effeminate figure of the "submissive" was often invoked in to highlight the cost of neglecting revolutionary action, as I will explore further in the next chapter. While the masculine idiom used by black and Mexican rebels, writers, and activists was steeped in specific political contests and histories of oppression, across these discourses, these politics often obscured women as agents of history and expressed a deep suspicion of gendered others, whether women or unmanly men.

In contrast to the framing of manhood rights within the U.S. nation, in protests around Rodriguez's lynching, and the uprising in south Texas, resistance was articulated through demands for national sovereignty. The rebels in south Texas, in particular, imagined their work within a broader Latin destiny in the Americas. The contrasting ideological byproducts of violent black subordination in the U.S. – the construction of "the Negro" as abject and docile as well as oppressed and potentially explosive – are reflected in Mexican responses to U.S. domination on both sides of the border. The Plan de San Diego rebels made black liberation an essential method and aim of their revolutionary project. In their initial manifesto they called for black people to join them in revolution, which they proposed to begin with the slaughter of all white men over the age of sixteen, a flourish that suggests the authors well understood the ingrained U.S. fears of black uprising. Indeed, as I will discuss in Chapter 5, in Texas these fears had historically been linked to suspicion of Mexicans as outside enemies.[62]

If Mexicans themselves in the nineteenth and early twentieth centuries often considered the oppression of African Americans as a potentially explosive source of social disorder to be harnessed, it was not necessarily because they were astute readers of the "hidden transcript" of black opposition.[63] Rather than a straightforward challenge to anti-black racism, such hopes and strategies might be read as part of a more complex response to U.S. domination that subverted and sometimes rearticulated its anti-black logic. As I will discuss in Chapters 3 and 5, for some Mexican writers, white Americans' anti-black violence made black men potential allies in armed struggle. Others, however, invoked blackness as a nationless, abject state which they sought to demonstrate they did not share. If looking at these historical moments together helps to illuminate the connective historical tissue between them, it also highlights that these connections can constrain as well as enable emancipatory politics.

In Chapters 2 through 5, I will examine the polysemous discourses of death, race, and manhood produced from the massacre in Slocum; the lynching of Antonio Rodriguez; the execution of the soldiers of the Twenty-Fourth Infantry; and, finally, in the uprising and repression in the Lower Rio Grande Valley. To provide a contextual framing for these discussions, I will first trace the construction of historical struggle, masculine power, and submission in a range of U.S. and Mexican theoretical and political texts, themes for which the figure of the slave was often a generative reference point.

Notes

1 "Not Race War: Just Murder," August 1, *New York Sun*, 1. On the Slocum massacre, the subject of Chapter 2, see E.R. Bills, *The 1910 Slocum Massacre: An Act of Genocide in East Texas* (Charleston: The History Press, 2014).
2 "Try to Spread Anti-American Feeling," November 17, 1910, *Montrose Democrat* (Montrose, PA), 4. On the lynching of Antonio Rodriguez and the resulting unrest in Mexico and Texas, see Harvey F. Rice, "The Lynching of Antonio Rodriguez," M.A. thesis (University of Texas at Austin, 1990). Monica Muñoz Martinez, *The Injustice Never Leaves You: Anti-Mexican Violence in Texas* (Cambridge, MA: Harvard University Press, 2018). Nicholas Villanueva Jr., *Lynching of Mexicans in the Texas Borderlands* (Albuquerque: University of New Mexico Press, 2017). Francisco A. Rosales, *"Pobre Raza!": Violence, Justice, and Mobilization among Mexico Lindo Immigrants, 1900–1936*, 1st ed. (Austin: University of Texas Press, 1999). Claudio Lomnitz, "Los Orígenes de Nuestra Supuesta Homogeneidad. Breve Arqueología de la Unidad Nacional en México," *Prismas* 14 (2010).
3 Those targeted by violence in Texas included both Mexican and U.S. citizens. The term ethnic Mexicans is therefore used to encompass all people of Mexican descent.
4 David Montejano, *Anglos and Mexicans in the Making of Texas, 1836–1986* (Austin: University of Texas Press, 1987), 116. As well as Montejano on the

uprising and repression, see Benjamin Heber Johnson, *Revolution in Texas: How a Forgotten Rebellion and Its Bloody Suppression Turned Mexicans into Americans* (New Haven, CT: Yale University Press, 2003). James A. Sandos, *Rebellion in the Borderlands: Anarchism and the Plan of San Diego, 1904–1923* (Norman: University of Oklahoma Press, 1992). Richard Ribb, "La Rinchada: Revolution, Revenge, and the Rangers 1910–1920," in *War Along the Border: The Mexican Revolution and Tejano Communities*, ed. Arnoldo de León (College Station: Texas A&M University Press, 2012). Trinidad Gonzales, "The Mexican Revolution, *Revolución de Texas*, and *Matanza de 1915*," in *War Along the Border: The Mexican Revolution and Tejano Communities*, ed. Arnoldo de León (College Station: Texas A&M Press, 2012). Charles H. Harris and Louis R. Sadler, *The Plan de San Diego: Tejano Rebellion, Mexican Intrigue* (Lincoln: University of Nebraska Press, 2013).

5 Committee on Foreign Relations, "Investigation of Mexican Affairs," ed. Sixty-Sixth Congress Second Session (Washington, D.C.: Government Printing Office, 1920).

6 "Find 30 Dead Mexicans," September 28, 1915, *Washington Post*, 2.

7 Robert V. Haynes, "The Houston Mutiny and Riot of 1917," *Southwestern Historical Quarterly* 76, no. 4 (1973): 430–31, n.53.

8 Richard Stokes, "Massacres by Mobs in East St. Louis Riots Blamed upon Epidemic of Desperate Crimes Committed by Colored Men From the South," July 8, 1917, *Washington Post*, 3. Charles L. Lumpkins, *American Pogrom: The East St. Louis Race Riot and Black Politics* (Athens, OH: Ohio University Press; London: Eurospan, 2008). Malcolm McLaughlin, "Ghetto Formation and Armed Resistance in East St. Louis, Illinois," *Journal of American Studies* 41, no. 2 (2007). Malcolm McLaughlin, *Power, Community, and Racial Killing in East St. Louis* (Basingstoke: Palgrave Macmillan, 2005).

9 On the white victims of Houston, see for example, "Mattes' Death to be Avenged, Battery A Says," August 25, 1917, *Chicago Tribune*, 2. "Paid Tribute to Officers Killed in Recent Mutiny," September 3, 1917, *Houston Post*. "'Race Rioters Fire East St. Louis and Shoot or Hang Many Negroes; Dead Estimated at From 20 to 75," July 3, 1917, *New York Times*, 6. "Soldiers Lynched to Appease South," 17 December 1917, *Brooklyn Daily Eagle*, 15. On the Houston Mutiny more generally see Robert V. Haynes, *A Night of Violence: The Houston Riot of 1917* (Baton Rouge: Louisiana State University Press, 1976). Adriane Lentz-Smith, *Freedom Struggles: African Americans and World War I* (Cambridge, MA: Harvard University Press, 2009). Garna L. Christian, *Black Soldiers in Jim Crow Texas, 1899–1917* (College Station: Texas A&M University Press, 1995).

10 Achille Mbembe, "Necropolitics," *Public Culture* 15, no. 1 (2003): 39. Michel Foucault, *Society Must Be Defended: Lectures at the College de France, 1975–76*, ed. Mauro Bertani, et al., 1st ed. (New York: Picador, 2003), 289.

11 Veena Das, "Violence, Gender, and Subjectivity," *Annual Review of Anthropology* 38 (2008): 285.

12 Paul M. Hart, "Beyond Borders: Causes and Consequences of the Mexican Revolution," in *War Along the Border: The Mexican Revolution and Tejano*

Communities, ed. Arnoldo de León (College Station: Texas A&M University Press, 2012), 8.
13 Rayford W. Logan, *The Negro in American Life and Thought: The Nadir 1877–1901* (New York: Dial Press, 1954). C. Vann Woodward, *The Strange Career of Jim Crow. Third Revised Edition* (New York: Oxford University Press, 1974), 72–74; Amy Kaplan, *The Anarchy of Empire in the Making of U.S. Culture* (Cambridge, MA, and London: Harvard University Press, 2002).
14 John M. Hart, *Empire and Revolution: The Americans in Mexico since the Civil War* (Berkeley: University of California Press, 2002), 261.
15 Fernando Coronil and Julie Skurski, "Dismembering and Remembering the Nation: The Semantics of Political Violence in Venezuela," *Comparative Studies in Society and History* 33, no. 2 (1991): 229, 331.
16 William D. Carrigan and Clive Webb, *Forgotten Dead: Mob Violence against Mexicans in the United States, 1848–1928* (New York: Oxford University Press, 2013); Muñoz Martinez, *The Injustice Never Leaves You*; Villanueva Jr., *Lynching of Mexicans in the Texas Borderlands*; Ken Gonzales-Day, *Lynching in the West, 1850–1935* (Durham, NC and London: Duke University Press, 2006).
17 For a useful introduction to borderlands scholarship, see: Benjamin Heber Johnson and Andrew R. Graybill, "Borders and Their Historians in North America," in *Bridging National Borders in North America: Transnational and Comparative Histories*, ed. Benjamin Heber Johnson and Andrew R. Graybill (Durham, NC: Duke University Press, 2010).
18 William D. Carrigan, *The Making of a Lynching Culture: Violence and Vigilantism in Central Texas, 1836–1916* (Urbana: University of Illinois Press, 2004).
19 Ibid., 31–32, 45.
20 Saidiya Hartman has used this phrase to capture how "black lives are still imperiled and devalued by a racial calculus and a political arithmetic that were entrenched long ago." Saidiya Hartman, *Lose Your Mother: A Journey Along the Atlantic Slave Route* (New York: Farrar, Straus and Giroux, 2007), 6.
21 Researchers examining the large proportion of white protestors at the 2020 demonstrations found that 45 percent of those questioned identified Donald Trump as a motivating factor in joining protests. Amy Harmon and Sabrina Tavernise, "One Big Difference about George Floyd Protests: Many White Faces," June 17, 2020, *New York Times*.
22 Stuart Hall, "Race, Articulation, and Societies Structured in Dominance," in *Black British Cultural Studies: A Reader,* ed. Houston A. Baker Jr., Manthia Diawara, and Ruth H. Lindeborg (Chicago: University of Chicago Press, 1996), 337.
23 David Theo Goldberg, "Racial Comparisons, Relational Racisms: Some Thoughts on Method," *Ethnic and Racial Studies* 32, no. 7 (2009): 1275.
24 Patrick Wolfe, "Race and the Trace of History: For Henry Reynolds," in *Studies in Settler Colonialism*, ed. F. Bateman and L. Pilkington (London: Palgrave Macmillan, 2011), 273. See also: Justin Leroy, "Black History in Occupied Territory: On the Entanglements of Slavery and Settler Colonialism," *Theory and Event* 19, no. 4 (2016). Ikyo Day, "Being or Nothingness: Indigeneity, Antiblackness, and Settler Colonial Critique," *Critical Ethnic Studies* 1, no. 2

(2015). Sharon Speed notes that Wolfe's conceptual division between histories of "bodily exploitation and territorial dispossession" is unhelpful for our understanding of the process of colonization in many parts of Latin America, including Mexico, where indigenous people, as Speed writes, were subject to regimes of labor extraction on "the very land that had been taken from them." Sharon Speed, "Structures of Settler Capitalism in Abya Yala," *American Quarterly* 69, no. 4 (2017): 785. Robin D.G. Kelley, "The Rest of Us: Rethinking Settler and Native," *American Quarterly* 69, no. 2 (2017). Kelley makes the important point that Wolfe's formulation ignores the processes of settler colonialism in Africa and within Europe itself. In South Africa, he notes, "They wanted the land *and* the labor, but not the *people* – that is to say, they sought to eliminate stable communities and their cultures of resistance," 269. Italics in original.

25 Abiel Abbot Livermore, *The War with Mexico Reviewed* (Boston, MA: American Peace Society, 1850), 11.
26 I take this term from Satnam Virdee, who, building on the seminal work of Cedric Robinson, argues that "capitalist rule advanced through a process of differentiation and hierarchical re-ordering of the global proletariat, including within Europe itself." Such an outlook, he notes, allows us to appreciate multiple and distinct modalities of racism. Satnam Virdee, "Racialized Capitalism: An Account of Its Contested Origins and Consolidation," *Sociological Review* 67, no. 1 (2019): 22.
27 "A Court Martial Tragedy," *Messenger* 2, no. 10 (1919): 23–24. Though they faced prejudice and nativist sentiment, the small Mexican population of Houston was not subject to public segregation as they were elsewhere in Texas. See: Tyina L. Steptoe, *Houston Bound: Culture and Color in a Jim Crow City* (Oakland: University of California Press, 2015), 85.
28 Daniel HoSang Martinez and Natalia Molina, "Introduction: Toward a Relational Consciousness of Race," in *Relational Formations of Race: Theory, Method, Practice*, ed. Daniel HoSang Martinez, Natalia Molina, and Ramón Gutiérrez (Oakland: University of California Press, 2019), 8. For other reflections on theorizing multiple racisms, see Antonia Darder and Rodolfo D. Torres, *After Race: Racism after Multiculturalism* (New York: New York University Press, 2004). Evelyn Nakano Glenn, *Unequal Freedom: How Race and Gender Shaped American Citizenship and Labor* (Cambridge, MA: Harvard University Press, 2002); Claire Jean Kim, "The Racial Triangulation of Asian Americans," *Politics & Society* 27, no. 1 (1999).
29 Gail Bederman, *Manliness and Civilization: A Cultural History of Gender and Race in the United States, 1880–1917* (Chicago: University of Chicago Press, 1995), 174.
30 Quoted in ibid., 115–16.
31 Jack London, *The Radical Jack London: Writings on War and Revolution*, ed. Jonah Raskin (Berkeley and Los Angeles: University of California Press, 2008), 109, 115.
32 Ibid., 114.
33 W.E.B. Du Bois, *Black Reconstruction in America 1860–1880* (New York: Free Press, 1992), 707, 630–31, 707. On violence during Reconstruction, see also:

Eric Foner, *Reconstruction: America's Unfinished Revolution, 1863–1877* (New York: Perennial, 2002). Leon F. Litwack, *Been in the Storm so Long: The Aftermath of Slavery* (London: Athlone Press, 1980, 1979). George C. Rable, *But There Was No Peace: The Role of Violence in the Politics of Reconstruction* (Athens, GA: University of Georgia Press, 1984). Kidada E. Williams, *They Left Great Marks on Me: African American Testimonies of Racial Violence from Emancipation to World War I* (New York: New York University Press, 2012).

34 C. Vann Woodward, *Reunion and Reaction: The Compromise of 1877 and the End of Reconstruction* (New York and Oxford: Oxford University Press, 1991), 214.

35 Heather Cox Richardson, *The Death of Reconstruction: Race, Labor and Politics in the Post-Civil War North, 1865–1901* (Cambridge, MA, and London: Harvard University Press, 2001), xiv.

36 Khalil Gibran Muhammad, *The Condemnation of Blackness: Race, Crime, and the Making of Modern Urban America* (Cambridge, MA, and London: Harvard University Press, 2010), 39, 32.

37 John S. Haller, Jr., *Outcasts from Evolution: Scientific Attitudes of Racial Inferiority, 1859–1900* (Carbondale: Southern Illinois University Press, 1995), 209. See also Felipe Smith, *American Body Politics: Race, Gender, and Black Literary Renaissance* (Athens. GA: University of Georgia Press, 1998), 43–44. Martin Summers, "'Suitable Care of the African When Afflicted with Insanity': Race, Madness, and Social Order in Comparative Perspective," *Bulletin of the History of Medicine* 84 (2010): 70–71; Daryl Michael Scott, *Contempt and Pity: Social Policy and the Image of the Damaged Black Psyche, 1880–1996* (Chapel Hill: University of North Carolina Press, 1997).

38 On the continual transmutation of black agency as crime, see Saidiya Hartman, *Scenes of Subjection: Terror, Slavery, and Self-Making in Nineteenth-century America* (New York and Oxford: Oxford University Press, 1997).

39 Walter White, *Rope and Faggot: A Biography of Judge Lynch* (n.p.: Knopf, 1929).

40 Robyn Wiegman, "The Anatomy of Lynching," *Journal of the History of Sexuality* 3, no. 3 (1993): 455. On gendered dynamic of lynching, see also Jacquelyn Dowd Hall, *Revolt against Chivalry: Jessie Daniel Ames and the Women's Campaign against Lynching*, rev ed. (New York: Columbia University Press, 1993). Amy Louise Wood, *Lynching and Spectacle: Witnessing Racial Violence in America, 1890–1940* (Chapel Hill: University of North Carolina Press, 2009).

41 The term Anglo is used in the U.S. Southwest to refer to white Americans in contradistinction to people of Mexican or Hispanic descent. Though often used interchangeably with "white," it also reflects the fact that some people of Mexican descent have historically resented the use of the term "white" in contradistinction to "Mexican," as it implied that Mexicans were not also part of the white race. Reflecting on the changes wrought in south Texas by the influx of Anglo American migration, the local author Jovita Gonzalez commented in 1930 that "The word 'white,' which the Americans use to differentiate themselves from the Mexican population, is like a red flag to a bull" to middle- and upper-class Mexicans. Classifying the "Spanish-Mexican together with the Indian

laborer," as segregation practices often did, Gonzalez wrote, was like classifying an "Anglo-American with an American negro." Jovita Gonzalez, "America Invades the Border Towns," *Southwest Review* 15, no. 4 (1930): 473, 475–76.

42 Mike Cox, *The Texas Rangers: Wearing the Cinco Peso, 1821–1900* (New York: Tom Doherty Associates, 2008), 46. Carrigan, *The Making of a Lynching Culture*, 23–24. Walter Prescott Webb, *The Texas Rangers: A Century of Frontier Defense* (Austin: University of Texas Press, 1991), 119–20.

43 Villanueva Jr., *Lynching of Mexicans in the Texas Borderlands*, 54–55.

44 Webb, *The Texas Rangers*, 478.

45 Walter Prescott Webb, *The Story of the Texas Rangers* (New York: Grosset & Dunlap, 1957), 112. On Anglo Americans' construction of Mexicans as "enemy others" in this period, see Miguel Antonio Levario, *Militarizing the Border: When Mexicans Became the Enemy*, 1st ed. (College Station: Texas A&M University Press, 2012). For a thoughtful overview of the important differences in the racialization of Mexicans in the United States and the settler colonial dispossession of Native Americans, see: Rosaura Sanchez and Beatrice Pita, "Rethinking Settler Colonialism," *American Quarterly* 66, no. 4 (2014).

46 Américo Paredes, *With His Pistol in His Hand: A Border Ballad and Its Hero* (Austin: University of Texas Press, 1958), 19.

47 Richard R. Flores, *Remembering the Alamo: Memory, Modernity, and the Master Symbol*, 1st ed. (Austin: University of Texas Press, 2002). Montejano, *Anglos and Mexicans in the Making of Texas*, 83.

48 Mike Milford, "The Rhetorical Evolution of the Alamo," *Communication Quarterly* 6, no. 1 (2013): 116–17.

49 J.W. Wilbarger, *Indian Depredations in Texas* (Austin, TX: Hutchings Printing House, 1890), iv, 14.

50 Lothrop Stoddard, *Re-Forging America: The Story of Our Nationhood* (New York: Charles Scribner's Sons, 1927), 257.

51 Smith, *American Body Politics*, 60.

52 Patricia A. Schechter, *Ida B. Wells Barnett and American Reform, 1880–1930* (Chapel Hill and London: University of North Carolina Press, 2001), 86, 81–84. Williams, *They Left Great Marks on Me*, 118–19. Lentz-Smith, *Freedom Struggles*, 44.

53 Angela Y. Davis, *Women, Race and Class* (London: Penguin Books, 1981), 11. Martin Summers, "Manhood Rights in the Age of Jim Crow: Evaluating 'End-of-Men' Claims in the Context of African American History," *Boston Law Review* 93, no. 3 (2013). On histories of black manhood and masculinity more generally, see Darlene Clark Hine and Earnestine Jenkins, *A Question of Manhood: A Reader in U.S. Black Men's History and Masculinity* (Bloomington: Indiana University Press, 1999).

54 Du Bois, *Black Reconstruction in America 1860–1880*, 702.

55 Herbert Shapiro, *White Violence and Black Response: From Reconstruction to Montgomery* (Amherst: University of Massachusetts Press, 1988), 41–42.

In the often-cited passage from *Notes on the State of Virginia*, Jefferson reflected on the dangers of slavery, a system that transformed half the citizenry into immoral despots and the other into enemies: "And can the liberties of a nation be thought secure when we have removed their only firm basis, a conviction in the minds of the people that these liberties are of the gift of God? That they are not to be violated but with his wrath? Indeed I tremble for my country when I reflect that God is just: that his justice cannot sleep for ever: that considering numbers, nature and natural means only, a revolution of the wheel of fortune, an exchange of situation, is among possible events: that it may become probable by supernatural interference! The Almighty has no attribute which can take side with us in such a contest." Thomas Jefferson, *Notes on the State of Virginia* (Richmond, VA: J.W. Randolph, 1853), 174.

56 Hart, *Empire and Revolution*, 311.
57 "En Defense de los Mexicanos," January 24, 1914, *Regeneración*, 2.
58 Consul Garrett to Secretary of State Lansing, August 26, 1915, National Archives and Records Administration (NARA) 812.00/15929, p. 2.
59 Claudio Lomnitz Adler, *The Return of Comrade Ricardo Flores Magón* (New York: Zone Books, 2014), 311; Héctor Domínguez-Ruvalcaba, *Modernity and the Nation in Mexican Representations of Masculinity: From Sensuality to Bloodshed*, 1st ed. (New York: Palgrave Macmillan, 2007). Benjamin H. Abbot, "'That Monster Cannot Be a Woman': Queerness and Treason in the Partido Liberal Mexicano," *Anarchist Developments in Cultural Studies* 1 (2018). Emma Pérez, *The Decolonial Imaginary: Writing Chicanas into History* (Bloomington: Indiana University Press, 1999).
60 Ibid., 68.
61 Ibid., 61–62.
62 See, for example, Paul D. Lack, "Slavery and the Texas Revolution," *Southwestern Historical Quarterly* 89, no. 2 (1985); Paul D. Lack, "Slavery and Vigilantism in Austin, Texas, 1840–1860," *Southwestern Historical Quarterly* 85, no. 1 (1981). William Carrigan, "Slavery on the Frontier: The Peculiar Institution in Texas," *Slavery and Abolition* 20, no. 2 (1999). Herbert Aptheker, *American Negro Slave Revolts* (New York: International Publishers, 1993), 52.
63 James C. Scott, *Domination and the Arts of Resistance: Hidden Transcripts* (New Haven, CT, and London: Yale University Press, 1990). Robin D.G. Kelley, "'We Are Not What We Seem': Rethinking Black Working-Class Opposition in the Jim Crow South," *Journal of American History* 80, no. 1 (1993).

1

Imagining slaves and sovereigns

This chapter will seek to offer insight into the constellation of ideas about race, manhood, resistance, and violence shaping the transnational social landscape in which anti-black and anti-Mexican violence unfolded in the 1910s. To this end I will examine how a range of white American, African American, and Mexican political figures, activists, racial theorists and scholars interpreted the New World histories of slavery and conquest. The narratives they constructed of the continental struggles of the past, from their varied vantage points within the present of U.S. imperialism and domestic apartheid, offered explanations for the violent relations of the new century. These narratives are deeply gendered. Of course, not insignificantly, they present historical struggles as being waged by, or inflicted upon, men. More than this, however, they often conceive of historical struggles as processes in which races' collective masculine vigor was expressed or proven impotent and in which races' manhood – a construction that encompassed not just the status of individual men within the imagined race but its collective status as a self-determined, sovereign people – was realized or deformed.

White U.S. Americans' origin stories of their nation's global ascendancy often included demonstrations of "the Mexican" and "the Negro's" supposed incapacity for history and civilization (the use of the always-male synecdoche capturing the inextricable entanglement of constructions of race and gender). "The stern stuff of manhood is not in them," Jack London asserted in 1914 in a contemptuous dismissal of the Mexican Revolution. Like many of his contemporaries, London rooted what he saw as the fruitless violence of the revolution in the inherent submissiveness of the Mexican masses, a trait that explained the country's entire dismal history. "[T]hey sit supinely back," he wrote, "and let the petty handful of leaders despoil them."[1] As we will see, notions of submission, docility, and consent – (non)men who "sit supinely back" – permeate narratives of enslavement and colonial violence offered by white American authors to explain the advancement of U.S. civilization and the turbulent degeneration or underdevelopment of other nations and peoples.

The African American and Mexican writers and political actors whose ideas are considered here offered their own narratives of New World history diametrically opposed to those which claimed the supremacy of white U.S. civilization. However, they also often perceived of struggles for freedom, social transformation, and nationhood through a masculinist frame. Discourses of manhood and virility permeated the politics of resistance against U.S. violence, imperialism, and Mexican dictatorship, as I will begin to examine here, in African Americans' anti-lynching activism and the Mexican anarchist movement in the borderlands. To greater and lesser degrees, the writers of both movements produced polemics that cast resistance in a narrow gendered frame that interpreted the absence of overt defiance as submission. Hence Ricardo Flores Magón, whose ardent commitment to destruction of capitalism and its racist social order was fundamentally opposed to London's commitment to "the white race," offered a remarkably resonant view of the dynamics of oppression and resistance: "To offer one's neck to the yoke without protest, without anger, is to castrate the most precious potencies of man."[2]

In tracing these different articulations of racial manhood and submission, I do not wish to suggest that they are identical or interchangeable. The use of manhood language by anti-lynching activist Ida B. Wells to expose white terror against black people, to denounce the inaction of the state, and to galvanize collective action to protect black lives and families, was not the same as the use of manhood language to justify murder, rape, terror, and the daily repressions of racial caste. Nevertheless, even liberatory invocations of manhood cast shadows that obscured and/or implicated women and those men who failed to embody its strict constraints. Not only are women excluded from the frame as historical actors but femaleness itself was constructed as a source of degradation. Hazel Carby has observed that "[r]ape has always involved patriarchal notions of women being, at best, not entirely unwilling accomplices, if not outwardly inviting a sexual attack."[3] Likewise, in the dichotomous logic of manly resistance and abject submission, those who fail to fulfill the demands of the manhood are often ascribed an effeminate receptiveness to domination that makes them "accomplices" in their condition.

The weight of transatlantic slavery hangs heavily in these narratives. The oppression and potential resistance of black men, their place in civilization, and their role as nation-builders (or destroyers), were, of course, necessarily contemplated through interpretations of slavery and its abolition. I will examine narratives of black people's struggles for freedom in the Americas produced by those who sought to indict the violent subjugation of black people under Jim Crow, as well as those who sought to affirm it. At the same time, as a social relation whose ideal-type consisted of total personal domination and absolute submission, slavery provided an "evocative and elastic metaphor" for imagining political struggle.[4] As we will see, a number of white Americans and Mexicans used slavery as a metaphor to contemplate their own revolutionary processes of man- and nation-making and to explore the threats of emasculating submission and the imperative of manly resistance. Such uses, however, never operated clear of the Americas' history of actual slavery, and as such continually tied constructions of racial blackness to gendered abjection.

New World narratives of black freedom

From the inception of U.S. nationhood, white Americans envisioned liberty as the hard-earned product of struggle. In framing their own independence from Britain as "an act of heroic resistance by a people threatened with slavery," François Furstenberg has argued that Americans could conceptualize slavery as "an act of individual choice – consent, even."[5] Rather than being hypocritically oblivious to the brutality of the institution they maintained as they used slavery as a metaphor for their own perceived oppression, Americans' day-to-day experience with actual slavery made the metaphor a powerful means of affirming the vital necessity of their struggle. George Washington, himself both revolutionary and enslaver, warned that Americans had to choose whether they were to be "Freemen, or Slaves" and whether they would choose "brave resistance, or the most abject submission." Submitting to "every *Imposition that can be heap'd upon us*," he wrote elsewhere, "*will make us as tame, & abject Slaves, as the Blacks we Rule over with such arbitrary Sway.*"[6] This analogic use of slavery both confirmed the historical worth of those who "threw off their chains" and made "the Blacks we Rule over" the paradigmatic embodiment of human debasement. The notion that men, as individuals and nations, earned freedom through their own self-determination continued to resonate in later constructions of gender and race.

On the dawn of the twentieth century, after white reactionaries had used terror and fraud to crush the structures of interracial democracy and as a steady pulse of lynching and acts of terror continued to police black existence, future president Woodrow Wilson reflected on the end of slavery. In *A History of the American People*, a work that, along with the novels of Thomas Dixon, provided source material for D.W. Griffith's anti-black epic *Birth of a Nation*, Wilson wrote: "It was a menace to society itself that the negroes should thus of a sudden be set free and left without tutelage or restraint." Those who strayed from former masters, he claimed, became vagrants and idlers, looking for pleasure instead of working. They "grew insolent, dangerous; nights went anxiously by, for fear of riot and incendiary fire." Wilson thus describes black people's embrace of liberty as a lack of self-governance rather than a realization of it; in yet another act of submission the former slaves "*yielded*" to the "impulse and excitement of freedom." Rather than a movement toward manhood or nationhood as with other peoples who "refused their chains," black desire for freedom is conceptualized as an abrogation of pleasure-seeking, immature beings. It was unfortunate, Wilson argued, that Northerners who lost their sons in the Civil War clung to the sentimental and fundamentally disastrous view that "[the negro was] the innocent victim of circumstances, a creature who needed only liberty to make him a man."[7]

Wilson's narrative of emancipated slaves turned insolent, idle, and corrupt by freedom captured the Southern ideology of race vigorously promoted by such organizations as the United Daughters of the Confederacy and the Confederate Veterans in print, oratory, and public monuments. According to this paradigm, which ultimately came to underpin a national common sense of the "Negro problem" at the turn of the century, slavery had been a beneficent institution that inculcated Christianity and civilization in its wards. The demise of this archaic but kindly institution left a disturbing and degenerating population of black people whose new criminality and increasingly volatile demands for equal citizenship (practices which often amounted to the same thing) demonstrated their incompatibility for it.[8]

The contentment and well-being of black slaves in captivity became a cornerstone of twentieth-century historiography as well as political and popular discourse. In a telling example, William Sydney Drewry, the only early twentieth-century historian to write an account of the Nat Turner rebellion, asserted that "slavery in Virginia was not such as to arouse rebellion, but was an institution which nourished the strongest affection and piety in slave and owner, as well as moral qualities worth of any age of civilization." (Drewry predictably explained away the Turner revolt as the project of a "wild fanatical negro.")[9] As Wilson's assessment of freedpeople makes clear, early twentieth-century discourses of the beneficence of slavery were not empty nostalgia but gave supposedly hard historical evidence to rationalize the structures of Jim Crow. The supposed health and contentment of black people under slavery were continually invoked in contrast with the disturbing degeneracy and criminality of those who needed more than liberty to make them men.

In 1907 the Northern sociologist John R. Commons also reflected on the peculiar history of black people in the United States, asserting that, while other races had been civilized through contact with American institutions, "the negro has been only domesticated." In contrast to the civilizing process in which able and vigorous individuals are assimilated, "domestication dreads and suppresses them as dangerous rebels." Though Commons thus hints at the repressive force of the institution, suggesting an environmental rather than purely biological explanation for black people's supposed civic incapacity, he also describes the end of slavery and the bestowal of citizenship on black men as a catastrophe:

> The very qualities of intelligence and manliness which are essential for citizenship in a democracy were systematically expunged from the negro race through two hundred years of slavery. And then, by the cataclysm of a war in which it took no part, this race, after many thousand years of savagery and two centuries of slavery, was suddenly let loose into the liberty of citizenship and the electoral suffrage.[10]

Freedom and citizenship are presented as unearned rights that the hapless and/or dangerous former slaves misuse and defile. Unlike other peoples, who birthed themselves into nationhood by throwing off their oppression, freedom was a status that the black race had not earned through blood – it "took no part" in the carnage through which white men freed it.

Like Wilson and many other American authors in the period, Commons's analysis ignored the actions taken by enslaved people to destroy slavery themselves. Steven Hahn writes that when the Union invaded the Confederacy, enslaved people launched "the largest slave rebellion in modern history," including the tens of thousands of formerly enslaved people who left plantations and farms and those who also took up arms in the Union Army to destroy slavery.[11] Rather, Commons writes, the freedmen were "let loose" into citizenship, an evocative phrase which had often been employed by white Americans imagining slave revolt. In 1836, for example, white Texan colonists were gripped by the fear that the "tyrannical" Mexican authorities were planning to foment slave uprising and would "let them loose" upon white families.[12] The image likens the assimilation into national institutions and suffrage to the dreaded chaos of slave insurrection. The unfettered black race, expunged of the qualities of potential manhood, "let loose" into the nation's body politic produced a "generation of anarchy and race hatred."[13] Rather than a realization of nationhood, black freedom is presented as a disintegration of it.

As the site of slave insurrection and black nationhood, Haiti had a rich symbolic presence in competing U.S. discourses of violence, black freedom, and their meaning for American civilization. In the early twentieth century, Haiti or "San Domingo", as it was often called, remained a frequent reference point for social actors from diverse political perspectives as they contemplated anti-black violence and African American resistance. For some white

Americans, "San Domingo" became a shorthand term for the impossibility of black politics and the catastrophic potential black uprising. Justifying the murder and fraud through which bands of paramilitaries in the state disenfranchised black citizens during Reconstruction, South Carolina Senator Ben Tillman asserted in a speech before the Senate that, had white men in his state been content to submit to the political empowerment of "ignorant and debased negroes, slaves five years before, and only two or three generations removed from the barbarians of Africa, the state of South Carolina to-day would be a howling wilderness, a second Santo Domingo." The continuing practice of lynching in the South, he suggested, was necessary to prevent this African barbarism from reasserting itself.[14]

Like Tillman, African Americans writing from the grim landscape of Jim Crow terror also saw in Haiti an America that could have been and still could be. Rather than an undoing of civilization, as they reflected on the revolution, they found within it a history and potential future for black men in America that upended the anti-black claims and exclusions of mainstream narratives of U.S. nationhood. I will examine these competing discourses of Haiti as a New World anti-history and Haiti as a history of New World transformation within two accounts of the revolution, each published by a U.S. author in 1914.

Echoing W.E.B. Du Bois's often-cited observation about the "problem of the color-line," in 1914, prolific eugenicist author Lothrop Stoddard wrote that "the 'conflict of color' ... bids fair to be the fundamental problem of the twentieth century." Indeed, for the United States, South Africa, and Australia, it would be the "gravest problem" they would face.[15] Strikingly, he wrote these words in the preface to a history on the Haitian Revolution, which he identified as being of "peculiar interest" to the white world's current "color question."[16] Stoddard declined to refer to the war in Haiti as a revolution in its own right, instead dubbing it "the French Revolution in San Domingo."[17] Nevertheless, like scholars with very different interpretations of the revolution, Stoddard recognized its fundamental importance for political struggles around the meaning of "race," writing that it was the "first great shock between the ideas of white supremacy and race equality."[18] From his standpoint as an apostle of white supremacy, rather than the birth of a nation, for Stoddard this "most noted attempt at negro self-government" represented the obliteration of one of "the finest of European colonies from the map of the white world." He emphasized the "black republic of Haiti" as emerging from the brutal massacre of the white population.[19]

Six years after *The French Revolution in San Domingo*, Stoddard published *Rising Tide of Color Against White World-Supremacy*, a widely read racial history of the globe that gave a eugenics-themed (and uncredited) recapitulation of ideas presented in Hegel's *Philosophy of History*. In his chapter on the "Black Race," he describes "the negro" as a "being" profoundly distinct not only from the white race but all races. Noting that "the Spaniards imported African negroes" into Latin America after the "Indians ... developed the melancholy trick of dying off under slavery," the "black peoples," Stoddard theorized, possessed a "superabundant animal vitality," which showed itself in their "ability to survive harsh conditions of slavery under which other races have soon succumbed."[20] Once again, alleged black fitness for slavery is linked to the disaster of black freedom. Stoddard sums up "the negro" as follows: "Everywhere his presence has spelled regression, and his one New World field of triumph – Haiti – has resulted in an abysmal plunge into the jungle-level of Guinea and the Congo." "Black peoples," he asserts, paraphrasing Hegel, "have no historic past" and thus "the negro tacitly admits that others are his masters."[21] While the exhaustive manner in which he researched the "French Revolution in San Domingo" works to belie both claims, this construction of the Haitian Revolution as a force of "regression" was continually evoked in U.S. political and cultural discourse.

As indicated above, Lothrop Stoddard was not the only American to publish a history of the Haitian Revolution in 1914. Theophilus Steward, who during the course of his life worked as a minister at the African Methodist Episcopal Church, an educator, author, and chaplain in the U.S. Colored Twenty-Fifth Infantry, also published an account. Where Stoddard understood race, and the inequality between races, as a driving force of modern history, Steward vehemently rejected the concept of race as an immoral "fiction." In a 1920 article entitled "The Race Issue, So-Called, a Social Matter Only," Steward wrote that this fiction had been invoked as an excuse for innumerable "horrid outrages" and the treatment of African Americans as "social outlaws."[22] Unsurprisingly, then, his understanding of what happened in Haiti and its significance for the modern world were very different from Stoddard's. Steward explicitly linked the Haitian and American Revolutions. He suggested that the Haitian Revolution, in fact, perfectly demonstrated the two essential doctrines of "true Americanism": "All peoples are fit for self-government. No people is fit to govern another." In practice, these doctrines were contradictory to American imperial exertions in this period and their ideological effluent. Steward thus uses the prism of the Haitian Revolution to reorient the meaning of "Americanism."

Comparing the patriots of Haiti with those of the young United States, he emphasized the even greater obstacles and challenges overcome by the former group of men. Noting that the American Revolution had been described by orators as a process in which a people "not yet a nation became a nation," as well as one of the "greatest creative efforts in history," Steward asked:

> If such eloquent language is necessary to portray the experiences of those who founded the American Republic, men, schooled in freedom and in the practice of government ... what language will be equal to the portrayal of the experiences of men who by their own arms have transformed themselves from slaves to sovereigns?[23]

Steward argued that while the achievements of Haitians were the heritage of all peoples, they were "the special heritage of the Negro Race," as it was through their ordeal that "the rehabilitation of the Negro Race has been accomplished." If men so low in the social scale and "so slightly separated from barbarism" could seize hold of their own destiny without aid or guidance, what might African American men similarly "dare to do for themselves"?[24] Steward's interpretation of Haiti as the "rehabilitation" and "transformation" of black race breathes a subtle indictment of black American men who had not yet fully transformed themselves to "sovereigns." Indeed, he insisted that participation in the U.S. military, not education or religion, was the only way to realize the potential of the race, hobbled by white bigotry as well as the "idleness, crime, vice, illiteracy, wretched female character, and the weakness and worthlessness of the so-called educated classes" among black people themselves.[25]

Though Steward thus placed Haiti within a framework of American ideals in his history and encouraged black men to uplift themselves through the U.S. military, there was an apocalyptic flavor to his theorizing of history. In his earlier work, Steward also prophesied a day of reckoning for the Anglo-Saxon nations of the world, whose age of dominance would soon be coming to an end. As Timothy Fulop writes, Steward's book *The End of the World* formed part of a broader and more diverse body of black millennial thought that envisioned a divinely ordained destiny for the black race and articulated strident critiques of the shortcomings of the United States as a Christian society. Steward posited that Anglo-Saxon nations would destroy themselves in fratricidal warfare, but that the non-European peoples of the world would create new nations, "walking in the light of one great god, with whom there are no superior or inferior races."[26]

While Steward did not counsel anti-state violence as the means through which to overcome the oppression of black men in America, neither did he rule out the real possibility of violent revolution to overthrow a civilization which outraged, lynched, murdered, raped, and robbed those it condemned as "social outlaws." "The enormous falsehood of inferior races must disappear," he warned, "and the enormous fraud practiced upon so large a body of mankind must cease." If consciences were not awakened and the truth of God not honored, Steward predicted, the world might be engulfed in violence of untold devastation.[27]

Read in light of these ominous visions of the future, Steward's conceptualization of Haiti's "bloody but ... brilliant" history clearly holds foreboding implications for the American nation. As well as demonstrating the "possibilities of the human race," it also demonstrated the moral necessity of violent resistance. "I regret also to be compelled to record," Steward wrote in his preface, "that [the Haitian Revolution] will again show that the way from slavery and disenfranchisement to real liberty is not to be trodden by the aid of the peaceable virtues alone."[28] Those who drew the sword to enslave or oppress, he observed, have more than once through history met their deaths at the "avenging sword" of their former victims. "The end of war cannot come, ought not to, until men learn to be just to their fellow men."[29] Thus for both Stoddard and Steward, Haiti was envisioned as one eruption of a broader global struggle over the future of white rule in the modern world – a struggle in which its utter demolition was possible.

As I will explore in the next chapter in the context of the massacre in Slocum, the themes of reckoning and annihilation, which had long featured in depictions of slave insurrection in the U.S. cultural imagination, were often articulated to predict or explain violence during the upheaval of Reconstruction and continued to be invoked the early twentieth century.

The energy in a black man's arm

As Steward's work begins to make clear, for a number of black writers, the Haitian Revolution as a struggle for freedom was simultaneously a people's struggle, as John Mercer Langston put it, to "gain their manhood."[30] As they reflected on the revolution, they found within it histories and futures for black men in America that defied the gendered and racist claims of standard narratives of U.S. nationhood. In an 1893 speech on Haiti delivered at the World's Fair in Chicago, Frederick Douglass asserted that Haitians had disabused the Christian world of the notion that the Negro was "a sheep like creature having no rights which white men were bound to respect ... The mission of Haiti was to dispel this degradation and dangerous delusion, and to give to the world a new and true revelation of the black man's character."[31] This revelation could have ambiguous consequences for the contemplation of black men in the present.

In an 1892 essay on lynching, Douglass alluded to the great lesson of the revolution – "the danger of goading too far the energy that slumbers in a black man's arm." He offered "gloomy predictions" on the eventualities of barbarism: "When men sow the wind it is rational to expect that they will reap the whirlwind. It is evident to my mind that the Negro will not always rest a passive subject to the violence and bloodshed by which he is now pursued." Americans should remember that "[t]he Negro was not a coward at Bunker Hill; he was not a coward in Haiti; he was not a coward in the late war for the Union; he was not a coward at Harper's Ferry, with John Brown."[32] In placing slave uprising – Haiti and Harper's Ferry – alongside Bunker Hill and the Civil War, this genealogy of black resistance insists upon the centrality of the freedom struggles of the enslaved to the emergence of American nationhood. However, while pointing to these historical instances of black heroism to imagine the terrible potential of a black whirlwind of resistance, Douglass's image of the Negro of the present is "a passive subject to…violence and bloodshed." In another essay on lynching, Douglass describes the dismal state of the black men brought before police courts: "Two hundred and fifty years of grinding slavery has done its work upon them. They stand before you today physically and mentally maimed and mutilated men." Though "deformed" and "distorted" by slavery, the Negro is "yet a man," Douglass argued, but it would take "time, education and training" to restore him.[33] The heroism of the black man of the past and the promised fury of the black man of the future demonstrate capacity for nationhood but also the debility of black men in the present.

The construction of Haitian nationhood as a feat of black manhood fit within a broader discourse of black writers who emphasized the emasculating effects of slavery and later caste violence. Militant activist and editor of black newspapers the *Globe* and the *New York Age*, T. Thomas Fortune described the incalculable appropriations of slavery. The "legitimized theft" of slavery cost African Americans not only centuries of lost wages but also inflicted upon them an "enervated and dwarfed manhood": "A billion dollars would have bought every slave in the South in 1860, but fifty billions would not have adequately recompensed the slave for enforced labor and debased manhood."[34] Arguing that all of history had taught that courage and intelligence were necessary for obtaining freedom, "as true of individuals as of nations or races," Fortune urged the Afro-American (his preferred term, which emphasized nationality) to emulate the struggle of poor Irish tenant farmers against landlordism.[35] Though he felt that slavery had drained courage and the "dynamic element" from the Afro-American character, as an undercurrent of restlessness pervaded the South, the time had come for black men, like the "Spartan helot, the Russian serf and the Irish peasant," to reassert themselves and reject the "wrongs heaped upon them." "When oppressed people begin to murmur, grow restless and discontented," he warned, "the oppressor had better change his tactics, or lock himself up, as does the cowardly tyrant of Russia."[36]

While Fortune and Douglass advocated women's rights, such rhetoric implicitly suggests that black men were particularly devastated by enslavement, and later racial caste, as they are denied the natural rights and sovereignty they are owed as men. If freedom was continually imagined as a matter of maintaining or realizing manhood, and the denial of political rights as emasculation, both the subjugation of black women and their presence as political actors are made secondary to the main stage historical struggle. Black women were imagined as being denied not self-determination and liberty by enslavement and racial caste, but the safe confines of marriage and chastity.[37] The rape and forced reproductive labor of enslaved women was frequently interpreted as a violation against black men's patriarchal rights. In *Souls of Black Folk*, for example, as he delineated the "deadweight of social degradation" borne by the Negro after emancipation, Du Bois cited the "red stain of bastardy, which two centuries of systematic defilement of Negro women had stamped upon his race." Carby observes that in such discourse "the illicit sexuality that Du Bois inscribes upon the bodies of black women contributes to rendering the male impotent," a central component in the "deformation" of black men's realization of manhood and their "patriarchal subordination in the national community."[38] As we will see, the figure of a mother "laid low by lust" and colluding with the oppressor would also appear in Mexicans' discourses of race and nationhood.

Though excluded from the heroic embodiment of black peoplehood, from the turn of the century black women were at the forefront of the fight against lynching, as writers and activists, as well as in confrontation with white lynchers. The gendered complexities of this situation are captured in the work of Ida B. Wells. Beginning her career as a journalist in Tennessee, Wells printed attacks on lynching, including an editorial in which she excoriated white men's sexual hypocrisy and suggested that the cases of "rape" they discovered were actually consensual relations between white women and black men. The editorial so enraged local white people that she was forced into exile upon threat of violence. In her 1891 tract "Southern Horrors," Wells urged direct action as the only means by which black people could successfully protect themselves against lynching, advocating the use of boycotts and labor strategies, emigration, and armed self-defense. As appeals to the white man's conscience would not instill "respect [for] Afro-American life," she called for "the Winchester rifle [to] have a place of honor in every black home," to provide the "protection which the law refuses to give." Wells herself resisted racism with force when white train conductors attempted to remove her from a first-class carriage, biting one of them on the hand when he refused to let go of her. Her unflinching militancy saw her shunned from the leadership of the nascent NAACP and the impact of her work continued to be side-lined by such male public figures as Du Bois and Walter White.[39]

As Kidada E. Williams argues, decades before the term "New Negro" entered black public discourse, Wells, Fortune, and other militant editors sought to construct a new identity through print culture and a collective movement among black people to challenge the consolidating forces of racial caste at the turn of the century. Immersed in a patriarchal society in which political rights and power were apportioned through gender, they proposed in particular that racist violence must be met by an invigorated black manhood determined to protect home and family. The concluding message of *Southern Lynching Horrors* is that the "[Afro-American] must act for himself."[40] Whereas Douglass gave foreboding warnings of potential black retaliation against white violence and the slumbering fury in the black man's arm, Wells referred to actual instances in which black men had successfully defended themselves against white mobs, disseminating a record of resistance among black and, inevitably, white readers. In an anonymous 1889 editorial in her paper the *Free Speech*, reprinted by the irate editors of a white paper in Memphis, she reported that black men set fire to Georgetown, Kentucky, in retaliation for a lynching there, applauding them for showing "the true spark of manhood by their resentment."[41]

However, just as Douglass and Theophilus Steward found much fault in contemporary black men as they delineated the glorious heritage of Haiti, the vision of a new black manhood could have ambivalent undertones. Newspaper editors called for black men to fight lynching unto death to protect their women and children, an ideal that was radical in its implications for racist social order but which nonetheless mobilized traditional notions of martial and patriarchal manhood. They were often disappointed in ordinary black men who failed to meet the grim demands of manhood and expressed this in print. Reporting an instance in which a pregnant black woman was brutally beaten by a white mob looking for her husband, who had fled, John Mitchell Jr., editor of the Richmond *Planet*, wrote that "[w]hen black men determine to die in defense of their homes, then these outrages will cease ... Colored men, make up your minds to die in defense of yourself and your families."[42]

Though Wells and other women activists highlighted the sexual violence and brutality inflicted by white men and mobs on black women and girls, an aspect of white violence often silenced in public discussions, the idealized patriarchal frame of resistant black manhood obscured much from view, including the black women who defended men and communities from white violence. In a number of recorded cases, women and girls were more active and prominent than men in collectively confronting white mobs.[43] Black women's resistance was acknowledged and admired by the *Chicago Defender*, but this admiration was expressed as a condemnation of black men, thus treating women's action as the product of men's gender deviance: "Since there are no men, women come to the front; protect the weaklings that still wear the pants from the lynch mobs."[44]

W. Fitzhugh Brundage writes that calls for armed action from Wells and other prominent editors and public activists, a number of them located in Northern cities, were often unreflective of the complex and varied realities of the people who were most vulnerable to violence. If black people did resist with force when they could, in some contexts such open defiance or even publicly criticizing mob violence could lead to violent white retaliation against entire communities. The standard of manly action, of fighting unto death to protect women and children, demanded in activist polemic devalues the multiple and often "inchoate" strategies of resistance and survival taken by people whose ability to use force was mediated by the differing resources and dangers presented by diverse and often bleakly repressive circumstances.[45]

Arguing that white men would not begin to respect black life out of compassion and conscience but only out of personal risk and economic interest, Wells made a powerful indictment of white men's justice and morality and the civilization they claimed to defend. However, she also suggests that the integrity of black manhood too was at stake in the fight against lynching. "Nothing, absolutely nothing, is to be gained by a further sacrifice of manhood and self-respect." The assessment of "further sacrifice" equates the absence of overt resistance with abject submission: "The more the Afro-American yields and cringes and begs, the more he has to do so, the more he is insulted, outraged and lynched."[46] Here the failure to exercise manly agency amplifies humiliation and oppression. Channeled through ideals of patriarchal manhood and self-determination, the militant language of self-defense holds black men at least partially responsible for the violence to which they are subjected.

The axe and the rifle: myths of nation and mixture

For early twentieth-century historians, politicians, and race theorists in both the U.S. and Mexico, comparisons of the modes of European colonization in North and Latin America were central to articulating the distinct racial natures and continental destinies of U.S. and Mexican peoples. For many Americans, Mexican racial mixture explained the supposed chaos that perpetually ravaged the country below the border. Mexican "mongrelcy" was significant not only for what it revealed about the nation's potential but also for what it revealed about its past. Again cribbing closely from Hegel, Lothrop Stoddard observed that Spanish conquest had predetermined

Latin America's unfortunate evolution: "That very word 'conquest' tells the story." In Stoddard's analysis, this process could not be more different from the pattern of colonization that prevailed in Anglo America: "the United States was *settled* by colonists planning homes and bringing their women."[47] In each case, the mode of interaction between Europeans and indigenous peoples was central to shaping national destiny. The settlement of the United States ensured racial purity through the presence of white women, in contrast to the sordid sexual morass that produced the mongrelized people of Latin America.

Relations between men in colonial encounters were also critical in determining the racial character of the resulting nations. In North America, Stoddard observed, "The Indians encountered were wild nomads, fierce of temper and few in number. After sharp conflicts they were extirpated, leaving virtually no ethnic traces behind." This virile war of extermination is contrasted with the feminized consummation between conquerors and conquered in Latin America, "the exact antithesis" of U.S. settlement. In Mexico, the "bold warriors" leading Spanish conquest descended upon densely populated regions and "with ridiculous ease … overthrew empires and lorded it like gods over servile and adoring multitudes."[48] The hardy and rugged pioneers in North America win their masculine contest with fierce Indians, while Europeans in Latin America enter into a decadent political and carnal domination of a racially degrading population.

Narratives of black fitness for slavery, whether by those extolling slavery's virtues for civilization before emancipation or those rationalizing black unfreedom afterwards, required the trivialization, denial, and pathology of slave resistance. Narratives of settlement, on the other hand, often emphasized and sentimentalized indigenous resistance. The masculine strength of white Americans' "red foes" is also made clear in Theodore Roosevelt's *The Winning of the West*. Intrepid American settlers "won and kept their lands by force," he writes:

> Their red foes were strong and terrible, cunning in council, dreadful in battle, merciless beyond belief in victory. The men of the border did not overcome and dispossess cowards and weaklings, they marched forth to spoil the stout-hearted and to take for prey the possessions of the men of might. Every acre, every rood of ground which they claimed had to be cleared by the axe and held with the rifle.[49]

Like white women, dreadful and merciless Indians ensured the race purity of settlement, with the former bearing white children and the latter honing settlers' manhood through the rigors of warfare. Such violence was definitive of the settlers' ancient heritage, Roosevelt argued. Their forefathers had "assimilated or exterminated the Celts" and they now repeated the process in the New World, but with more extermination and less assimilation. "It was quite otherwise in the countries conquered by Cortes, Pizarro, and their successors," Roosevelt reflected. "Instead of killing or driving off the natives as the English did, the Spaniards simply sat down in the midst of a much more numerous aboriginal population."[50]

The violent relation between native and European in Latin America, bloody though it may have been, was of the wrong type – both on account of the Spaniards' unmanly indulgence in mastery (they "simply sat down") and the Indians' unmanly submission. Stoddard writes that, rather than refusing to submit and fighting to extinction like the "wild" Indians in the U.S., the Indians of Mexico, who had attained a "degree of civilization," were paralyzed with terror in their encounter with Europeans. The "Indian males" – pointedly Stoddard does not use the word "men" – are pressed into "slave-gangs" or "slaughtered," while Indian women are appropriated wholesale by the Conquistadores.[51] The grotesque racial impurity that now plagued Latin America was the historical product not only of Indian women's sexual submission but, necessarily, of the "Indian males'" abject physical and political submission to white men. Rather than being a racially purifying force like the violence of Anglo settlement, the undisciplined violence of Spanish conquest is a force of racial corruption.

As I will discuss in Chapters 3 and 5, Americans with imperialist interest in Mexico or those justifying anti-Mexican violence in Texas often conflated the figures of the Mexican and the Indian. In other contexts, however, Americans drew distinctions between the "partially civilized Indians" of Mexico who fell into a worshipful subjection to their conquerors and the "wild Indians" of North America who fought to extinction. These distinctions worked to explain the genocidal dispossession of stateless indigenous peoples and the expropriation of Mexican territory in the nineteenth century. Mexican men were neither fierce, free savages nor themselves masterful and resourceful producers or enforcers of civilization. Mexican ancestry evidenced a sexual and social decadence: the blood of submissive Indians and that of dissolute conquerors, without the iron strength to guard their racial purity or build civilization in the wilderness. In marked contrast to his description of the constant "ebullition" of the Mexican nation, deformed by its dual heritage of Spanish and Indian cruelty, early twentieth-century Texan historian Walter Webb described the Plains Indian as existing in a pristine landscape, driven by pure instinct:

> His home was the wild prairie and the broad high plain where roamed millions of buffalo and countless droves of deer, and smaller game. He loved these things with devotion and fought for them with all his ferocious cunning. His tactics in war were in thorough keeping with his primitive nature.[52]

As their own Indian ancestors had been "civilized, sedentary, agricultural and ... [as] docile as sheep" in comparison, it was no wonder that Mexicans, like the Spanish before them, had been unable to control the Comanche and Apache in the borderlands. The "task of subduing them" was left to the energetic white Americans, whose mastery of natural lands and natural peoples demonstrated their racial fortitude.[53] Webb asserted that the frontiersmen on the Plains learned they could never "surrender to an Indian," who in turn refused to surrender himself: "If one cannot surrender, then one must flee or fight, and in the end must die rather than fall alive in the hands of the enemy." Reflecting on this passage, María Josefina Saldaña-Portillo observes that in such accounts the white man's conquering of the environment was accomplished through miming the Indian's primal masculine traits.[54] These narratives also effaced the genocidal violence of American expansion through implying that the Indian made the masculine choice of death before submission. As I will examine further in Chapter 5, these discourses of Indians' "extirpation" complemented those in which white men imagined themselves to have mimetically inherited the traits and powers of their "vanished" adversary, their fabricated like-Indianness becoming a key element of constructions of white masculine power.[55]

Reflecting on the uneven ideological outcomes of New World struggles, Chicano folklorist Américo Paredes wryly observed in 1958 that in the Southwest "one finds Americans of Mexican descent attempting to hide their Indian blood by calling themselves Spanish, while Americans of other origins often boast of having Comanche, Cherokee, or other wild Indian blood, all royal of course."[56] While the Mexican's deluge of Indian blood in the U.S. imagination signified his racial trajectory of submission, degeneracy, and inability to maintain the land which he had lost to white Americans, the strain of Indian blood or the "like-Indianness" of the rugged white American signified his racial triumph over a now virtually mythical enemy, the embodied trace and distinctive habitus of his completed conquest of the continent.

Writing against the aggressive tide of U.S. and European ideologies of race, and under the recurring threat of invasion that plagued Mexico's existence as a nation, Mexican intellectuals also stressed their historical differences from the United States. By the mid-nineteenth century, James Sanders writes, the Mexican public sphere was awash with proud assertions of Mexico's national principles of racial equality and universal male citizenship, which differentiated their society so dramatically from their aggressive northern neighbor. A Mexico City newspaper, for example, asserted that Mexico stood for "the cause of human liberty," whereas the United States, a slave nation, "exploits a man and marks him with a brand of servitude as if he were a beast." Later in the century this egalitarian republicanism increasingly gave way to racialized discourses of modernity that measured a people's progress in terms of "industrialization, science (and scientific racism), technological development and state power," rather than rights and democracy.[57] Yet, even as they used and adapted some of the logic from the period's U.S. and European racial thought, Mexican intellectuals developed their own stories of race and national progress.

At the end of the nineteenth century, the historian and liberal politician Vicente Riva Palacio asserted that Mexico's true history began in the children of the conquerors and of the women of the conquered land. *Mestizos* were the "germ of a new people" that "would come to acquire the indisputable right of its autonomy, forming a new nationality." Unlike North Americans, who were the same racial material as their English forebears, Mexicans were "entirely new on the face of the earth." Thus, Riva Palacio envisioned a unique biological basis for Mexicans' New World sovereignty.[58] Such ideas gained new verve with the Mexican Revolution, as thinkers theorized the emergence of the Mexican nation in self-conscious contradiction to the version of scientific racism promulgated in the United States as well as by the dictatorial regime of Porfirio Díaz.[59] Just as Riva Palacio highlighted the mestizo's unique vigor and resistance to disease in contrast to the Indian's susceptibility to decay, twentieth-century Mexican intellectuals positioned the mestizo as uniquely situated to defend the young Mexican nation. In his 1916 work *Forjando Patria* (*Forging Fatherland*), Mexican anthropologist Manuel Gamio described a new nation of "virile races of iron and bronze," melded in the "great forge of America." Gamio viewed the mestizo class as imbued with vigorous revolutionary agency. The mestizo was "the eternal rebel, the traditional enemy of the class of pure blood or foreign blood, the author and director of uprisings and rebellions," who in the recent revolution had been able to harness the "latent energies" of the indigenous class, directing them to revolutionary triumph.[60]

These discourses of mestizo nationhood were distinctly gendered. As Linnete Manrique points out, the agent of nation-building was always figured the mestizo, never the mestiza.[61] While there were celebrated masculine figures of indigenous resistance mobilized in Mexican political discourses in this period, as we will see in Chapter 3, the most iconic female figure of Mexican founding myths, Malinche, the Aztec woman who served as the interpreter for Spanish conquistador Hernán Cortés, has been despised as a whore and traitor to her people. In a parallel to the figure of the black woman whose sexual relations with her enslaver defiled black manhood, Malinche's imagined sexual submission to Cortés enabled the conquest. *Malinchista* in Mexican Spanish is used to refer to someone who sells out their people or who seeks to simulate foreigners. The male product of "mixture" is celebrated but the female figure who enables the mixture is imbued with disgust.[62] Ironically, then, nationalist revulsion for Malinche reverberates with the same logic of U.S. imperialist discourses of Mexican racial history that makes subjection to colonial domination a source of shame and complicity.

As its title indicates, in his famous essay *The Cosmic Race*, Mexican philosopher José Vasconcelos envisioned mestizaje as a process of human history that exceeded the narrow confines of nationalism. Responding to the looming horizon of scientific racism, Vasconcelos rejected the biological theory of eugenics that insisted upon racial purity and the superiority of white race. The "official science," through which "we have come to believe in the inferiority of the mestizo, the unredemption of the Indian [and] the damnation and irreparable decadence of the Black," he wrote, was merely ideology "conceived by our enemies" to justify their own imperialism and humiliate Latin Americans.[63] Vasconcelos inverted the imperialist claims of American and European race science to position race mixing as a future-making process through which a new "synthetic" race that would fuse the strengths and beauty of all races and nations. As I will discuss in Chapter 3, this vision had explicit anti-black features. The Americas, he claimed, was predestined, "kept in reserve for five thousand years," to be the site at which this new and superior race would be fused. Like Theophilus Steward, Vasconcelos envisioned the imminent doom of white men's world dominance, suggesting that their racism was ultimately a destructive force: "Anglo-Saxons are gradually becoming more a part of yesterday. The Yankees will end up building the last great empire of a single race, the final empire of White Supremacy." Their drive to conquer and annihilate the indigenous peoples they encountered on the American continent proved "their limitation and is an indication of their decadence." In contrast, Latin Americans were at the global vanguard of the new racial future.[64]

Though positioning Latin American mixing as a progressive alternative to American racism, in appropriating indigeneity as an essential ingredient in mestizo citizen-subjecthood, Vasconcelos relegated the "pure" Indian to the nation's prehistory. Like U.S. ideologies of race and nation, for Vasconcelos history began with the arrival of Europeans. His declaration, for example, that the "Indian has no other door to the future except through mixing," constructs a pre-modern indigenous figure whose only salvation is through melding into Hispanic civilization, culturally and bodily. Despite their fundamental differences, then, twentieth-century Mexican race ideologies bear a family resemblance to those of the U.S. In Mexico, indigeneity was claimed as an essential racial building block of the new energetic mestizo man and the nation he defends. In the United States the "vanished" Indian became a symbol for the authentic American nation, his annihilation the whetstone of American manhood. In each ideology, "the Indian" was the conduit to someone else's modernity.

"Slavery," submission, and the Mexican Revolution

In 1910, Mexicans, including peasants, industrial workers, miners, and middle-class liberals, set in motion the first revolutionary process of the twentieth century. The long and bloody struggle for both internal social transformation and external national autonomy that followed produced "the first great postcolonial constitution of the century." Over the course of the revolution, dispossessed workers and peasants asserted communal rights to land and self-determination over the neo-colonialist demands of U.S. capital.[65] Many Americans assessing the revolution presented it as the latest eruption of chaos to result from the nation's unpromising beginnings in conquest and racial mixture. Stoddard described Latin American revolutions as "senseless" outbursts in which, in contrast to the American Revolution, "the plundered people grow more and more abject in poverty and slavishness."[66] To undercut any potential reading of their present action as a demonstration of racial vigor, Jack London claimed that only a fraction of the dispossessed Mexican masses were fighting, the vast majority content to linger passively as their leaders despoiled them. On the other hand, he wrote, "It is impossible to conceive of twelve million Americans, gnawed by the land hunger, arming and sending into the field one-fourth of one percent of their number to fight for land."[67]

In some Americans' assessments, Mexicans might work to overcome their historical training in degradation and "slavishness," with careful U.S. guidance. The journalist Arthur Stanley Riggs asserted that the underlying reason for Mexico's present condition could be traced to Spain's despotic colonial rule. "[T]he oppression had been so severe and of such long duration," he wrote, "that, before the people could recover what must have been their original manhood and reason, new oppressors from among themselves arose to tyrannize, exploit and disregard them." Under Díaz, the Mexican people "were slaves, they were spineless, passionless, senseless ignoramuses only fit to be kicked about and used."[68] Riggs submitted this description of Mexicans' pathetic state to the reader to support his plea for America's "peaceful armed occupation" of Mexico. Just as the U.S. occupation of the Philippines had miraculously transformed "8 million Filipino tribesmen into a nation," so too could American teachers perform a similar miracle in Mexico.[69]

Though opposed to occupation, President Woodrow Wilson also presented the Mexican Revolution as a chance to make men and nation out of "slaves." The historian Alan Knight observes that Wilson framed the revolution in "grand historical terms; no people, he asserted, had won freedom without fighting for it themselves."[70] In his 1916 speech accepting the Democratic nomination for the presidency, Wilson asserted the sacred right of Mexico's "15,000,000 oppressed men, overburdened women, and pitiful children," to overthrow their "virtual bondage." That he delivered this speech about the sacredness of emancipation and liberation from within the shadow of Jim Crow was a moral inconsistency that did not go unnoticed. In a statement condemning the president's conspicuous silence on anti-black terrorism and his implementation of segregation among federal government employees, the Colored Advisory Committee of the Republican National Committee noted that "[t]he President has expressed himself as in sympathy with the 'enslaved men and women of Mexico,' but has found no words of sympathy for the colored citizens of America." They contrasted Wilson's pious justifications for his refusal to invade Mexico with his administration's 1914 invasion of "the Black Republic of Hayti," thus linking the occupation of Haiti and the subjection of black people at home.[71]

Indeed, Wilson's assessment of the emancipation of "enslaved" Mexicans was strikingly different from his earlier assessment of African American freedpeople after the Civil War, described at the beginning of this chapter. Rather than potential nation-builders, he described the freedpeople as a "laboring, landless, homeless class … a host of dusky children untimely put out of school," whose inclusion in the national polity was contrary to "the natural order of life."[72] Though Wilson was keen to acknowledge the historical meaning of the Mexican Revolution, it was not out of faith in Mexicans' racial fitness. "I do not believe the Mexican peons are at present as capable of self-government as other people," he commented, "ours for example." As the occupiers of the large state bordering the American nation, Mexicans presented a very different kind of problem for it from that of a sub-population whose subjugation was deemed necessary for the maintenance of social and political order. Wilson's commitment to the United States' global destiny as a bringer of peace and civilization, including the development of a capitalist democracy germane to American interests in Mexico, was enriched by an affirmation of Mexicans' potential for democratic enlightenment and eventual realization of nationhood. Nevertheless, as the Colored Citizens Advisory Committee statement suggested, the conspicuous affirmation of "enslaved" Mexicans worked to further exclude "colored citizens" from the domains of normative peoplehood: "'Humanity' for which the President has expressed such great love, does not include the Colored Race."[73]

Mexican radicals also used the evocative themes of slavery, submission, and manhood in making the case for the necessity and sanctity of the Mexican Revolution. For the Mexican anarchist Ricardo Flores Magón, co-founder of the Partido Liberal Mexicano (PLM), the Mexican Revolution was one front of a wider international struggle against capitalism. Like Ida B. Wells, Ricardo and his brother Enrique printed radical denunciations of the powers that be in their newspaper that made them targets of repression. After a stint of imprisonment in Mexico City, the brothers fled Mexico for Los Angeles in 1904. From there they forged ties with U.S. labor and radical groups and published the PLM's magazine *Regeneración,* which had a transborder readership and provoked the ire of U.S. authorities. The PLM membership included some 350 local groups organized in communities across the Southwest of the U.S. and the north of Mexico. As its members were often illiterate, the editorial columns of *Regeneración* would be read aloud at meetings.[74] Capturing the impact of the PLM among working-class and impoverished Mexicans, the powerful Chihuahuan landlord Enrique Creel complained bitterly that if the industrial workers in his state had to pay a "25 centavos tax to the government ... they would have cried to high heaven, but many of them have deprived their children of bread in order to send five pesos to the Flores Magóns."[75] Though the Flores Magón brothers originally presented themselves as reform liberals, in 1911 they made their anarchist politics explicit, declaring themselves against "Capital, Authority and the Church," all of which strangled the human spirit.

Like his fellow exile Wells, Ricardo Flores Magón believed in the power of the rifle to transform social relations. He highlighted the manner in which the Mexican ruling class utilized scientific racism to justify the repression of the people, while foreigners enriched themselves on Mexican land and labor. "To ... Díaz and the men who are in power, there is no race that is lower, stupider, lazier, more vicious, more immoral or more antithetical to civilization than the Mexican race." Flores Magón summarized the problem and the solution in strident terms: "Do we Mexicans deserve this? Maybe we do, because we've not known how to punish our oppressors. But it is time to open our eyes, comrades. The Winchester will give us the right to be respected."[76] As we will see, however, Flores Magón made much more explicit and constricting links between manhood, respect, and armed action than did Wells.

Like other radical thinkers before them, Flores Magón and other *Regeneración* writers used the powerful metaphor of slavery to expose the exploitative and coercive nature of capitalism.[77] In a 1911 piece, Flores Magón delineated the unifying slavery of the global working classes, asserting that humanity was divided between capitalists and workers: "The worker, then, is a slave everywhere. A slave in Russia, a slave in the United States, a slave in Mexico, a slave in Turkey, a slave in France – a slave literally everywhere."[78] Flores Magón did not envision liberal democratic nationhood as the end goal of the breaking of Mexico's chains. For him, the nation was a "scourge," a structure of the rich that worked only in favor of the rich; it was, he told his readers, "the cop armed with a club who kicks us ... who puts a rope around our necks." The Mexican Revolution was a fight for land and liberty but it was not a fight for a flag; Flores Magón envisioned a day when all flags would fall, to be replaced by the red banner of the world's disinherited.[79]

Though Flores Magón rejected bourgeois nationalism, his political imagination worked through the understanding of revolutionary power as an inherently masculine force and resistance as an activity essential to the realization of manhood. As Benjamin H. Abbot notes, the PLM's emancipatory project genuinely if imperfectly demanded women's social equality. Yet Flores Magón and other PLM writers "exalted a revolutionary masculinity characterized by productive labor and violent defense of independence, while denigrating effeminacy and homosexuality as its antithesis."[80] In keeping with the broader Mexican revolutionary culture, virile women who fought for the revolution could be appreciated and idealized, in print or visual art. In a parallel with the tactics of the *Chicago Defender* who ridiculed the men of the community in which women had confronted the lynch mob, this admiration of fighting women was often expressed in order to shame men for their inaction. Depictions of effeminacy in men, on the other hand, connoted "falseness, weakness, foreign corruption or colonization."[81] In his much-cited address to revolutionary women, Flores Magón mapped women's social inequality by including them equally in the shame of slavery: "If men are slaves, you will be too. Shackles do not recognize gender ... You cannot separate yourselves from the degradation of oppression."[82] Though women were equally degraded, just as the idealized revolutionary was a man, so was the paradigmatic figure of oppression the male who had sacrificed his virility.

Calls to revolution in *Regeneración* were given force as much by their visceral denunciation of the individual that submitted to oppression as their denunciation of oppression itself. "The submissive," read a 1907 article, "are those who lack sufficient moral development to subordinate their self-preservation to the demands of human dignity; those who flee sacrifice and danger, yet sink themselves in opprobrium ... The submissive are traitors to progress, the contemptible stragglers who retard the march of humanity."[83] Imagining the revolutionary struggle as one exerted against the undertow of an unmanly submission to slavery and immoral attachment "self-preservation," Flores Magón articulated his own version of "death before bondage" rhetoric. Echoing George Washington, he asserted to his readers that they must necessarily make a choice between "shackles, misery, humiliation before foreigners" and "liberty, economic improvement, the raising up of the Mexican citizenry, the noble life of the man who is master of himself." The correct choice was clear: "Those who refuse to support the cause of liberty deserve to be slaves."[84]

Flores Magón does not directly reference transatlantic slavery in his ruminations on the enslavement of the world's workers. However, one only has to consider the Spanish word for slave-driver – *negrero* or "driver of blacks" – a term often employed in the pages of *Regeneración*, to see how profoundly transatlantic slavery shaped modern imaginaries of domination. Demonstrating the elasticity of the slavery metaphor in various political lexicons, Mexican writers used the term to refer to a variety of perceived capitalist oppressors, be they Mexican or American. A 1911 piece in *Regeneración* decried bourgeois landowners as "*negreros*" because they "appropriated the land and subjected humanity to wage slavery."[85] Though slavery is thus invoked as a general condition of most of humanity, the term *negrero* stubbornly links subjection with blackness, illustrating how the imagery of slavery in American modernity was at once endlessly flexible and yet ineluctably tied to the captivity of Africans and their descendants.

When Flores Magón does think specifically about slavery as a historical social relation, his assessments are revealing. In a 1910 piece entitled "'Chains of the 'Free,'" he compares the plight of the modern worker to the generic slave of "the past." Describing the wage as the chain of the free, as it worked to legitimate the robbery of the worker of the full fruits of his labor, the piece insists that the worker today is as much a slave as the chattel slaves of yesterday. Yet Flores Magón then rejects this equivalence by suggesting that, in fact, the chattel slave of the past had it better than the modern worker. The worker has even more burdens than the chattel and is given none of the care that was given, Flores Magón imagined, to the slave as chattel object. In an assessment that revives the construction of the contented slave, and from which the coercive terror of slavery is entirely erased, he writes:

> The slave was happier than the free worker ... As the slave costs the owner money, the owner was careful with the slave, he had him work in moderation, he fed him well, he sheltered him when it was cold, and if he fell ill, he entrusted him to the care of doctors.[86]

Though meant to indict the wage system rather than to defend the institution of slavery, Flores Magón's depiction of the chattel slave as cared for and content in relation to the worker/slave of capitalist modernity nevertheless implicitly suggests the chattel slave's disqualification from the forces of revolutionary progress. While the enslaved proletariat class had the potential to demonstrate "war-like vigor" through revolution, the "happiness" of the well-fed chattel seemed to suggest a stagnating acquiescence in objecthood.

While he does not here reference racial blackness directly, in continually reasserting the shame of "slavery" and the submission of degradation, in suggesting that those held in the yoke of oppression have to "choose" their freedom, Flores Magón iterates the same logic that undergirds direct expressions of racism in labor and radical movements. In 1911, Flores Magón wrote an appeal to Samuel Gompers, leader of the American Federation of

Labor (AFL), urging the federation to support the Mexican Revolution, a "cause as just and holy as ever history recorded." The letter, published in 1911 in Emma Goldman's periodical *Mother Earth*, identified American "money power" – "[t]he Standard Oil Co., the Guggenheims, the Southern Pacific Railway, the Sugar Trust ... all that Wall Street autocracy" – as those forcing Mexico into "unspeakably atrocious slavery," with the connivance of the Díaz government. Appealing to the shared oppression of Mexican and American "workingmen," both of them chained by capital, Flores Magón urged Gompers to recognize that "the slavery against which we are fighting is the slavery your American Federation of Labor was organized to fight."[87]

Just months before Flores Magón petitioned him for support highlighting the common slavery of U.S. and Mexican workers, Gompers had come under fire in the black press. Reports emerged that he had given a speech in St. Louis suggesting he wanted to exclude black people from the labor movement. To defend himself, Gompers denied the charges and clarified that in the speech in question he had merely explained that as African Americans were "but a little more than half a century from a condition of slavery," they could not be expected to have "the same conception of their rights and duties as other men of labor have in America." An earlier article examining the shortcomings of black men as workers in the AFL's official publication, the *American Federalist*, noted that "the negro" was "the happiest and most contented individual imaginable," and therefore would offer his labor in any circumstances, "no matter how degrading."[88] Of course, Flores Magón and the PLM are not implicated in Gompers's racism or exclusion of African Americans from shared struggle. PLM members in Lehigh, Oklahoma, sought to form alliances with "American, Italian, Polish and Negro companeros." At a later meeting they recorded that black allies were present who spoke in favor of the revolution. Several black men were included in the force with which the party occupied the city of Mexicali in 1911.[89] Nevertheless, the interplay between the PLM's masculinist framing of slavery and resistance and Gompers's explicit use of racist imagery exemplifies the manner in which discourses of "just and holy" slave rebellion in the twentieth century continued to exclude the descendants of enslaved African Americans.

At times the construction of black docility seeped into *Regeneración* itself. In 1913 a group of twenty ethnic Mexicans, some of whom were activists in the PLM, attempted to ride from Texas to Mexico to aid fight against the rival revolutionary forces of Venustiano Carranza. These men were stopped by Texas Rangers and arrested for violating neutrality laws, later to be convicted by an all-white jury and sentenced to between nine and ninety-nine years in prison. The PLM launched an impassioned defense of the men. One group of ethnic Mexicans from San Marcos, Texas, wrote to Governor Oliver Colquist threatening that if any of the men should be hung, they would make Texas answer for the injustice.

Celebrating the revolutionary self-assertion of these men, whom it likened to the Jacobins of the French Revolution, the following editorial appeared in *Regeneración* in December: "Capitalism believed that the Mexican proletariat in Texas was a mass of peons that would forever remain prostrated at the feet of the masters who rule that barbarous state. The government thought that those 'greasers' would be as submissive as the blacks under the yoke of the barbarous cowboys."[90] The passage is striking in that it draws a parallel, as many white Americans did, between prostrated peons and submissive blacks. The editorial suggests then that the Mexican proletariat, in its threat to take armed action should their comrades be executed, had demonstrated to the world that it was neither a "mass of peons" nor like "the blacks." While Mexicans had defied capitalists and masters, black men remain in submission. In conceptualizing one historical yoke of oppression shared by both African Americans and Mexicans in Texas, the passage also suggests that the same methods of resistance are equally available to all who would grasp them. This notion is belied by the fact that the confrontation in this instance emerged from Mexicans crossing the border to join an army in a country they considered their own, a situation clearly without parallel for African Americans. The prostration of "the black," then, is implicitly presented as a lack of vigorous revolutionary resolve.

In the narratives of U.S. nation-making produced by the early twentieth-century Americans considered here, gendered notions of vigor, docility, submission, and manliness were essential to the explanatory racial divisions drawn between those who thrust civilization forward and those who could not keep pace. Though employed for very different purposes, radical and anti-racist discourses that reiterated freedom as the realization of manhood and oppression as a shameful state of emasculation created their own exclusions and denunciations. Such framings narrowed the range of people, activities, and sentiment that could be made legible as politically and historically meaningful. Reflecting on the difficulties presented to the black radical tradition by the figures of the domestic laborer, welfare mother, and sex worker, Saidiya Hartman observes: "Strategies of endurance and subsistence do not yield easily to the grand narrative of revolution."[91] The reduction of resistance to manly agency, a matter of choice, will, resolution to act and unbendable masculine essence, furthermore, fundamentally serves to distort and obscure the often ravaging conditions in which people "make their own history."[92]

As the masculinist framing of historical action served to naturalize the subordination of women and abjection as a female quality, it also had a particular anti-black verve. As we have seen, from the nation's inception, the relation of slavery offered a potent means for thinking through the meaning of freedom and the consequences of domination, making constructions of blackness potent ingredients in ideological repertoires of gender and power. Even where not explicitly invoked, in a social world indelibly shaped by transatlantic slavery and the ongoing violence of its incomplete abolition, discourses of blackness often hovered in close proximity to contemplations of power and political self-assertion. When Flores Magón differentiated the "enslaved" proletariat from the happier "slave of the past" or when Woodrow Wilson declared the right of enslaved Mexicans to wage revolution, because only those who had fought for freedom were truly free, they implicitly reasserted a logic that denied historical agency to enslaved African Americans and their descendants. As we will see in the next two chapters, legacies of enslavement and abolition run through both the August 1910 massacre of African Americans in Slocum, Texas, and the lynching of Mexican Antonio Rodriguez in Rock Springs three months later.

Notes

1. Jack London, "Troublemakers of Mexico," June 13, 1914, *Colliers*, 13–14.
2. London famously said, "I'm a white man first, and only then a socialist." London, *The Radical Jack London*, 98. "Clarion Call to Arms," June 1, 1907, *Regeneración,* in Ricardo Flores Magón, Mitchell Cowen Verter, and Chaz Bufe, *Dreams of Freedom: A Ricardo Flores Magón Reader* (Oakland: AK Press, 2006), 150.
3. Hazel V. Carby, *Reconstructing Womanhood: The Emergence of the Afro-American Woman Novelist* (New York and Oxford: Oxford University Press, 1987), 39.
4. David Brion Davis, *The Problem of Slavery in the Age of Revolution, 1770–1823,* (New York: Oxford University Press, 1999), 467.
5. François Furstenberg, "Beyond Freedom and Slavery: Autonomy, Virtue, and Resistance in Early American Political Discourse," *Journal of American History* 89, no. 4 (2003): 1296.
6. Ibid., 1301, 1302. On the use of slavery as metaphor in the Age of Revolution, see also Michel-Rolph Trouillot, *Silencing the Past: Power and the Production of History* (Boston, MA: Beacon Press, 1995), 85–86.
7. Woodrow Wilson, *A History of the American People, Volume V: Reunion and Nationalization* (New York and London: Harper & Brothers Publishers, 1902), 18, 22.
8. See, for example, John David Smith, *An Old Creed for the New South: Proslavery Ideology and Historiography, 1865–1918* (Carbondale: Southern Illinois University Press, 2008). David W. Blight, *Race and Reunion: The Civil War*

9 William Sidney Drewry, *Slave Insurrections in Virginia, 1830–1865. A Dissertation, Etc.* (Washington, D.C.: Neal company, 1900), 44.
10 John R. Commons, *Races and Immigrants in America* (New York: Macmillan Company, 1907), 34–35.
11 Steven Hahn, *A Nation under Our Feet: Black Political Struggles in the Rural South, from Slavery to the Great Migration* (Cambridge, MA, and London: Belknap, 2003), 7.
12 Lack, "Slavery and the Texas Revolution," 188–89.
13 Commons, *Races and Immigrants in America*, 35.
14 "Congressional Record, January 21," ed. Second Session, Fifty-Ninth Congress (Washington, D.C.: Government Printing Office, 1907), 1440.
15 T. Lothrop Stoddard, *The French Revolution in San Domingo* (Boston, MA, and New York: Houghton Mifflin Company, 1914), vii.
16 For a useful historiography of the revolution that includes a discussion of both Stoddard and Steward, see Carolyn E. Fick, *The Making of Haiti: The Saint Domingue Revolution from Below* (Knoxville: University of Tennessee Press, 1990), 2–8.
17 Michael O. West and William G. Martin, "Haiti, I'm Sorry: the Haitian Revolution and the Forging of the Black International," in *From Toussaint to Tupac: The Black International since the Age of Revolution*, ed. Michael O. West, William G. Martin, and Fanon Che Wilkins (Chapel Hill: University of North Carolina Press, 2009), 102 n.51.
18 Stoddard, *The French Revolution in San Domingo*, viii; Theodore Lothrop Stoddard, *The Rising Tide of Color against White World-Supremacy* (London: Chapman and Hall, 1920), 91–92.
19 Stoddard, *The French Revolution in San Domingo*, viii, 344–50.
20 Ibid., 14.
21 Ibid., 141–42, 91–92.
22 Albert George Miller, *Elevating the Race: Theophilus G. Steward, Black Theology, and the Making of an African American Civil Society, 1865–1924* (Knoxville: University of Tennessee Press, 2003), 137.
23 Theophilus G. Steward, *The Haitian Revolution, 1791 to 1804; or, Side Lights on the French Revolution* (New York: Thomas Y. Crowell Company, 1914), viii–ix.
24 Ibid., v.
25 Ibid., 6.
26 Timothy E. Fulop, "'The Future Golden Day of the Race': Millennialism and Black Americans in the Nadir, 1877–1901," *Harvard Theological Review* 84, no. 1 (1991): 99.
27 Miller, *Elevating the Race*, 138.
28 Steward, *The Haitian Revolution*, 6.
29 Ibid., vii.

30 Matthew J. Clavin, *Toussaint Louverture and the American Civil War: The Promise and Peril of a Second Haitian Revolution* (Philadelphia: University of Pennsylvania Press, 2010), 44.
31 Frederick Douglass, "Lecture on Haiti. The Haitian Pavilion Dedication Ceremonies Delivered at the World's Fair, in Jackson Park, Chicago, Jan 2d, 1893," in *African Americans and the Haitian Revolution: Selected Essays and Historical Documents*, ed. Maurice Jackson and Jacqueline Bacon (New York: Routledge, 2010), 209.
32 Frederick Douglass, "Lynch Law in the South," *North American Review*, no. 155 (1892): 22–23.
33 "Southern Barbarism," speech on the occasion of the Twenty-Fourth Anniversary of Emancipation in the District of Columbia, Washington, D.C., April 16, 1888, reprinted in Phillip Foner and Yuval Taylor, eds, *Frederick Douglass: Selected Speeches and Writings* (Chicago: Lawrence Hill Books, 1999), 700.
34 Timothy Thomas Fortune, *Black and White: Land, Labor and Politics in the South* (Good Press, 2019), 40–41.
35 Tommy J. Curry, "The Fortune of Wells: Ida B. Wells-Barnett's Use of T. Thomas Fortune's Philosophy of Social Agitation as a Prolegomenon to Militant Civil Rights Activism," *Transactions of the Charles S. Peirce Society: A Quarterly Journal in American Philosophy* 48 no. 4 (2012): 464–65.
36 Ibid., 464. Fortune, *Black and White*, 98.
37 Saidiya Hartman, "The Belly of the World: A Note on Black Women's Labor," *Souls* 18, no. 1 (2016): 166–67.
38 Darlene Clark Hine, "Rape and the Inner Lives of Black Women in the Middle West: Preliminary Thoughts on the Culture of Dissemblance," *Signs* 14, no. 4 (1989): 917, 912. Outlining the manner in which the impact of oppression has often been measured in terms that seems to weigh the loss of men's patriarchal rights heavier than the violation of women's persons, Darlene Clark Hine observes that until the end of the twentieth century "when historians talked of rape in the slavery experience they often bemoaned the damage this act did to the Black male's sense of esteem and respect." Hazel V. Carby, *Race Men* (Cambridge, MA: Harvard University Press, 1998), 33.
39 Ida B. Wells-Barnett, *Southern Horrors: Lynch Law in All Its Phases* (Frankfurt: Outlook Verlag, 2018), 24. Schechter, *Ida B. Wells Barnett and American Reform*, 43, 167–68. Joy James, "Profeminism and Gender Elites: W.E.B. Du Bois, Anna Julia Cooper, and Ida B. Wells-Barnett," in *Next to the Color Line: Gender, Sexuality and W.E.B. Du Bois*, ed. Susan Gillman and Als Eve Weinbaum (Minneapolis and London: University of Minnesota Press, 2007), 80–87.
40 Williams, *They Left Great Marks on Me*, 119; Wells-Barnett, *Southern Horrors*.
41 Philip Dray, *At the Hands of Persons Unknown: The Lynching of Black America* (New York: Modern Library, 2002), 59.
42 Williams, *They Left Great Marks on Me*, 118–19.
43 Ibid., 129, 31. Schechter, *Ida B. Wells Barnett and American Reform*, 114–15, 48–49.

44 Williams, *They Left Great Marks on Me*, 149.
45 W. Fitzhugh Brundage, *Lynching in the New South: Georgia and Virginia, 1880–1930* (Urbana: University of Illinois Press, 1993), 205. Brundage describes how, far from being a unified practice, lynching encompassed a range of different practices carried out by different actors. The attitude of white authorities, white planters, and white public varied dramatically. The ability of people to resist with force depended on the demographic context as well as the relationship of the lyncher to the rest of the white community; in situations where individual white men were exercising violence on a personal vendetta, the wider white population and authorities were less likely to become involved, making self-defense a potentially viable option. In cases in which thousands of people had gathered for the ritual murder of a victim accused of rape or murder, armed self-defense was impossible.
46 Wells-Barnett, *Southern Horrors*, 24.
47 Stoddard, *The Rising Tide of Color against White World-Supremacy*, 105. Italics in original. Hegel wrote that the fundamental distinction between them was that "South America was conquered, but North America colonized," Georg W. F. Hegel and J. Sibree (trans.), *The Philosophy of History* (New York: Cosimo Classics, 2007), 84.
48 Stoddard, *The Rising Tide of Color against White World-Supremacy*, 105.
49 Theodore Roosevelt, *The Winning of the West* (New York: G.P. Putnam's Sons, 1889), 110.
50 Ibid., 12.
51 Stoddard, *The Rising Tide of Color against White World-Supremacy*, 105–6.
52 Webb, *The Texas Rangers*, 11.
53 Ibid., 14, 8–9.
54 María Josefina Saldaña-Portillo, *Indian Given: Racial Geographies across Mexico and the United States* (Durham, NC, and London: Duke University Press, 2016), 11.
55 David Anthony Tyeeme Clark and Joane Nagel, "White Men, Red Masks: Appropriation of 'Indian' Manhood in Imagined Wests," in *Across the Great Divide: Cultures of Manhood in the American West*, ed. Matthew Basso, Laura McCall, and Dee Garceau (New York: Routledge, 2001), 114.
56 Paredes, *With His Pistol in His Hand*, 21.
57 James E. Sanders, "Race and Nation in the Age of Emancipations," in *"All the Inhabitants of this America Are Citizens": Imagining Equality, Nation, and Citizenship in an Atlantic Frame*, ed. Whitney Nell Stewart and John Garrison Marks (Athens, GA: University of Georgia Press), 164–65, 166, 174.
58 D.A. Brading, "Social Darwinism and Nationalism in Mexico," in *Nations and Their Histories: Constructions and Representations*, ed. Susana Carvalho and Francois Gemenne (Basingstoke: Palgrave Macmillan, 2009), 116–17.
59 Alan Knight, "Racism, Revolution and *Indigenismo*: Mexico, 1910–1940," in *The Idea of Race in Latin America, 1870–1940*, ed. Richard Graham (Austin: University of Texas Press, 1990), 86, 84–85.
60 Ibid., 86.

61 Linnete Manrique, "Making the Nation: The Myth of M*estizajes*," *Anthropol* 5, no. 3 (2017): 6.
62 Natividad Gutiérrez, *Nationalist Myths and Ethnic Identities: Indigenous Intellectuals and the Mexican State* (Lincoln: University of Nebraska Press, 1999), 150–52.
63 José Vasconcelos, *The Cosmic Race: A Bilingual Edition* (Baltimore, MD: Johns Hopkins University Press, 1997), 34.
64 Ibid., 18–20.
65 David Craven, "Lineages of the Mexican Revolution (1910–1940)," *Third Text* 28, no. 3 (2014): 223, 226. For a helpful overview of the revolution, see Hart, "Beyond Borders."
66 Stoddard, *The Rising Tide of Color against White World-Supremacy*, 121.
67 Mark Cronlund Anderson, *Pancho Villa's Revolution by Headlines* (Norman: University of Oklahoma Press, 2000), 137–38. John A. Britton, *Revolution and Ideology: Images of the Mexican Revolution in the United States* (Lexington: University Press of Kentucky, 1995), 27–28.
68 Arthur Stanley Riggs, "A Tonic for Mexico: A Plea for Peaceful Armed Occupation," *Forum* 62 (1919): 428–29.
69 Ibid., 437, 432.
70 Alan Knight, "U.S. Anti-Imperialism and the Mexican Revolution," in *Empire's Twin: U.S. Anti-Imperialism from the Founding Era to the Age of Terrorism*, ed. Ian R. Tyrrell and Jay Sexton (Ithaca, NY, and London: Cornell University Press, 2015), 105.
71 "Address to the Colored Voters by the Colored Advisory Committee of the Republican National Committee, Adopted in New York on October 6, 1916," *Crisis* 13, no. 1 (1916), 5. For more on the Wilson administration's occupation, the rampantly racist rhetoric of the occupying forces, and the resistance of Haitians to the occupation, see: Laurent Dubois, *Haiti: The Aftershocks of History* (New York: Metropolitan Books, 2012). Knight writes the administration viewed occupying Mexico as a more difficult prospect than smaller nations like Haiti and Nicaragua. Knight, "U.S. Anti-Imperialism and the Mexican Revolution," 117.
72 W. Wilson, "The Reconstruction of the Southern States," July, 1901, *Atlantic*. Jennifer Keene, "Wilson and Race Relations," in *A Companion to Woodrow Wilson*, ed. Ross A. Kennedy (Oxford: Wiley-Blackwell, 2013), 136.
73 Benjamin T. Harrison, "Wilson and Mexico," in *A Companion to Woodrow Wilson*, ed. Ross A. Kennedy (Oxford: Wiley-Blackwell, 2013), 196. See also, Gareth Stedman Jones, "The Specificity of US Imperialism," *New Left Review*, no. 60 (1970): 80–81. "Address to the Colored Voters by the Colored Advisory Committee of the Republican National Committee," *Crisis*, 5.
74 Elizabeth McKillen, *Making the World Safe for Workers: Labor, the Left, and Wilsonian Internationalism* (Urbana: University of Illinois Press, 2013), 32–33. W. Dirk Raat, *Revoltosos: Mexico's Rebels in the United States, 1903–1923*, 1st ed. (College Station: Texas A&M University Press, 1981), 27–29. Sandos, *Rebellion in the Borderlands*, 42–43, 58–59. For more about the life and thought

of Flores Magón, see: Lomnitz Adler, "The Return of Comrade Ricardo Flores Magón"; Flores Magón, Cowen Verter, and Bufe, *Dreams of Freedom*.
75 Friedrich Katz, *The Life and Times of Pancho Villa* (Stanford: Stanford University Press, 1998), 45.
76 Lomnitz Adler, "The Return of Comrade Ricardo Flores Magón," 311.
77 Davis, "The Problem of Slavery in the Age of Revolution, 1770–1823," 467.
78 "Class Struggle," March 4, 1911, *Regeneración*, in Flores Magón, Cowen Verter, and Bufe, *Dreams of Freedom*, 187–88.
79 Lomnitz Adler, "The Return of Comrade Ricardo Flores Magón," 300–1.
80 Abbot, "'That Monster Cannot Be a Woman,'" 11. As Abbot shows, this could be made graphically explicit in Magón's anti-queer attacks on former comrades who fell out of his favor.
81 Domínguez-Ruvalcaba, *Modernity and the Nation in Mexican Representations of Masculinity*, 40–41. See also, Pérez, *The Decolonial Imaginary*, 55–74.
82 "To Women," September 24, 1910, *Regeneración*, in Flores Magón, Cowen Verter, and Bufe, *Dreams of Freedom*, 61.
83 "Clarion Call to Arms," June 1, 1907, *Regeneración*, in ibid., 150.
84 "Manifesto to the Nation: The Plan of the Partido Liberal Mexicano," 1906, in ibid., 127.
85 "Bandidos y Negreros," May 29, 1911, *Regeneración*, 2.
86 "Chains of the Free," October 22, 1910, *Regeneración*, in Flores Magón, Cowen Verter, and Bufe, *Dreams of Freedom*, 182.
87 Ricardo Flores Magon, "An Appeal of Mexico to American Labor, March 11, 1911," *Mother Earth* 6, no. 2 (1911): 46.
88 "Gompers Says He Has Been Misrepresented," January 5, 1911, *New York Age*, 1. Samuel Gompers, "The Negro in the A.F. of L," *American Federationist* 18 (1911): 35.
89 Johnson, *Revolution in Texas*, 63. Ben Vinson III, *Flight: The Story of Virgil Richardson, a Tuskegee Airman in Mexico* (New York: Palgrave Macmillan, 2004), 156.
90 "Estamos Listos," December 13, 1913, *Regeneración*,1. Lomnitz Adler, "The Return of Comrade Ricardo Flores Magón," 418–23. Lomnitz Adler credits the article to Antonio de P. Araujo, a Mexican-born journalist and activist who was the editor of the magazine at the time because Flores Magón was in prison.
91 Hartman, "The Belly of the World," 171.
92 Here I reference Karl Marx's often cited formulation that men make their own history, but not under circumstances of their choosing.

2

This land of barbarians

In the last essay he wrote before his death, Frederick Douglass excoriated the cries of black rape recently emanating from the perpetrators and abettors of "Southern barbarism." He pointed out the suspiciously sudden nature of the proclaimed rape epidemic and traced the evolving nature of the South's series of imagined Negro problems after emancipation. During Reconstruction, as "Negroes were slain by scores," he wrote, "the justification was said to be Negro conspiracies, Negro insurrections, Negro schemes to murder all the white people, Negro plots to burn the town and to commit violence generally." It was only after the tales of insurrection and the outrages of "Negro domination" no longer offered defensible excuses – as no uprising ever erupted and as black political participation was murderously repressed – that the South raised the "heart-rending cry of the white women and little white children."[1] By the time of Douglass's writing, the charge of black rape had gained the status of truth in both the North and the South: "Its perpetual reiteration in our newspapers and magazines," he wrote, "has led men and women to regard [the Negro] with averted eyes, dark suspicion and increasing hate." Thus the "sweet voices" of Northern women, as well as the howls of negrophobic demagogues, lamented the plight of white Southerners, menaced by a colored race, as one such Northern woman put it, hovering over their women and children "like the locusts of Egypt." This shift from insurrection to rape illustrates the turn of the century's deepening dissimulation of struggles over labor, land, resources, and political rights into the "problem" of black people's supposed racial abnormality.

In contrast to the widely accepted construction of black rape, allegations that black people were plotting to rise up and murder all the white people, as Douglass suggests, were met with considerable cynicism. In 1910, white men massacred African Americans in Slocum, a small unincorporated town on the outskirts of Palestine, Texas, claiming they were acting upon intelligence that the local black population was conspiring to kill white people. The tales of black conspiracy were quickly dismissed and the violence of the white men roundly condemned. On August 1, the *Times Democrat of New Orleans*, which generally took a blithe attitude toward lynching, rebuked the Texas "rioters": "White supremacy is in danger nowhere in Texas, so far as we have been informed, and at this distance we know of no other case adequate to condone the horrible slaughter which is reported."[2] In a period in which manly racial vigor and the thirst for domination were seen by many as key features of an Anglo-Saxon American race acquiring territories and imposing its will around the globe, the violence of white mobs in some scientific and popular interpretations was portrayed as unfortunate, even criminal, but possibly inevitable. As in discussions of the lynching of supposed black rapists, many commentators also framed the killing in Slocum in terms of civilizational incommensurability.

The coverage of Slocum reflects the wider U.S. discourse of racist violence in which claims of white people's endangerment were frequently intermixed with assertions of white wrath and power. I will trace these themes of white endangerment and white wrath from the struggle to consolidate a new racial order after the end of slavery, examining constructions of "race war," uprising, extermination, and degeneration, in national media and scholarly texts, as well as within a celebratory local history of Anderson County. Felipe Smith writes that at the close of Reconstruction, as Americans contemplated the future of the free black population, the possibilities they imagined included "separate white and black Americas, the wholesale expulsion of black Americans from the country, or the acceleration of a process of extinction that would solve the 'Negro problem' once and for all."[3] If explicit suggestions of black annihilation were the terrain of radical racists in the early twentieth century, mainstream scientific discourses of black degeneration and a steady news stream of racial punishment worked to reinforce the construction of black people's supposed inability to adapt to citizenship.

Though the particular killing of the unarmed victims in Slocum was condemned, these condemnations were often shaped by a bigger picture of black guilt. "The passion and emotion" of Southern depictions of the black rape epidemic in the early twentieth century, Khalil Gibran Mohamed observes, were disinfected by the ostensibly objective data of social scientists who produced seemingly detached and conclusive statistical evidence of black criminality. Like the racial demagoguery of South Carolina senator and lynching apologist Ben Tillman and the virulently anti-black novelist Thomas Dixon, scientific studies of race in the incipient years of Jim Crow identified the emancipation of black people from slavery as generating the new problem of "black crime."[4] In these narratives, as I will explore below, white violence was often presented as a natural response of the advanced white race to the uncivilized transgressions of the black race. Therefore, even when the innocence of particular black victims of white violence was emphasized and brutality denounced, many white commentators viewed the problem of racist violence as stemming from the presence of black people within white civilization. After Slocum, even as the threat of black insurrection was discounted, contemplations of punishment, discipline, and the imperative for black improvement pervaded some mainstream responses to the massacre. In their responses to the massacre in Texas, black writers, religious leaders, and readers around the nation made their own assessments of white violence and American civilization, contemplating what potential futures might be wrought by persecution and resistance.

July 30, 1910: the massacre

Palestine, county seat of Anderson County, Texas, was not named after the Holy Land but the town in Illinois from whence came its white settlers. In 1936, local historian Pauline Buck Hohes published *A Centennial History of Anderson County Texas* to celebrate the courage and perseverance of those colonists who had endured the bloody travails of turning a wilderness into a nation, tracing the fruits of their efforts into the present day. She hoped that her modern readers would be inspired to carry forward the same "courage, determination, [and] persistence" exerted by the pioneer "when clearing his land or fighting the Indians." No other history, she enthused, could be "more honorable, more romantic." In 1836, as the Lone Star flag was raised over a land finally free from Mexican oppression, "there were 30,000 Anglo-Americans in Texas. The Mexican population numbered 3,470, and the Indians 14,200."[5] Black people do not figure in Buck Hohes's quantification of populations present at Texas's emergence among the world's nations. She does, however, elsewhere in the book, quantify the value of slave property: "before [the Civil War] broke out, there were 1,917 slaves in Anderson County, whose value reached the sum of $1,085,760. The combined value of the land, horses, and cattle at the same time was but little over half that amount!" It was entirely unsurprising, she wrote, that at the outset of the Civil War the citizens of Anderson County were "aghast at the thought of losing this wealth."[6] The importance of slavery to the colonists, as she explained for her twentieth-century readers, was not merely economic but existential as the settlers braved the frontier.

> Naturally, they brought their slaves; they were to occupy large tracts of land; the slaves were necessary to cultivate it. The average Southerner, before the war of 1861–5 could not envision an existence devoid of slaves. The housewife had never learned to cook and scrub, no more did the husband till the soil. Nature (to their thinking) created the negro for menial tasks.

With the parenthetical addition of "to their way of thinking" and the qualifying "before the war," Buck Hohes carefully historicizes slavery, but reaffirms its natural role in the cultivation of civilization.

Twenty-six years before her history was published, on a morning left out of its pages, armed white men stalked through the roads, marshes, and woods of Slocum, a rural community outside Palestine. On the first day of killing, three young men, Charley Wilson, Lusk Holley, and Cleve Larkin, walked from the home of Wilson's grandmother to that of his mother to tend livestock. They met a group of six or seven white men on the road who opened fire without addressing them. Cleve Larkin, eighteen years old, was dead. Charley Wilson, though wounded, made it to his mother's house. Lusk Holley also survived and later attempted to flee to Palestine with his older brother Alex and a neighbor. On their way, they encountered a larger group of armed white men, traveling in single file. The man leading them whistled and the men opened fire. As Holley lay bleeding on the ground, pretending to be dead, his brother killed, another group of white men passed. The killing continued late into the night. In the morning, it began again, extending into neighboring Houston County.[7]

In the many newspaper accounts to come, several incidents were reported to have sparked the white men's wrath. First, Reddin Alford, described as "a white man" and sometimes also as "a cripple," and Marsh Holley, the father of Lusk and Alex, identified simply as "a negro" in most press coverage, entered into a dispute over a promissory note that Alford had endorsed for Holley. Alford had been forced to pay the note, the story went, and Holley then refused to repay the debt and "grew insulting." Some coverage of the violence also reported a second incident as a contributing factor. Several days after the dispute over the promissory note, this account claimed, a different white man, James Spurger – later indicted for his part in the killing – was called upon to do county road works duty and indignantly refused because the overseer of the work crew was a black man.

In reality, Abe Wilson, Charley Wilson's father, the supposed black overseer, had merely been asked by the (white) Houston County road maintenance supervisor to help notify local people that help was needed with county road maintenance.[8] "On top of all this," the *Shreveport Times* reported – the weight of the phrase "all this" incongruously attached to the seemingly inconsequential matters of a debt of $70 and a message about road works – "came the discovery ... that the negroes were holding secret meetings." These nightly assemblies were held "for the purpose of rising and killing the whites."[9] At their secret meetings, held in a schoolhouse in the woods, it was said, the "negroes" plotted to kill some or all of the white people, depending on the telling, and to burn their property. They were armed and prepared.[10] When the white people found out about their nefarious plans, they resolutely made their own preparations. In some versions of the story the white people were enlightened about the plot by a faithful "old time negro," an invention that invokes the warm relations of slavery, invoking the contrast frequently made in the period's plantation nostalgia between the "faithful slaves" of the past and their "degenerate progeny."[11] Calls were made to the surrounding communities to ask for reinforcements to quell the uprising. At some point, some of the white men cut the telephone wires, an action seemingly at odds for a people who feared themselves to be under siege.

W.H. Black, the sheriff of Anderson County, was candid about what he and his deputies found, and did not find, upon their arrival in Slocum. They found bodies. Black estimated that between fifteen and twenty people, all black, had been killed, but this, he stressed, was a conservative estimate. Truly, it would be difficult to know "just how many were killed, because the dead are scattered all over the woods. Some will probably never be found."[12] Black and his men also found "the greatest excitement prevailing throughout that section of the country":

> Men were going about and killing negroes as fast as they could find them and, so far as I have been able to ascertain, without any real cause. These negroes have done no wrong that I could discover. There was just a hot-headed gang hunting them down and killing them.[13]

Black estimated the killing mob to be between 200 and 300 men. Contrary to the reports that "hundreds of negroes, armed to the teeth" were descending upon the area, Black and his deputies found no trace of the black invaders. After searching the houses of local black families for arms, they found only nine single-barreled shotguns, none of which had been fired recently. The killings were outrageous enough that the Anderson County Grand Jury indicted seven white men for the murder of five black men, a move conspicuously out of proportion with the reported scale of both perpetrators and dead, but nevertheless unprecedented in east Texas.[14] Despite the indictments and the outrage articulated by newspaper editors across the country, however, the killings quickly dissolved from national consciousness. Even the fate of the accused murderers two weeks after the violence went unreported in many of the papers that had reported the killings themselves.

On August 13, three black ministers, J. Milton Waldron, J. Anderson Taylor, and W.J. Howard, representing the Colored Ministers Union, a group of more than 150 ministers from Washington, D.C., signed a letter to President Taft. Having already sent a telegram to Taft on August 1, urging action against the "wholesale murder of innocent and unarmed men" in Texas, they now sent a longer statement addressed to the "President and the American People." On the cover page, they mourned the murder of "20 or more innocent and unarmed colored men near Palestine" and beseeched the president to use the powers of his office to "suppress lynching, murder and other forms of lawlessness in this country." "Unless something is done to make human life more valuable and law more universally respected," they concluded, intimating at a fearful reckoning, "we feel that our beloved country is doomed to destruction at no distant date."

The response from the Department of Justice, to whom Taft forwarded the petition, was brief. It stated that the protection of life and property was a matter for state authorities and that as the minsters' letter referred to "general conditions," there was nothing specific that the Department of Justice could investigate. The assertion that the letter reflected "general conditions" unintentionally underscores the constancy of anti-black violence.[15] In any case, the claim that there was nothing specific to investigate was seemingly belied by the nation's newspapers, which had offered vivid and alarming accounts of mass killing. Headlines describing the violence included: "Whites Kill 18 Negroes" (*Boston Globe*); "Hunting Down Negro like Beast [sic.] in Texas" (*Albuquerque Journal*); "Whites Engaged in a Negro Hunt" (*Tampa Tribune)*; "Bloodthirsty Whites Slay Scores of Blacks" (*Salt Lake Herald-Republican*); "Butchery of Negroes" (*Watchman and Southron,* Sumter, South Carolina).

Though each of these headlines graphically announced the mass killing of black people, the press also treated it as impossible to measure and account for. The number of black people killed in Anderson County was variously reported as "at least a score," "from 18 to 40," "more than 20," or simply unknowable.[16] Should the Attorney General have surveyed press accounts of the violence, the varying death tolls would have given the events a usefully intangible quality. As I will discuss later in this chapter, the narratives of the massacre oscillated over the few days it held the press's attention between tales of armed battles between Negroes and white men and a slaughter of helpless black victims. All versions in the white press, however, concluded with the mass destruction of black life.

The Palestine Board of Trade quietly attempted to justify the killing by refuting all of the sensational embellishments of the race war story but maintaining nevertheless that the rumors of black uprising had been "neither confirmed nor disproven." In its statement the Board also avoided mentioning that the majority of the victims had been shot in the back, a detail reported by the *Palestine Daily Herald* two days earlier.[17] Many others, however, were more incredulous about the claims of a plotted uprising. An editorial printed in the *New York World* (and reprinted in the black paper, the *New York Age*) skewered the fantastical narratives of nefarious Negro plots to "burn barns and do other evil deeds" and the "unprepared and outnumbered whites" who "defended themselves so promptly that two or three dozen Negroes are reported dead." The efforts of the white men armed to protect law and order and restore peace, it noted sarcastically, were "impeded because it is impossible to find the Negro army that threatened the community. This difficulty may arise from the fact that nearly all the Negroes have fled from the region."[18] Yet even those editorials in white papers that condemned the "slaughter" or ridiculed the supposed black uprising did not demand federal intervention to protect black people in Texas.

In *The Red Record*, an exposé of lynching, Ida B. Wells noted that in the first decade after the Civil War, news would be transmitted from the South of insurrections planned by Negroes but swiftly and "vigorously resisted by white men." "It was always a remarkable feature in these insurrections and riots," she observed sardonically, "that only Negroes were killed during the rioting, and that all the white men escaped unharmed." Such derision had met claims of black insurrection emanating from the South for nearly half a century and was not limited to black authors. An editor in Rhode Island, for example, commented in 1876 that, "For some strange reason it always turns out that negro uprisings and negro massacres result in the killing of a large number of blacks and few or no whites."[19] As the Attorney General's response, or lack thereof, begins to suggest in the case of the massacre in Slocum, that the stories of black uprisings used to justify acts of terrorism were unbelievable did not engender urgency on behalf of state authorities. Indeed, the circulation of clearly fabricated or dramatized accounts might have enabled their inaction. Elaine Parsons argues that during Reconstruction, the circulation of fantastical depictions of Ku Klux Klan activities, such as Klansmen drinking blood from skulls or operating within massive underground chambers, helped diminish any sense of national responsibility to take action. In a process which the Klan themselves consciously encouraged by employing macabre methods and imagery, the guerrilla war waged against freedpeople was made to seem "spectral, ambiguous and indeterminate."[20] With its burst of voyeuristic indifference, the press coverage of killings in Slocum fit into a broader cultural landscape in which black threat and black vulnerability were continually constructed as both banal and spectacular, whose constant manifestations were predictable (a set of "general conditions") but always indefinite.

The front-page story printed in the *New York Times* is full of ambivalence, capturing the dynamics of transgression and vulnerability that seemed to inhere continually in constructions of black race. Under the headline "Score of Negroes Killed by Whites," the story details reports of Negroes arming themselves. The white people of Slocum grew uneasy and sent word to Palestine and other locations to send white men with arms and ammunition because "the negroes were advancing on the place and trouble would follow." The story quickly makes clear, however, who bore the brunt of the "trouble" that ensued: Eighteen Negro bodies had already been discovered, with more believed to be "scattered over a large area." As the story drew to its close, it summarized the current situation: "Not one white man was hurt, and at a late hour this evening everything is quiet and no further trouble is feared by the officers."

The report notes that several hundred white men from the "large posses" that arrived at Slocum from the surrounding area had returned home. However,

> others remain at the scene of the trouble, as people of that section of the country are terrorized and fear another outbreak. The negroes of Palestine have been very quiet to-day, and this evening scarcely any can be seen on the streets, which are crowded with groups of men discussing the many killings, but no further trouble is anticipated by the officers.

It is notable that "negroes" are implicitly differentiated from "people" and "men" in the passage. It is furthermore striking that the people being referred to as fearing further outbreaks of violence are the white people who cried uprising, rather than the black people whom those posses had stalked, murdered, and driven from their homes. The lack of credibility of the rumors of black uprising and the unlawfulness of the white men's killing is acknowledged in the passing statement that a district judge had called for a Grand Jury to be convened to "probe the killing of the negroes." Yet the lines between perpetrators and victims, terrorizers and terrorized, is markedly blurred in this image of the now-pacified town. White men, some of whom perhaps had themselves been involved in the massacre, linger in the streets to discuss the mass killing of their fellow citizens whose bodies still lay "scattered"; law enforcement relax in the knowledge that "no further trouble" is expected; the "people" remain fearful though the "negroes are quiet." And of course, "Not one white man was hurt."[21]

As many slaves, so many enemies: uprising fears and genocidal fantasies[22]

The *Seattle Republican*, a black newspaper edited by Horace R. Cayton, derided the reports of "uprising" in Slocum:

> Down in Texas another bloody uprising on the part of unruly Negroes has been reported and it necessitated the killing of some fifty or more of them on the part of the humane whites in order to preserve the peace. It is very remarkable that the Negroes of the United States should periodically so far forget where they are as to make efforts to drive the whites from the land and take possession of the same for themselves, but if the press of the country can be relied upon they will do it.[23]

Though Cayton thus implies that press reports attributed an economic or territorial motive to the "unruly Negroes," the stories of uprising produced in the media coverage of Slocum were absent of any apparent motivation apart from burning the property of white people and/or killing them. Indeed, it is striking that news reports did not seem to question why the black conspirators would be motivated to kill. Neither does the possibility of the white men's economic motivations for the massacre enter into the press coverage. Texas politician Jerry Sadler, who grew up in Anderson County in the shadows of the killings, would later reflect in his memoirs that the violence was motivated by the fact that the black people targeted owned desirable farmland. In his full-length history of the massacre, E.R. Bills notes that the African American population of southeastern Anderson County was reduced by more than half after the massacre, suggesting that the violence thus fits into a broader pattern of racial expulsion in the early twentieth century.[24]

Of the more detailed descriptions of the supposed black plot, the one which appeared in the *Houston Post* read: "It was reported to the white men that the results of these meetings was to effect that on Saturday night, July 30, negroes would advance in a body and kill every man, woman and child in the community." Whether the men who started the killing believed that a black uprising was imminent, the fear was apparently deeply felt in the white community more widely. Women and children had been moved to local schoolhouses under armed guard, while "the majority of the men went to the front to quell the uprising." Even on August 1, when an unknown number of black people lay dead, among the white people in Palestine only the "braver families" had returned home.[25] Despite the fact that the rumored black insurrectionists were nowhere to be found, when Sherriff Black's men arrived in Palestine, the local white people continued to welter in the throes of "excitement": "Everybody seemed to be almost scared to death. Everybody was armed with shotguns. They had the women and children all bunched up in places and were guarding them. Many people were so scared and excited that they could hardly tell their own names."[26] The imagined uprising of lurking black people overcome with the apparently senseless desire to kill white people bears an unmistakable resemblance to previous generations of white anxiety emerging from slavery as well as from its abolition.

The carceral-domestic relation of "family governance," as pro-slavery social theorist George Fitzhugh described the relations of slavery, presented an image of enslaved people as wholly contained within the master's patriarchal authority.[27] At the same time, and continually undercutting enslavers' confident assertions of perfect dominance over slaves, the presence of a captive class lodged with violence in their homes engendered nightmares of retaliation, subversion, and disintegration. In 1822 in the wake of the Denmark Vesey conspiracy, a South Carolina publicist warned that "constant vigilance was required against the Negroes, the JACOBINS of the country ... they are the ANARCHISTS and the DOMESTIC ENEMY: the COMMON ENEMY OF CIVILIZED SOCIETY, and the BARBARIANS WHO WOULD, IF THEY COULD, BECOME THE DESTROYERS OF OUR RACE."[28] Such anxiety was expressed by Stephen Austin, "Father of Texas," in 1830. As the Mexican government sought to restrict the importation of slaves into Texas in order to limit American colonization, Austin wondered what the colony might look like without slavery. His reflections capture both enslavers' extractive vision of the world and the paranoid quality of their nightmares. By 1910, he commented, the white people of the South would be terribly outnumbered and yet his compatriots were uninterested in contemplating a Texan future without slavery, believing that without it the land would revert to its "original uselessness": "It is in vain to tell a North American that the white population will be destroyed some fifty or eighty years hence by the negroes, and that his daughters will be violated and Butchered by them."[29] That white men carried out a massacre in 1910, the same year of Austin's foreboding vision, explaining their killing with narratives of "rising blacks," illustrates not an essential or ahistorical fear of blackness but how the ongoing violent subjugation of black people continued to fuel nightmares of retributive destruction.

In her history of Anderson County, Pauline Buck Hohes includes a brief account of an "uprising of the negroes" in 1860 in Tennessee Colony, a town approximately thirty miles from Slocum. The slaves that Texans deemed so essential to their existence allegedly plotted to poison the wells to kill all of the white people. Hundreds of slaves, she notes, were whipped in "richly merited punishment."[30] The incident that Buck Hohes described was part of a wider spate of reported slave conspiracies across Texas to poison and burn. In August 1860, the *Daily Picayune* argued that what Texans were witnessing was not concerted effort at permanent insurrection against the authority of the whites; rather it was "wanton mischief." The black plotters had no real plans for liberating themselves and "no definite idea of what [they] were to gain for themselves":

> Doubtless, the uppermost idea was that of unrestrained riot, the luxury of unbounded license, in the immediate gratification of every animal appetite, the orgies of idleness, gluttony, and lust. But there does not seem to have been a directing mind or definite purpose, beyond the saturnalia of the hour, where they should go, and what they should do after the success of their murderous purposes, in order to escape the iron grasp of punishment.[31]

Michel-Rolph Trouillot writes of slave rebellion in the New World more generally that if planters and managers could not ignore slaves' resistance, they could trivialize and pathologize it. Here the nightmarish possibility of resistance is "drained of its political content."[32] The would-be insurrectionists are aroused by perverse appetites with no other possible outcome than meaningless destruction and the inevitable "iron grasp of punishment."

Despite the clear continuity between fear of slaves rising before emancipation and fear of former slaves taking vengeance afterwards, Eric Foner suggests that we should not interpret the latter as purely the lingering pathological fears of former enslavers. The insurrection anxiety during Reconstruction, he writes, reflected "the revolutionary transformation in social relations wrought by emancipation," in which the established power relations of the previous order had been swept away and those of a new one not yet fully come into being.[33] These new circumstances in which black and white people found themselves breathed a frenetic new life into the imagery of black insurrection that haunted earlier generations of slave owners. When rumors swirled that the freedpeople would rise on Christmas Day in 1865, amid tensions around black hopes for their own land and reluctance to sign planters' contracts for the next year, white people feared not merely that the insurrectionists would seize the land they coveted but that they would "massacre the whites."[34] The mistress of a plantation in South Carolina listened to the freedpeople singing in their quarters and imagined "a horde pouring into our houses to cut our throats and dance like fiends over our remains."[35]

An editorial printed in Tennessee and Alabama in 1867 reported that black leaders were going from plantation to plantation, urging laborers to join them for "vengeance." Their planned "Reign of Terror" had marked out white women and children as the victims. Though condemning the radical Republicans as "Jacobin demagogues," the editor expressed confidence that the military, controlled by the more conservative General Grant, would provide a "vigorous exercise of power as will give these black fiends to understand that the land is not wholly theirs." However, if "the negro insurrections" were not stamped out, the whole of the South would be set ablaze, from one end to the other.[36] The black desire for land is refracted in this bloody vision – the freedpeople need to learn that "the land is not wholly theirs," but effaced through the imagined aim of orgiastic destruction. The monstrous apparitions of uprising that white people conjured allowed them to invade freedpeople's homes, disarm them, brutalize them, and punish their leaders, to try to force them, Leon Litwack writes, to "[revise] their notions about the prerequisites of freedom."[37] The creation of the black insurrectionist driven by the carnal desire for murder, like the subsequent creation of the black rapist, denies the possibility of black politics.

Fears, real or affected, of black uprising were articulated alongside what Caroline Emberton has called the "genocidal fantasies" that some former slaveowners engaged in when confronted with the cataclysm of emancipation. While planters used every means necessary to re-establish their hegemony in the post-war world and solidify new social relations conducive to the exploitation of black labor, for some slaveowners in the throes of emancipation the end of slavery signaled the necessary end of those who had been slaves. As the wife of one ex-planter in Savannah, Georgia, asserted, "with their emancipation must come their extermination." Rather than merely musing on such an eventuality, another woman, enraged at the freedpeople in her midst and her own impoverished circumstances after the war, longed to take an active role, writing in a letter to a friend, "I want the power of annihilation." Emberton argues the terror waged by white people in this period, which might seem contrary to the interests of those who depended upon black labor, expressed the "assailants' vision for a reconstructed Southern society," the righting of "a world turned upside down."[38]

The dark prediction of black annihilation came to be a running refrain of black uprising talk. Of the imagined uprisings plotted for Christmas in 1865 a South Carolina planter predicted that the insurrection would drive white people to "begin the work of extermination." Conservatives warned that the radical doctrines of those who would give the freedpeople political equality with former masters would spark a "spirit of exterminating violence toward the black race," who would become as rare as "Indians and buffalo."[39] Another South Carolinian confidently dismissed the danger of black insurrection in 1867, precisely because its outcome would be so certain:

> The negro may die out ... but, as long as our people treat the negro with justice and prudence, they need not dread the Bogey-Bugaboo of "blood-thirsty" ... freedmen. The negroes are not fools ... there is no reason to believe that they have any idea of beginning a movement that would infallibly cause their almost instantaneous extermination.[40]

While discourses of black race and the problem it posed to the white people of the South and the nation more generally would shift in important ways by the twentieth century, they continued to be inflected with intimations of "extermination."

Terror in Anderson County

The violence of Reconstruction ripped through Texas on an astounding scale; General Phillip Sheridan, commander of the federal forces in Texas and Louisiana after the war, wrote that there were "more casualties occurring from outrages perpetrated upon Union men and freedmen in the interior of the state than occur from Indian depredations on the frontier." Reflective of the disorienting social upheaval of the period, Foner notes that violence against freedpeople during Reconstruction was justified through charges of "impudence" more often than criminality. Seemingly any assertion of black authority, self-worth, or social agency could be interpreted as an "impudent" arrogation of white men's authority, with freedpeople whipped for not yielding the sidewalk to white people (which would remain a common "offense" through the twentieth century), for using a title, men not removing their hats and women dressing up as if "they thought something of themselves."[41] Between 1865 and 1868, the Freemen's Bureau recorded 1,000 murders of black people in the state of Texas, with listed justifications including "using insolent language," "refusing to call him master," or in another case because one white man "wanted to thin out" the black population.[42] Palestine and Anderson County more widely were in a state of "near anarchy," with a situation so intolerable for freedpeople and their Unionist allies that the county tax collector wrote to the governor in 1869, pleading, "Do something for us, for *God Sake*." In Palestine, white people attacked a saloon where black people were dancing and threw several men out of the upper-story windows, apparently enraged that freedpeople were enjoying themselves.[43]

As the South contracted in violence, for some observers in the North, growing weary of calls from black Southerners and their allies for federal intervention, the terror that freedpeople were subject to cast a poor light on black men's capacity for citizenship and manhood. Echoing the same logic that held enslaved people responsible for their enslavement, a judge in Albion Tourgee's account of Reconstruction in North Carolina lectured that in order to survive as a self-governing community, the freedmen and the white Unionists in the South must join forces to "assert themselves" and put down the "lawless violence" of their assailants. "The capacity of a people for self-government is proved, first of all, by its inclination and capacity for self-protection," he wrote. Should legal routes fail, men must take matters into their own hands. "If people are killed by the Ku-Klux," he asked, "why do they not kill the Ku-Klux?" These sentiments were also voiced by the Massachusetts congressman Benjamin Butler when asked by a delegation of African Americans for a contribution toward purchasing arms to be sent to besieged freedpeople in the South. If black people could not defend themselves, he told them, they were not "worthy to be freemen." He later wrote a friend that "so long as they submit to be killed by every marauding white man who will do so, so long there will be no help." He himself, of course, would "take to killing equally" if he were in their position.[44]

Black newspaper editor T. Thomas Fortune, whose father was active in Reconstruction politics, offered a different reading of the gendered meaning of the period's violence that emphasized black men's efforts to uplift themselves through labor and white men's unmanly and parasitic violence. In a searing passage in his 1884 work *Black and White: Land, Labor and Politics in the South*, he wrote that after the war the black men "went manfully to work" to better themselves and the ravaged country around them. On the other hand,

> the white men of the South, the capitalists, the land-sharks, the poor white trash, and the nondescripts, with a thousand years of Christian civilization and culture behind them, with the "boast of chivalry, the pomp of power" ... organized themselves into a band of outlaws ... and deliberately proceeded to murder innocent men and women for POLITICAL REASONS and to systematically rob them of their honest labor because they were too accursedly lazy to labor themselves.[45]

In stark contrast, in his discussion of Reconstruction violence, which was far more mainstream than Fortune's, Woodrow Wilson painted a picture of humorous youthful mischief in *History of the American People* as he reflected on the emergence of the Ku Klux Klan. His portrait of the so-called "Invisible Empire of the South" presented a fearful and childlike black race. "It threw the negroes into a very ecstasy of panic to see these sheeted 'Ku Klux' move near them in the shrouded night; and their comic fear stimulated the lads who excited it to many an extravagant prank and mummery." As the objective of the Klan moved from mummery to "silenc[ing] or driv[ing] from the country" the members of the Reconstruction regime, white and black, they found that "[t]he negroes were generally easy enough to deal with: a thorough fright usually disposed them to make utter submission, resign their parts in affairs, leave the country, – do anything their ghostly visitors demanded." Those white men who were allies to the freedpeople and were also targeted by the Klan "were less tractable." Wilson acknowledges that not all black people dissolved into "utter submission," but in a back-handed manner that suggests the exception proves the rule: "and here and there even a negro ignored or defied them."[46]

Wilson's description reflects the mingling of comedy and terror, and the production of comedy from terror, entailed in the tactics of the Ku Klux Klan during Reconstruction and its depiction in the press. Comic sketches of the Klan terrifying gullible black people proliferated in anti-Republican papers. Though such stories often centered on "false alarms" – in which skittish black characters are scared into insensibility by what they take to be the Klan but in which they come to no harm – they were often printed alongside reports of actual Klan violence. Thus, Andrew Silver argues, they "served both to condition the reception of terror as comic and to temper the tone of articles detailing real instances of Klan torture and murder." The differentiation between the comic vignettes and the news of actual terrorism was blurred by the fact that articles reporting real acts of terror committed by the Klan were often written in a humorous tone, focusing on "black fright and flight as the primary means of evoking laughter."[47]

In her centennial history of Anderson County, Pauline Buck Hohes offered an account of Reconstruction that also filtered terrorism through comical anecdote of black flight, transforming the struggle to define a new political and social order into white men's easy chastisement of an inept and wayward race. While black freedom is presented as holding real menace, the ability of the county's white men to re-establish racial discipline is not seriously threatened:

> The negroes, liberated and given the rights of citizenship were inclined to become a menace to civilization. Unlettered and their imagination fired with their new importance, to live amongst them promised to prove dangerous. The misguided sympathy felt for them by Republicans led to measures being taken that were galling to the South and harmful to the negro himself.

Buck Hohes offers the standard early twentieth-century Lost Cause narrative of Reconstruction. The trouble was provoked by "carpetbaggers," immoral Northern white men looking to manipulate "the negroes" for their own gain, who swarmed into Texas. Conflating the desire for political life and citizenship with an unspecified danger to white women, she writes that as the "negroes were instructed to their rights, etc" it "grew hazardous for white women to walk the streets alone." Thus, the white men of the South were prompted to take matters into their own hands, organizing the "famous Ku Klux Klan" in order to address the menace.[48]

Rather than detailing the murder, assault, and sexual terror deployed to subjugate the freed population, Buck Hohes related a humorous "fright and flight" anecdote. George Mitchell, one of Anderson County's "leading citizens," described disciplining the black men who participated in the Loyal League, a grassroots organization that mobilized black voters.[49]

> We took long rolls of paper painted red and white and stuck them over the ears of our horses and put white paper masks on the horses' faces with holes for their eyes. Then we disguised ourselves in white with red dunce caps and set out to intercept the negroes on their way to the lodge ... When we were ready to try our scheme, I took cayenne pepper and put some in the nose of each horse. You should have heard the snorting! Then we charged out into the road, right into the midst of the procession of Loyal Leaguers. The result was the breaking of the meetings permanently.[50]

In contrast to the Texas pioneers' terrible and bloody clashes between savage Indians and barbarous Mexicans, the work of disenfranchising black men is not imagined as masculine heroics but as easy punishment administered to insolent racial children.

While the ostensibly light-hearted anecdote effaces the blood of Reconstruction, Buck Hohes's stern certainty in asserting the necessity of punishment leaves the traces of the terrorism she carefully seeks to soften:

> Today, after more than seventy years has passed, it is still felt that the step taken was necessary and wholesome for the negroes themselves. By its means the negroes were intimidated. They calmed down and behaved, and in time the new relations between ex-slave and former master adjusted themselves and the two races found that they could live and work harmoniously in the same section without either harming or imposing on the other.[51]

Just as Buck Hohes blurs the terror of Reconstruction violence, she erases the killing in Slocum from her account of Anderson County history altogether, though her account covers the years in which it took place. In what is said and what is not said, she tacitly admits and fundamentally denies black citizenship. Black people's liberation and exercise of political rights are designated a harmful imposition on the white race and a threat to civilization. The supposed "harmonious" relations that prevail when "the negroes ... calmed down" clearly entail subordination. And yet, though she details the killing of rebellious slaves, as well as marauding Indians and Mexicans in the lost but seminal days of frontier life, white citizens' mass killing of fellow citizens, either during Reconstruction or in 1910, could not apparently be made palatable for inclusion in this celebratory account of the county's history. Nevertheless, the recollection of white men's "wholesome" punishment of black impudence reasserts underlying relations of power upon which black people in the twentieth century must carefully tread.

Twentieth-century discourses of extermination and extinction

From the end of the nineteenth century, social scientists produced theories of black race that gave a new context to racist violence. As noted in the Introduction, numerous scientists began to suggest that outside of the protective care of slavery, America's black population were degenerating, physically, mentally, and morally. In his much-cited statistical work *The Race Traits and Tendencies of the American Negro*, German statistician Frederick Hoffman predicted that the black race was on track to die out gradually, "unless a fundamental change takes place." Charting black and white rates of scrofula, venereal disease, yellow fever, cancer, intemperance, and so on, across various U.S. states, the Caribbean, and colonial Sierra Leone, Hoffman concluded that the "excessive mortality" of the black race was rooted "not in the *conditions of life*, but in *the race traits and tendencies*." Key among the race traits in question was the "immense amount of immorality" among

Negroes. Indeed, the "downward tendencies of the colored race," he asserted, "can only be arrested by radical and far-reaching changes in their moral nature." Hoffman's assessment of the situation rearticulates the "self-help" ethos of free labor ideology through the prism of race science. If they were to survive, the black race must stop "clamoring for aid and assistance from the white race" and take charge of their own evolutionary trajectory to become sexually continent, thrifty, and economically efficient.[52] It was a matter of concern for all Americans, Hoffman suggested, as "races ... on the downward grade ... have invariably become useless if not dangerous factors in the social as well as political economy of nations."[53]

Other sociological and popular theories offered concepts of "excessive mortality" from a different angle, asserting that black racial abnormality incited deadly white fury. In a paper examining whether "race friction between blacks and whites" was inevitable, Mississippi sociologist Alfred Stone argued in 1907 that "racial antipathy" was "practically universal on the part of the white race toward the negro" and was particularly strong in its Anglo-Saxon branch. The institution of slavery engineered the white and black races into relations of "mutual amity," a harmony made possible through the symbiosis of white mastery and black acceptance, which held antipathy at bay; but race hatred naturally reasserted itself when this institutionalized hierarchy between races was dissolved and black men sought citizenship. The "essential elements" of race friction, Stone argues, were "a demand for and a denial of racial equality." Like Hoffman, Stone used a transnational framework to demonstrate black abnormality. Surveying the examples of Jamaica and South Africa, he asserted:

> [T]he white man when confronted with a sufficient number of negroes to create in his mind a sense of political unrest or danger, either alters his form of government to be rid of the incubus, or destroys the political strength of the negro by force, by evasion, or by direct action.[54]

In 1903, Thomas Dixon delivered essentially the same sentiments in popular form in a public lecture in Cleveland, Ohio. The time was growing near, he asserted, when the black race would no longer be needed. When "the presence of the negro becomes burdensome to the white man ... the latter will try to suppress the negro. The negro will resent this, and war in its most horrible forms will ensue." The war, however, would not be an equal contest; for "the negro, it will be a fight for existence." There were already counties in the South, he pointed out, where the white people had staged "uprisings" to drive the black people out. When asked by an audience member whether he was speaking literally or figurative about race war, Dixon answered ominously, "There can be no misinterpretation of my words." The "sanguinary race war" he foresaw "will blot out thousands of lives" and force "the negro" from the continent altogether. The only way to avoid the torrent of bloodshed would be for black people to leave the country voluntarily.[55]

White commentators offering much less dramatic assessments of racialized violence also seemed to presume the natural tendency for white men to lash out at "negroes." After a spate of rumors across the South about "Before Day clubs," secret black organizations imagined to plot the nocturnal murder of white people, an observer in Florida lamented that the

> lawlessness of one or two negroes in a community is made an excuse of suspecting that all negroes in that community are banded together to do an injury of some sort to white people. As a general thing there are always a few hot-headed white men who want to make a raid on the negroes.[56]

Likewise, the Anderson County sheriff's description of the Slocum killers as "just a hot-headed gang" disparages the men's lack of self-control, their reckless brutality, but also naturalizes the violence as the unrestrained passion of white men.

Like Alfred Stone, James E. Cutler, a Northern sociologist who wrote a history of lynching in the United States and acted as a consultant to military intelligence on the subject of "Negro subversion," also theorized that the presence of the black race drove white men to violence. Rather than obnoxious demands for racial equality, Cutler identified the problem as an abnormal black criminality that subverted the conventional restraints of advanced civilization. The attempt to apply a judicial system developed for "a highly civilized and cultured race" to an inferior race, Cutler posited, had led to the breakdown of law and order in the management of Negro crime. The government should have instead made "special provision for the control of the negro population in the Southern States" after slavery.[57] It was the white man's inability "to understand the motives, impulses and characteristics resulting in heinous crimes by negroes" that led to the lynch mob's unfortunate adoption of torture, burning, and cruelty to punish these crimes. Cutler reflected:

> The fact is lost sight of that the colored race in the United States is a child race, in the sense that it is attempting to accomplish by absorption in the course of a generation or two, all that the white race has been able to develop and establish only after centuries of effort.[58]

In administering justice to black people, white people had acted similarly to "the unreasonable father" who laid down rules for a child as if that child had the maturity of an adult, "and then punishes him with capricious and savage severity when he disobeys or fails to attain the standard that has been set for him."[59] The muckraking Northern journalist Ray Stannard Baker passionately condemned lynching as an act of savagery that "brought the white man down to the lowest level of the criminal negro." He also evoked the white man as a father figure to the black race. Given that all the responsibilities and powers of government both in the North and the South and the entire apparatus of justice was in white hands, he exclaimed, "How keen is the need, then, of calmness and strict justice in dealing with the Negro!" Arguing that white men's participation in lynching only further inculcated criminality in the Negro who saw that murder continually went unpunished, he asserted, "A criminal father is a poor preacher of homilies to a wayward son."[60] Whatever warmth the relations of father and son might connote, the analogy also emphasized the ultimate weakness of the underdeveloped black race before the dreadful power of the manhood of the white race.

These notions of black degeneracy and disturbance permeate the white media coverage of the massacre in Slocum. Even the press that dismissed the uprising story and condemned the violence rearticulated a black civilizational deficit, subtly reasserting black racial guilt even while they lamented the innocence of some or all of the victims. For example, the *Houston Post* reported that the local consensus was that "there were a few negroes in the community who deserved punishment for recent minor misdeeds" – these vague "misdeeds" remain unnamed – though it was clear now that no uprising had occurred and a "grave mistake had been made." In an article reprinted in the national magazine *Literary Digest*, the *Houston Chronicle* decried the "indiscriminate butchery of negroes because of some crime committed by an individual member of the race":

> With all the faults of the individuals the negro race is not a bad race. Fidelity, loyalty and courage are not uncommon traits. And the negro is the satellite of the white man. You could not drive him away from the white man, in whose shadow he flourishes, and the white race is not yet ready to dispense with the negro; certainly it cannot afford to dispense with him by the assassination route.[61]

Again, the author does not state which crime had been committed by an "individual member of the race" in this case. However, while "indiscriminate butchery of negroes" is denounced, the suggestion that "some crime" had been committed, as well as the reference to "all the faults of the individuals," insinuates an underlying problem of black guilt. Ominously, while the "assassination route" is rejected as a workable option, it is nonetheless articulated as a possibility.

Also in the *Literary Digest*, a *Boston Globe* writer warned that violence driven by "insensate negrophobia" would create deep and long-lasting rifts. The "worst enemy of the South," the writer declared, "is the professional negro-hater who indiscriminately assails a race for the misdeeds of a few of its members."[62] The writer, like their Houston-based colleague, does not attempt to specify what "misdeeds" might have been committed that resulted in the murder of the people of Slocum. However, the familiar assumption that "a few" were guilty of something implicitly confirms white violence as a response, albeit brutal and excessive, to supposed manifestations of black abnormality. Like other American newspapers, the *Globe* could be relied upon to demonstrate that some "negro," somewhere, was guilty of, and being punished for, something. In the discourse around Slocum and, as we will see, in discussions of the pogrom in East St. Louis and the Houston Mutiny seven years later, ostensibly unrelated stories of blackness – whether accounts of the acts of rape, murder, or conspiracy supposedly perpetrated by black people, accounts of lynching, massacres, or expulsions perpetrated against them, or, as was frequently the case, some mixture of both – were physically clustered together on the same newspaper pages, textually mingling black guilt and black suffering, white endangerment and white wrath.

In the few days that Slocum occupied the national gaze, the stories of killing were published alongside stories of black men being lynched, "hunted," or expelled in other parts of the country.[63] Though editors did not draw explicit verbal links between the stories, their proximity made clear their imagined relationship. Negroes everywhere raped and brutalized. Negroes everywhere were abjectly subject to extreme violence and bodily punishment. The *Boston Globe*'s reporting on August 2 is illustrative of the symbiotic construction. Underneath its story that eight white men had been arrested for the Slocum murders ("Eight Negroes Killed") were a series of unrelated reports of black people pursued or executed from around the South. In Mobile, Alabama, a posse led by the local sheriff had a "negro," accused of assaulting a white woman, "surrounded in a marsh, whither he was trailed by bloodhounds." Then came: "Another Negro Shot" in Defuniak, Florida, bringing the estimated "number of negroes lynched" in that city for the alleged assault and murder of a white child to four. And finally, an account from Pelham, Georgia, of black men shot by police: "One Negro Dead, One More Dying."[64] Thus, the violent death of the people in Slocum, "innocent and unarmed," was linked to the destruction and imminent death of black men hunted, lynched, and shot by law enforcement for rape, murder, and disorder. Dangerous bestial blackness, hunted and punished, and helpless blackness, hunted and tormented, are implicitly presented as variant expressions of the same "Negro Problem."

Battles and black generals

Over the course of the three days that it occupied national attention, the massacre in Slocum was told through a shifting range of narratives, often in the same newspapers. Before the county sheriff issued the statement clarifying that a massacre rather than a "race war" had transpired, there was a spate of stories imagining dramatic pitched battles. Before the narrative shifted from the theme "race war" to "butchery," a number of stories produced striking images of threatening black masculinity. The *New York Sun* observed that these Negroes were the "new generation who refuse to accept white domination." Peace had been difficult to maintain, the *Sun* told its readers, because many of the white men in the area were from the "North and West where they are unaccustomed to handling negroes."[65] The black men in these stories were presented as virile and organized, if outmatched. In its vivid picture of the "Races at War," the *Herald* described "a camp of 300 negroes, each armed and thirsting for vengeance for the killing of twenty-four of their number in clashes with white men last night." Opposing these "armed and vengeful blacks" were newly arrived Texas soldiers and an encampment of 200 or 300 white men. While there was a momentary peace at the time of writing, "the black men declare there will be more fighting" and they met the white men's attempts to "parley" with bullets.[66] The *Chicago Tribune* increased the numbers of combatants considerably, asserting that 500 white men were "giving battle" to 1,000 black men. The black fighters were "generaled by a giant fanatic of their own race who rides back along their battle line, shouting encouragement to his men and defying the concentrated fire of the entire force of whites."[67]

In several of the narratives that presented the killings as a battle, out-of-state writers depicted a frontier imagery. An Oregon paper described the "desperate race war" in the "Lone Star State" with language reminiscent of that used in previous decades to describe "Indian attacks": "three hundred armed negroes terrorize the settlers." A paper in Arkansas reported that the "whites were superior … [in] arms and leadership," soon routing "the blacks," but that the latter were nevertheless "well armed, and being led by some of the most daring blacks of the Southwest … it is believed that only the arrival of the militia will prevent further bloodshed."[68] In New York it was reported that "Some two hundred country negroes took to the warpath."[69] A more florid account likened the conflict to the rugged masculine adventures of settlement: "All of Texas is aroused. Not since the days when Mexican marauders swept across the border or when the Texas rangers fought pitched battles with 'bad men' has feeling and excitement run so high."[70] The *Palestine Herald* singled out this particular narrative as an example of the "lying reports" being produced by outsiders, suggesting a distinct discomfort with imagined black militias being inserted into the state's romantic mythology of masculine frontier warfare.

The unmissable theme throughout the Slocum discourse, even within these stories of armed black defiance, was the impending doom of the black men. The whole countryside was aroused and "an attempt to exterminate the negroes was feared."[71] Though the *Chicago Inter Ocean* claimed that black men were "reported to have expressed their intention of cleaning out the entire white community," the fate of the white community is assured: "Whites are flocking to Slocum determined to wipe out every negro in the neighborhood." In this endeavor they were making considerably more progress than their opponents:

> Within a short time after the first row the whites of the entire country about had started a war of extermination against the negroes. Scores of blacks were pursued by mobs. In some instances they barricaded themselves in their settlements; when captured they were shot to death or lynched.[72]

The dynamic here reflects a broader tumultuous oscillation in the telling of Slocum across place and across the few days in which it made national headlines. While the emphasis on black vulnerability became much more pronounced on August 1, with many papers carrying the comments of Sheriff Black that the "negroes were being hunted like sheep," even in reports describing a "war" and the Negro conspiracy to "clean out all the whites," the scale of black dying was always told as greater than that of "the whites." This confidence in the supposedly inevitable outcome of "race war" would be deeply shaken seven years later, as I will discuss in Chapter 4.

Sowing and reaping

In their petition to President Taft, cited at the outset of this chapter, the Colored Ministers Union were restrained, particularly in relation to the interventions of other black observers, discussed below. However, their warning that, if left unchecked, the violence of Texas could signal the imminent "destruction of our nation" also places the specter of a reckoning on the horizon, a recurring theme in the discourse of race violence. On the eve of the Civil War, Frederick Douglass offered an apocalyptic forecast for a nation that built itself on bondage. "The republic has put one end of the chain upon the ankle of the bondman, and the other around its own neck." While the land was now poised to "weep and howl, amid ten thousand desolations brought upon it by the sins of two centuries," the nation might be purified, if the slaves' "cry of vengeance" were incorporated into the fight for the Union.[73] The clear implication of Douglass's warning, however, is to remind his audience of the potential of the oppressed Negro both to build and to destroy.

Thirty-three years later and near death, Douglass contemplated the hell unleashed on an emancipated people in a nation that had "fallen in love" with naming its own brutality, lawlessness, apathy, and prejudice a "Negro problem." One again he invoked the biblical image of the man who chained the ankle of his fellow without heeding that the other end of the chain was about his own neck. In their statement on Slocum addressed to the president and the American people, the Colored Ministers Union emphasized their long friendship with the white people of the South. In his essay on lynching, Douglass did not temper his warning. He gave white readers the prospect of a whirlwind of destruction:

> As we sow we shall reap, is a lesson that will be learned here as elsewhere. We tolerated slavery and it has cost us a million graves, and it may be that lawless murder now raging, if permitted to go on, may yet bring the red hand of vengeance, not only on the revered head of age, and upon the heads of helpless women, but even the innocent babes in the cradle.[74]

After the lesson of a million dead had gone unheeded, black violence is not promised as a regenerative force that might cleanse the nation of blood but one that will simply destroy. Unlike the cleansing violence wielded by free and militarized black men that Douglass imagined in 1862, here the "red hand of vengeance" is not tied to self-actualized manhood but disembodied; it is voracious rather than regenerative. The terrible imagery – "even the innocent babes in the cradle" – recalls the familiar horrors of imagined slave uprising. Here vengeance is not the senseless expression of black barbarism but the tragedy of civilization's violence turned in upon itself.

Like their white counterparts, the editorial staff of the African American newspaper the *Chicago Defender* used considerable imagination in reporting the violence at Slocum. They described a thrilling battle scene under the headline "200 Whites [were] Killed and Many Wounded":

> The white had been so cruel in their treatment towards the Negroes that it became unbearable. [The Negroes] were forced to protect themselves, they organized 300 strong and demanded to be let alone and treated as peaceful citizens. The whites had started what they called a war of extermination and the fight was on. These sturdy farm hands proved to be real men and it would have been the extermination of the domineering whites had not the state militia been called out, [and] of course they joined their brethren, the white. Then the Negroes gave them a taste of what a black man can do when goaded to it; they fought a pitched battle, 300 Negroes against 1,500 whites. The Negroes entrenched themselves and 15,000 could not have taken those entrenchments had their ammunition not have gave out, and even then the single ones among them held the works until the married men had made good their retreat. Then and not till then did they surrender. Thus proving their unflinching manhood, and loyalty when the test was made. The estimate loss of whites killed and fatally wounded reached the 200 mark while the Negroes lost but 30 all told. Those taken prisoners were 120 single men, the others are free, thanks to the willing sacrifice of their comrades. We are all awaiting the fate of those captured in this land of barbarians of ancient days.[75]

They inverted the dynamics of the white papers; in their account the black men were vastly outnumbered by white men, and the white dead vastly outnumbered the black. Rather than a single "fanatic" general, the black men are uniformly "unflinching," the sacrifice of the single men and the sense of familial duty of the married men demonstrating not just bravery but the highest standard of moral manhood.

The location of the conflict, and the reader, in "this land of barbarians of ancient days" historically reorders the standard racialized teleology of American nationhood. Unlike the previously examined narratives which situated the violence as an episode of white men's ongoing struggle to manage a discordant race, or as latter-day eruption of the nation's wild frontier, the *Defender* thus places black men as a vanguard of civilizing violence in a terrain of pre-modern white barbarity. While the image of disciplined, orderly, martial black manhood contrasts with the shapeless force of vengeance Douglass foresaw, the *Defender* article nevertheless notably projects the agency of its "real men" beyond self-defense. Goaded into action, the "whirlwind" of black manly energy would have spelled the "extermination of the whites" if it had not been checked by the forces of the state. The constructed fears of black conspiracy and white slaughter are recast as the vanquishing of peaceful citizenry over domination. Unlike Douglass and the Colored Ministers Union, the *Defender* writer did not prophesy a possible future of destruction if mob rule was not contained but imagined a completed feat of black retribution. Though it reorders the standard anti-black narratives of the white press, this fantasy retelling of the massacre mirrors the white press in erasing the actual victims and survivors from narrative view.

The *Defender's* inventive narrative dramatized a sense of defiance more widely articulated. Echoing the image of morally upright and unbending black manhood, a black speaker from Savannah told his Boston audience that black men should "go forth with a Bible in one hand and a six-shooter in the other." Branding the speech a "violation of hospitality and the law," the *Boston Globe* condemned this "prophet of racial warfare," advocating instead the "calm fortitude, wise avoidance and noiseless perseverance of Booker T. Washington" as the only acceptable means for black people to slowly erode the "huge mountain of prejudice" against them.[76] At least one black reader was incensed by the *Globe*'s censure. "Do you advise patient annihilation?" the anonymous writer demanded in a letter to the editor. "Would you in Massachusetts stand for such outrages? Do you indorse the Texas butchery? What is fair for one is equally fair for the other. Unless you put down the outrages by law the negro by every right of manhood must defend himself at any cost."

The response of the *Globe*'s editor to this "colored citizen of Boston" is telling. "We had no intention of denying to any man, black or white, the universal right of self-defense," the editor asserted, but rather had only ventured to offer black people the "warning of experience." The experience the editor wished his black readers to remember was their own. From "the evil day they were dragged from their native forests down to the latest lynching," "brute force" had been at the root of all of black people's misfortune. The writer confirms the inevitability of anti-black violence, implicitly asserting the irreconcilable racial distance from those around them: "[negroes] continue to be in a conflict where overwhelming numbers are against them." The particularity of the Negro's historical and racial circumstances, then, considerably tempered the initially asserted "universality" of the manhood right to defense.

> While the negro should be jealous of his rights, he must beware of brooding over his wrongs. If he will only compare himself with himself, instead of with a people who had the start of him by several centuries in the slow and arduous ascent of the heights of independence and education, he will find much to rejoice for and everything to hope for at the hands of Father Time.

While the editor wants to assure "the negro" that he can hope to achieve full civilized humanity, his current lag in this regard is stark and definitive. Though acknowledging the "many and burdensome grievances" black people suffered, the suggestion that their resolution would be found in the "hands of Father Time" intimates that as they come closer to the standards of white civilization, they will cease to be subject to white violence.

Those who could be found

In 1984, G.J. Hayes, a white man born in 1910, described the traces of the massacre that haunted his childhood. Troubled by the silence around the killings, Hayes lobbied the county historical commission to install a marker at the site of the massacre. "I know you know there is a plaque about the Indian Massacre in which 3 people were killed," he wrote. "What you don't have that I am sure many of the white people are very much ashamed of is that a much greater massacre occurred which you do not mention." His father, a local doctor who had sheltered a black woman in the family's attic during the killing, insisted that the number of dead was far higher than eighteen. Eighteen was a number "put out by the whites who became extremely ashamed of themselves and had to play it down." Hayes also claimed that the father of a childhood friend had ridden with the killing mob. When this man found out that the uprising was "a false alarm," Hayes wrote, he committed suicide. Others seemed less troubled. Decades after the killing, Hayes spoke to two men who told him that they had dug a pit in a local playground and buried eight or nine people in it, knowing that the children's play would "wipe out the evidence of them being buried."[77]

As Monica Muñoz has pointed out, the administrators of official public memory in twentieth-century Texas "marked the landscape with racially coded narratives of progress," erecting markers at sites where Native Americans carried out raids and massacres against white settlers.[78] The commemoration of setter martyrdom enshrined the innocence of white pioneers and thus sanctified their bloody and triumphant struggle to create nation out of nature. Whether or not Hayes was correct in reading shame into silence, the white brutality that left uncounted black dead was difficult to assimilate into national narratives of civilization's generative violence. For many white observers, the pogrom was rationalized as a lamentable outcome of the tendency of "hot-headed" white men to lash out in frenzy, or the unfortunate lack of development of the black race, or the inevitably violent combination of the two. For black observers, the violence was another expression of the voracious force of unfreedom at the core of U.S. nationhood. In either case, if "Indian massacres" confirmed the righteousness of the civilization settlers wrought from the wilderness, the murders at Slocum betrayed a disturbing wilderness corroding civilization from within.

Two days after the killing, the *Houston Post* published a brisk description of the arrangements underway in Anderson County for the mass burial of "the bodies of those negroes who could be found" in a common, unmarked grave. The article noted that many of the white people, apparently still uneasy, planned to spend another night under guard in the schoolhouses. It predicted, however, that "[t]omorrow is expected to see the last vestige of the trouble – one of the bloodiest in the history of Texas – wiped completely away." In the early hours of the morning, a small group of black men under the supervision of Texas Rangers dug a burial trench at the property of Dick Wilson, a victim of the massacre, in which an unspecified number of victims were buried. This action was necessitated, the *Post* commented, by the interests of public health. What forces of corruption might be unleashed by the bodies of the dead were the "vestiges" of white men's killing not "wiped completely away"? "Despite the efforts of these volunteers," the *Post* noted,

> not all of the victims' bodies were found. In many cases, relatives of the negroes discovered the whereabouts of a body and dragged it to a secluded spot during the hours of the night. On account of the fact that several bodies have been disposed of, the exact number of negroes killed will never be known.

White death, on the other hand, was, as ever, reassuringly quantifiable: "No white man was injured during the trouble."[79] The description of the families' actions as a "disposal" and the discussion of mass burial as a "public health" matter belie the weight of the crime committed. Indeed, it is the actions of "the negroes' relatives," the article suggests, that prevent a full accounting of the killing. That none of the papers printing accounts of "dead negroes just scattered around everywhere" or of "poor barefooted fugitives" fleeing from the white mob sought to find out the names, ages, or biographies of the dead, that the Attorney General was apparently content for their remains to be disappeared in an unmarked grave, demonstrate the deep national ambivalence to black suffering. Nevertheless, the actions of these people who searched in the night in a landscape of terror to recover the bodies of their loved ones from the forces of murder and erasure emanate through the language that seeks to deny their meaning.

Notes

1 Frederick Douglass, *Why Is the Negro Lynched? Reprinted with Permission from the Ame Church Review for Memorial Distribution, by a Few of His English Friends* (Bridgewater: John Whitby and Sons, 1895), 14, 12, 13.
2 "Race riot in Texas," August 1, 1910, *Times-Democrat*, 8. The day before, the paper had approvingly reported how a group of "infuriated citizens" had "avenged [a] girl's death" by lynching two black men. "Girl's Death Is Avenged," July 31, 1910, *Times-Democrat*, 1.
3 Smith, *American Body Politics*, 3.
4 Muhammad, *The Condemnation of Blackness*, 53, 85.
5 Pauline Buck Hohes, *A Centennial History of Anderson County Texas* (San Antonio: Naylor Company, 1936), vii, 5.
6 Ibid., 50.
7 Bills, *The 1910 Slocum Massacre*, 13–16. "Situation in Hand, the Law Effective," August 1, 1910, *Palestine Daily Herald*, 1. E.R. Bills has written the only full-length monograph on the Slocum Massacre. It gives a detailed account of the local conflicts leading up to the killing, including the names of the individual actors involved and the amount of the promissory note. Bills worked with Constance Hollie-Jawaid, the great-granddaughter of Alex Holley who was killed in the massacre, as well as other descendants of victims, to pressure the Texas State Historical Commission to erect a marker commemorating the killing. David Martin Davies, "Slocum Massacre Texas Historic Marker Dedicated," January 18, 2016, on Texas Public Radio, www.tpr.org/post/slocum-massacre-texas-historic-marker-dedicated (accessed February 1, 2021).
8 "Negroes Shot by Whites in Wild Frenzy," August 1, 1910, *Shreveport Times*, 3. Bills, *The 1910 Slocum Massacre*, 12–13.
9 "Race Riot Near Palestine, Texas; Eighteen Negroes Reported Killed," July 31, 1910, *Shreveport Times*, 1.

10 "Race War, 27 Dead," July 31, 1910, *Baltimore Sun*, 1. "Negroes Are Killed in Texas Race Riot," July 31, 1910, *Los Angeles Times*, 1.
11 Mississippi congressman B.G. Humphrey reflected on the unfortunate differences between "the negro who grew to manhood in slavery and the negro who has grown to manhood in freedom" in an article titled "Faithful Old Slaves; Degenerate Progeny." Blight, *Race and Reunion*, 284.
12 "Bloodthirsty Mob in Texas," August 1, 1910, *Paducah Sun* (Paducah, KY), 8. Excerpts of Black's statement were printed in numerous papers around the country, including the *New York Times* and the *Washington Herald*.
13 "Bloodthirsty Mob in Texas," August 1, 1910, *Paducah Sun*, 8.
14 The grand jury determined that "seven negroes ... and no white men" had been killed during the trouble. There was insufficient evidence to make charges for the murders of John Hayes and Alex Holley. "Seven Men Are Indicted on Charge of Murder," August 18, 1910, *Palestine Daily Herald*, 3. Bills, *The 1910 Slocum Massacre*, 68–69.
15 Ibid., 81, 83.
16 "4 Rioters Arrested," *Evening Sun* (Baltimore, MD), August 1, 1910, 1. "Score of Negroes Killed by Whites," July 31, 1910, *New York Times*, 1. "Not Race War: Just Murder," August 1, 1910, *New York Sun*, 1. Given that several hundred white men were involved and that the killing went on for several days, Bills suggests that the number of victims could be in the hundreds. Bills, *The 1910 Slocum Massacre*, 117. In 2019, the descendants of the victims continued to face resistance from residents to their efforts to uncover mass graves. The Texas State Historical Commission would only agree to name eight victims on the historical marker. Michael Barajas, "Where the Bodies Are Buried," *Texas Observer*, July 15, 2019, www.texasobserver.org/where-the-bodies-are-buried (accessed February 1, 2021).
17 "Reports Denounced by Palestine Citizens," August 3, 1910, *Palestine Daily Herald*, 3. "Situation in Hand, the Law Effective," August 1, 1910, *Palestine Daily Herald*, 4. The front-page story in the *Herald* on the same date was "No Votes for Negroes," about the disenfranchisement of 14,000 "illiterate negroes" in Oklahoma.
18 "The Newest 'Race Riot,'" August 4, 1910, *New York Age*, 4.
19 Ida B. Wells, *The Red Record* (Cirencester: Echo Library, 2005). "The Day," December 12, 1876, *Newport Daily News* (Newport, RI), 2.
20 Elaine Frantz Parsons, "Klan Skepticism and Denial in Reconstruction-Era Public Discourse," *Journal of Southern History* 77, no. 1 (2011): 89–90. In the case of Slocum, it is revealing that a century later, Anderson County officials objected to the erection of the historical marker because of "lack of evidence." County Commissioner Greg Chapin commented that there was a lack of reliable evidence: "It's all hearsay ... Everything has contradicted itself totally ... as far as how many were killed – how many weren't killed. How many blacks. How many whites." Davies, "Slocum Massacre Texas Historic Marker Dedicated," Texas Public Radio.
21 "Score of Negroes Killed by Whites," July 31, 1910, *New York Times*, 1.

22 "As many slaves, so many enemies" is the observation made by the Roman philosopher and slaveholder Seneca. Orlando Patterson, *Slavery and Social Death* (Cambridge, MA: Harvard University Press, 1982), 339.
23 "Perfect Peace Preserved," August 5, 1910, *Seattle Republican*, 1.
24 Jerry Sadler and James Neyland, *Politics, Fat-Cats and Honey-Money Boys: The Mem-Wars of Jerry Sadler* (Santa Monica, CA: Roundtable Publishing, 1984), 7–8. Bills, *The 1910 Slocum Massacre*, 77.
25 "The Dead Buried," August 1, 1910, *Houston Post*, 1–2.
26 "Negroes Shot by Whites in Wild Frenzy," August 1, 1910, *Shreveport Times*, 3.
27 Craig Thompson Friend, "'The Crushing of Southern Manhood': War, Masculinity, and the Confederate Nation State, 1861–1865," in *Masculinities and the Nation in the Modern World: Between Hegemony and Marginalization*, ed. Pablo Dominguez Andersen and Simon Wendt (New York: Palgrave Macmillan, 2015), 23.
28 Orlando Patterson, *Rituals of Blood: Consequences of Slavery in Two American Centuries* (Washington, D.C.: Civitas/CounterPoint, 1999), 191. See also Alan Taylor, *The Internal Enemy: Slavery and War in Virginia, 1772–1832* (New York: W.W. Norton & Company, 2013). Vesey was the leader of a planned insurrection in South Carolina and executed in July of 1822.
29 Andrew Torget, *Seeds of Empire: Cotton, Slavery, and the Transformation of the Texas Borderlands, 1800–1850* (Chapel Hill: University of North Carolina Press, 2015), 154–55.
30 Buck Hohes, *A Centennial History of Anderson County Texas*, 236.
31 William W. White, "The Texas Slave Insurrection of 1860," *Southwestern Historical Quarterly* 52, no. 3 (1949): 280–81.
32 Trouillot, *Silencing the Past*, 83.
33 Foner, *Reconstruction*, 120, 122–23.
34 Litwack, *Been in the Storm so Long*, 425–72. Rable, *But There Was No Peace*, 23–24.
35 Litwack, *Been in the Storm so Long*, 426.
36 "The Alabama Warning," December 19, 1867, *Home Journal* (Winchester, TN), 1.
37 Litwack, *Been in the Storm so Long*, 428. On black people's struggle for land during Reconstruction, see James S. Allen, "The Struggle for Land During the Reconstruction Period," *Science & Society* 1, no. 3 (1937).
38 Caroline Emberton, *Beyond Redemption: Race, Violence and the American South* (Chicago: University of Chicago Press, 2013), 187–88. On some white Southerners' "eagerness" for black extinction, see also Litwack, *Been in the Storm so Long*, 276.
39 Rable, *But There Was No Peace*, 23.
40 "Bogey-Bugaboo!" November 7, 1910, *Charleston Daily News* (Charleston, SC), 2.
41 Foner, *Reconstruction*, 430.
42 Ibid., 120, 122–23.

43 James Smallwood, Barry A. Crouch, and Larry Peacock, *Murder and Mayhem: The War of Reconstruction in Texas*, 1st ed. (College Station: Texas A&M University Press, 2003), 43, 112. Barry A. Crouch, "A Spirit of Lawlessness: White Violence; Texas Blacks, 1865–1868," *Journal of Social History* 18, no. 2 (1984): 224.
44 Albion Tourgee, *A Fool's Errand, by One of the Fools* (New York: Fords, Howard, & Hulbert, 1880), 211–12. Litwack, *Been in the Storm so Long*, 436–37. Emberton, *Beyond Redemption*, 166.
45 Fortune, *Black and White*, 166–67.
46 Wilson, *A History of the American People*, 60, 65.
47 Andrew Silver, *Minstrelsy and Murder: The Crisis of Southern Humor, 1835–1925* (Baton Rouge: Louisiana State University Press, 2006), 56–57. This tradition was still apparent in 1910. As it described the carnage in Slocum, the *Houston Post* included an account of one victim who had supposedly been "scared to death." Instead of offering easily attainable details about actual victims, this fabrication, clearly designed to undercut both the ferocity of white terrorism as well as the tragedy of black people's deaths, was given its own subheading: "Negro Dies of Fright." "The Dead Buried," August 1, 1910, *Houston Post*, 1–2.
48 Buck Hohes, *A Centennial History of Anderson County Texas*, 52. Crouch writes that only a small portion of the more than 1,5000 recorded instances of anti-black violence were committed by the Klan in Texas. Nearly 70 percent were perpetrated by individuals. Crouch, "A Spirit of Lawlessness," 220.
49 William L. Richter, *Historical Dictionary of the Civil War and Reconstruction*, 2nd ed. (Lanham, MD: Scarecrow Press, 2012), 665–66.
50 Buck Hohes, *A Centennial History of Anderson County Texas*, 52–53.
51 Ibid., 52.
52 Frederick L. Hoffman, "The Race Traits and Tendencies of the American Negro," *Publications of the American Economic Association* 11, no. 1, 2, and 3 (1896): 95, 328. Italics in original.
53 Ibid., viii.
54 Alfred A. Stone, "Is Race Friction Growing and Inevitable," *American Journal of Sociology* 13, no. 5 (1908): 686–87. For more on Stone's paper and its reception, see Muhammad, *The Condemnation of Blackness*, 84–85.
55 "Will Be Driven Out," February 23, 1903, *Akron Beacon Journal* (Akron, OH), 6.
56 "'Before Day' Clubs," September 24, 1904, *Miami News*, 4.
57 James Elbert Cutler, *Lynch-Law: An Investigation into the History of Lynching in the United States* (New York: Longmans, Green, and Co., 1905), 226.
58 J.E. Cutler, "Capital Punishment and Lynching," *Annals of the American Academy of Political and Social Science* 29 (1907): 183.
59 Ibid., 183, 274.
60 Bederman, *Manliness and Civilization*, 52. Ray Stannard Baker, *Following the Color Line: An Account of Negro Citizenship in the American Democracy* (New York: Doubleday, 1908), 215.
61 "The Texas Race Riot," August 13, 1910, *Literary Digest*, 41, no. 7 (1910): 226.

62 Ibid.
63 Reports of angry white people driving black people from their towns or counties also appeared regularly in the national press in the early twentieth century. On ethnic cleansing, see Elliot Jaspin, *Buried in the Bitter Waters: The Hidden History of Racial Cleansing in America* (New York: Basic Books, 2007). James W. Loewen, *Sundown Towns: A Hidden Dimension of American Racism* (New York: New Press, 2005). In 1910 the press reported the expulsion of the black populations of Coleman, Texas, "Negroes Driven from Texas Town by Race Rioters," April 25, 1910, *Los Angeles Herald*, 1; Davis, Oklahoma, "Drive Negroes out of Town," August 26, 1910, *Lindsay News* (Lindsay, OK), 1; and Delaware, Oklahoma, "Negroes Driven out of Delaware," August 28, 1910, *Morning Tulsa Daily World*, 1.
64 "Eight Whites in Texas Jail"; "Surrounded in a Marsh"; "Another Negro Shot"; "One Negro Dead, One More Dying," August 2, 1910, *Boston Globe*, 9.
65 "Fourteen Men Dead in Texas Race War," July 31, 1910, *New York Sun*, 1.
66 "Races at War," July 31, 1910, *Washington Herald*, 1.
67 "Texas Race War Costs 25 Lives," July 31, 1910, *Chicago Tribune*, 1.
68 "Bloody Race War in Texas," July 31, 1910, *Arkansas Democrat*, 1.
69 "Desperate Race War Breaks Out in Lone Star State and Rangers Rush to Scene," July 30, 1910, *Daily Capital Journal*, 1. This was published next to a story from New York about "Innocent Negroes Beaten" by a score of white men and boys armed with clubs because they "ventured into the surf" at Coney Island. "Fourteen Men Dead in Texas Race War," July 31, 1910, *New York Sun*, 1. The term "warpath" was also printed in the coverage of the *Detroit Free Press*. "18 Negroes Die in Riot," July 31, 1910, *Detroit Free Press*, 1.
70 "Race War in Texas," August 5, 1910 *Times-News* (Nephi, UT), 5; "Race War in Texas," August 4, 1910, *Spanish Fork Press* (Spanish Fork, UT), 4; "Bloody Race War Raging in Anderson County, Texas," July 31, 1910, *Jackson Daily News* (Jackson, MS), 1. "Investigating Hayti," July 31, 1910, *Jackson Daily News*, 1.
71 "Ten Negroes Are Killed in Texas Race Riots," July 30, 1910, *El Paso Herald*, 1.
72 "Score Killed in Race War; Towns Aflame," July 31, 1910, *Inter Ocean* (Chicago), 2.
73 Foner and Taylor, eds, *Frederick Douglass: Selected Speeches and Writings*, 450.
74 Douglass, *Why Is the Negro Lynched?*, 34–35.
75 "200 Whites Killed and Many Wounded in Race War in Texas," August 6, 1910, *Chicago Defender*, 1.
76 "Patience, Not the Pistol," August 3, 1910, *Boston Globe*, 6.
77 G.J. Hayes, letter to Eliza H. Bishop, March 2, 1984, Houston County Historical Commission, the Slocum Massacre, www.teachslocummassacre.org/telegrams-and-letters (accessed February 1, 2021).
78 Muñoz Martinez, *The Injustice Never Leaves You*, 244–45.
79 "The Dead Buried," *Houston Post*, August 1, 1910, 1–2. The *Post* mistakenly lists Dick Wilson's name as Willets. Bills, *The 1910 Slocum Massacre*, 22.

3

The Mexican has a country

On November 13, 1910, Mexican President Porfirio Díaz, then three decades into a seven-term presidency on the very brink of its demise, sent a telegram to U.S. President William Taft. It thanked Taft for his promise to "investigate the incident of the burning at the stake of the Mexican Rodriguez in Texas."[1] Ten days earlier, twenty-year-old Antonio Rodriguez had been taken from the jail in the town of Rock Springs by a mob of Texans who substituted a mesquite pyre and gasoline for a trial and sentence. Rodriguez was accused of killing a woman only ever identified in the press by her husband's name ("Mrs. Lem Henderson") or, in some cases, his occupation ("the wife of a local rancher"). It was not the burning itself that dominated Díaz's attention, but the explosion of anti-American riots that erupted when news of the incident reached Mexico. After meeting with Díaz, Henry Lane Wilson, the American ambassador to Mexico, reported to Washington that the Mexican president was "deeply grieved and very indignant," not at Rodriguez's murder but at the rioters' disregard of his authority. He was certain that "revolutionists," already conspiring against him in every section of the republic, were using the burning as a "convenient cloak" to incite further unrest. He promised to mercilessly repress any further anti-American demonstrations. New demonstrations seemed unlikely, Wilson noted, unless the Mexican populace should be further inflamed by fresh reports of an impending lynching in Oklahoma, where local posses were currently searching for a Mexican national accused of killing the local police chief.[2]

In the weeks after Antonio Rodriguez was burned alive in Texas, stories of Mexican rage filled U.S. papers. Beginning on the evening of November 8, Ambassador Wilson reported that a mob, which he estimated at more than 1,000, made up primarily of "university students, shopmen and the better class of artisans," took to the streets. Chanting "Death to the Yankees" and "Down with the gringos," they attacked the offices of an American-owned newspaper, before continuing on to the Mexican Foreign Office. The next day, the "incendiary speeches" and "tumultuous" marches continued. This time, Wilson claimed, demonstrators attacked American houses and businesses, "[insulting and maltreating] no less than a dozen American citizens," including his own son, who sustained minor injuries. When the demonstrators arrived at an establishment where an American flag was on display, they pulled it down, "tore it into pieces, trampled and spat on it" in front of a number of American citizens. "[D]uring the occurrence," Wilson noted, "no less than ten Mexican policemen stood by, mute and inactive witnesses of the outrage." Adding further to the insult, when the demonstrators convened in front of *El Diaro del Hogar*, an anti-government newspaper, to make yet more "inflammatory speeches," some of them posed for photographs with "torn portions of the American flag in their hands."[3]

President Taft sent a telegram to Díaz that he had the utmost confidence in the Mexican president's sincere desire to "allay all trouble between the two countries and in his determination to suppress unlawful violence or insults to American in Mexico," just as Taft's government would use "all efforts we can to punish our criminals in Texas."[4] American newspapers informed their readers of the "mob's" attack on the "Stars and Stripes" and the Mexican foreign minister promised that those guilty of "offering insult to the flag" would be punished.[5] That the offense of desecrating an American flag was indirectly likened to the offense of burning a Mexican person alive illustrates the highly uneven international terrain in which the conflict unfolded.

As an examination of protestors' statements and Mexican press around the lynching reveals, Mexicans were acutely sensitive to the racialized implications of their northern neighbor's peculiar "national folkways," as Walter White of the NAACP referred to lynching. The front-page editorial of the Catholic daily *El País* on November 8 wondered why no representative of the Mexican government had as yet raised their voice "about an act not only terribly cruel, brutal, iniquitous" but also "profoundly humiliating for the Mexican people; since as we know, this criminal act, which in the land of the yankee they call lynch law, only is applied to inferior and degenerate races." The Americans' lynching and the inaction of the Mexican state highlighted the humiliating gulf between the "special considerations that keep the yankee on Mexican soil and the degrading, cruel system faced by sons of Mexico on the other side of the Rio Bravo. This is a form of slavery even more frightening than the Roman conquest."[6] Notably, the editorial likened Mexicans' form of slavery to that practiced in the distant Roman Empire rather than the enslavement of Africans in the Americas, which would have rearticulated the linkage between the "sons of Mexico" and imagined racial degenerates.

That the national humiliation of the lynching was perceived to be more profound because of its association with "inferior races" – and one "inferior race" in particular – begins to reveal the shifting symbiosis between race and nation in the Americas. This is made clearer in another piece in *El País*. It commented that if an American were burned in any part of the Mexican Republic, 500 newspaper columns would be insufficient to describe all of the "hostile demonstrations and lamentable" excesses that would follow. It was time that Mexico's neighbors learned that "the rights of the Mexican in the eye of law and civilization are as good as those of an American." To emphasize the point, the writer reflected on the situation of "the negro," who was thus differentiated not only from "the Mexican" but also from "the American":

> The negro is lynched with impunity because he has no country. But the Mexican has a country and both in the human and brute creation the mother never stops to think of what strength she possesses when it is a question of defending her offspring. And this unreasoning impulse is what makes a mother sublime.[7]

Clearly "having a country" had practical significance. Mexican citizens victimized by mobs had recourse to diplomatic avenues of recompense and protection that African Americans did not, a fact that Americans, white and black, also commented upon.[8] After the lynching the *Springfield Republican* lamented the international headaches caused by "our white savages": "They have grown so accustomed to lynching Negroes, even by the slow torture of fire, that they recklessly use the method on foreigners who can justly claim the protection of treaty rights."[9] What actions should or would be taken by the American and Mexican governments, with what consequences, was a subject of debate in both countries. However, the "sublime" effects of having a country extended beyond juridical questions of consular protections. The assertion that the Negro "has no country" erases the U.S. citizenship of African Americans, however constrained it might be, reinscribing racial blackness as without history, nation, or civilization. It also suggests the urgency some Mexicans felt to tether Mexican race to these markers of humanity.

In their responses to the violence of the lynching, the riots, and the revolution, Mexicans and Americans imagined nationality as a transcendent quality, differentiating men from barbarians and civilization from savagery. In U.S. narratives of their own expansion and imperialism, the imbrication of race and nation worked to affirm the distinction of American men and country. The Anglo-Saxon race with its singular manly capacity for self-government endowed the American nation with a historical destiny. In contrast, as we saw in Chapter 1, Mexican racial difference, read inferiority, signified the deformed nature of the Mexican nation. This mutual degradation of race and nation operated to subordinate Mexicans within the United States and also to assert Americans' rights within Mexico.

In protesting the lynching, Mexicans also waged a passionate defense of what a group of Mexico City students described as their "outraged nationality." For some Mexicans, the lynching was an outrage not just because the mob had cruelly murdered Rodriguez but also because it had inflicted this crime against the representative of a fellow nation. Their defense of race and nation was staked upon exposing the hollow pretenses at U.S. claims to civilizational superiority as well as establishing their own ancestral pedigree. As I will explore in the second half of the chapter, in the discourse of the Rodriguez protestors, blackness was imagined with revealing ambivalence. The protestors identify Americans' anti-black violence as the "rotten core" of U.S. civilization and sometimes express affinity with African Americans. At others they assert Mexican manhood, honor, and resistance through differentiating Mexicans, "who have a country," from the putative nationlessness of black race. This troubling use of blackness reflects how U.S. anti-black racism has shaped Mexicans' experience and understanding of race. It also reflects, not unrelatedly, that Mexicans have often expunged Africans from their narratives of national and racial identity.

Lynching, nation, and race

Antonio Rodriguez was far from the first person of Mexican ethnicity to be lynched in the United States. In recent decades a number of scholars have undertaken archival research to recover the history of anti-Mexican mob violence in the United States, a history largely effaced from U.S. cultural and scholarly memory. In their foundational work, William D. Carrigan and Clive Webb have been able to confirm the lynching of 597 Mexicans in the Southwest between 1880 and 1930, recognizing that the true number would be impossible to calculate. Given their relative proportions in the wider population, Carrigan and Webb calculate that African Americans and Mexicans in the United States had "roughly the same chance" of being murdered by a lynch mob during these years. This calculation is based on their total of 3,346 African American victims. However, more recent research from the Equal Justice Initiative puts the total number of anti-black lynching in the years between 1877 and 1950 at 4,084.[10] While the lynching of Rodriguez laid bare deeply ingrained patterns of violence and contempt, it was not itself typical of anti-Mexican violence in the United States. A crowd estimated in some reports to be in the thousands gathered to watch Rodriguez die. Mexican lynching victims, Carrigan and Webb note, were not typically killed in ritualized daylight public spectacles, but murdered "in the middle of the night, or in remote ranchlands, hidden gulches, and deserted roadsides."[11] As a case in point, in the lynching that catalyzed the Plan de San Diego uprising in south Texas five years later, armed men took Adolfo Muñoz, accused of murder and horse theft, from the custody of a Texas Ranger who had made the highly suspect decision to transfer Muñoz from San Benito to Brownsville in the middle of the night. The supposed ambushers hanged Muñoz from a tree by the roadside.[12]

While the appropriation of Mexican land and exploitation of Mexican labor engendered specific American practices and discourses of anti-Mexican violence, the Rodriguez lynching, with its spectacular performance of brutality, was also given meaning from the nation's unique culture of anti-black terrorism. Scholars estimate that during the years between 1880 and 1940 as many as 500 public torture lynchings were enacted in the United States, primarily in the Deep South. The practice, which developed conterminously with the hardening of Jim Crow, was distinguished by its use of publicity, ritual, and abnormal cruelty and attendance by large crowds. Nearly all victims of these spectacles of terror were black.[13] Carrigan and Webb delineate a number of important practical factors to which the more clandestine nature of typical anti-Mexican lynching could be attributed: the greater possibility of federal intervention due to protest on behalf of the Mexican government, the greater ease with which intended victims could escape because of the presence of the border, and thin population density in the Southwest compared to the South.[14]

It is also necessary to examine public torture lynching as a particular product of a former slave society asserting a new order of racial caste. Orlando Patterson suggests the torture lynchings are best thought of as sacrificial rituals of society in a state of liminality, practiced against a domestic enemy whose aberrant presence as a now masterless slave presented a threat to the very foundations of civilization.[15] Sociologist of crime and punishment David Garland draws a historical connection between the use of burning in spectacle lynchings to a specific class of seventeenth- and early eighteenth-century public executions, which again emphasizes the notion of black people as a class of domestic enemy. While burning in this period was no longer inflicted upon women convicted of witchcraft, American colonists used public burning for the crime of *petit treason*, against two classes of offenders – slaves who killed their owners or plotted revolt, and, less commonly, wives who killed their husbands. Whereas high treason entailed an offense against the sovereign, *petit treason* entailed a perverse attempt to reverse "the traditional hierarchy of the household," a criminal act of "treachery in private life" against the authority of the private household that "proceeded from the same principle" of treachery against "king and government."[16] The burning of black victims reinforced the ideology of racial patriarchy that emerged from slavery, in which the subjection of black people to the authority, discipline, and punishment of individual white men, comes before and above their subjection to the state. Slavery advocate George Fitzhugh notably theorized that in "family government," "slaves, wives, and children have no other government; they do not come directly in contact with the institutions and rules of the State."[17]

In his well-known historical sociology of slavery, Patterson defines the condition of the enslaved person as one of social death, achieved through a process of natal alienation: "Alienated from all 'rights' or claims of birth, he ceased to belong in his own right to any legitimate social order. All slaves experienced, at the very least, a secular excommunication."[18] The maintenance of slavery necessitated the severance of all human social ties, thus denying bonds of ancestry across time, as well as the immediate family hierarchies of gender and generation among enslaved people. In an illustrative example, a woman who had been enslaved in New Orleans later recalled being whipped "because I said to missis, 'My mother sent me'. We were not allowed to call our mammies 'mother'."[19] As slavery denied captives' rights to their families it also denied their capacity for history and homeland. The "loss of native status" eradicated the possibility of a slave forging legally meaningful attachment to "localities other than those chosen for him by the master."[20] Stripped of geographical or cultural referent, as Du Bois pointed out, Europeans and their descendants transformed the Spanish word "Negro" from a descriptive adjective to "the substantive name of a race." Often denied even a capital letter to denote a sense of peoplehood, "Negro" emerged "to tie color to race and blackness to slavery and degradation."[21] As Jared Sexton writes, "neither the native nor the foreigner, neither the colonizer nor the colonized ... [t]he nativity of the slave is not inscribed elsewhere in some other (even subordinated) jurisdiction, but rather nowhere at all."[22] As we will see, it was precisely this state of being from nowhere at all, a race without country or ancestry, that some Mexicans suspected the lynch mob ascribed to Antonio Rodriguez and which they vehemently sought to deny.

Border dialectics of Mexican race and nation

Mexican responses to the lynching and their defense of Mexican race and nation need to be understood within a transnational historical context. Reflecting on the long, "interpenetrated" border between the United States and Mexico, Claudio Lomnitz argues that in Mexico the conceptualization of a singular Mexican race was fueled both by the need of the state to form a national subject and by the U.S. racialization of Mexican nationality initiated in the Mexican–American War. The Rodriguez demonstrations, he suggests, marked the solidification of a national racial identity in Mexico, a process forged through the "border dialectics" of the nineteenth and early twentieth centuries. Unprecedented numbers of Mexicans came into the United States in the decades before the revolution, pushed by the impoverishing effects of the Díaz regime's ruthless program to modernize Mexico through the privatization of land and engagement of foreign investment, a project which had proven highly lucrative for U.S. capitalists and a narrow class of Mexican elite. After the revolution began, thousands more Mexicans fled across the border to seek refuge from the violence and social upheaval. Traversing the border gave Mexicans a new understanding of Mexican race.[23] As one example, José Vasconcelos, who produced the treatise on Mexican race discussed in Chapter 2, was profoundly affected by his experiences growing up on the border. Attending American schools in Eagle Pass, Texas, he received regular lessons on American views of Mexicans' "semi-savagery." "There is no race, we think," he would write later in an essay to fellow Latin Americans, "until the day that crossing the U.S. border reveals that we have already been classified, and before being given the opportunity to define ourselves."[24]

It is important also to remember that border crossing was not unidirectional. From the mid-nineteenth century, U.S. finance, mining, industrial, railroad, and agricultural capitalists had descended upon the country, consummating the United States' first imperial relationship beyond its continental boundaries. Newspaper magnate William Randolph Hearst, who owned an estimated 7 million acres of Mexican land, commented, "I really don't see what is to prevent us from owning all of Mexico and running it to suit ourselves." By 1910, Americans owned almost 27 percent of the nation's land and around 40,000 U.S. colonists lived in Mexico.[25] Just as crossing the "magic threshold of the border" transformed Mexicans of all classes into racialized subjects in the United States, it also transformed "virtually any white American into a kind of aristocrat" in Mexico. U.S. landowners in Mexico took full advantage of established Mexican institutions of forced labor. A firm which ran rubber, henequen, and hardwood plantations in Campeche, for example, employed private police to ensure their bonded laborers could not leave company property until their "debts" were repaid.[26] Americans also replicated segregated labor practices of the Southwest in their Mexican industries, paying their "native" employees less than American migrants carrying out the same jobs and organizing Mexican and American workers within separate social spaces. Encounters with American capital and colonists meant that Mexican race was given "pragmatic and tangible" meaning for Mexicans in the Republic, particularly those working in the border regions, in the mining and oil industries, and within the national rail network, which was largely owned by American operatives.[27]

Reflecting these "border dialectics," Mexican protestors denounced anti-Mexican racism within the United States and the country's imperial abuses within Mexico. In an imagery reminiscent of Frederick Douglass's warning to white Americans about the lynching of black men, an editorial in *Regeneración* written by an English-speaking "comrade" suggested that Americans subject to protest in Mexico City were reaping the whirlwind of their violent abuse of Mexicans on both sides of the border. "[I]f our leeches down there do behave like conceited, arrogant and ignorant barbarians in a conquered land, let them take their medicine, even if some of the innocent should have to suffer with the guilty."[28] A Mexico City editorial put the lynching in broader historical trajectory, asserting that "putrefying claws ... fastened upon, upper California, Texas, New Mexico, etc" continued to mar the "pure blue heaven of Anahuac." The editorial urged the Mexican people to "remember what has been done to you by the hungry condor of the North": "Demand justice, Mexicans, the insolence of the blond barbarian, the dollar giant, the pigmy of human understanding must be punished."[29] The Rodriguez lynching thus incited an outpouring of Mexican rage because it so graphically demonstrated the extremes of brutality to which Mexicans might be subject in the United States, as well as making salient the social and economic impunity with which Americans operated in Mexico.

A Mexican citizen of Mexico: U.S. constructions of Mexican race and nation

As the protests erupted against the lynching, the rancor of the Mexican press offended American officials in Mexico and incensed the Associated Press. Newspapers across the country reprinted what one editor referred to as the "violent expressions of animosity towards the people of the United States" circulating in the Mexican press.[30] Like the protest itself, U.S. responses to Mexican rage reveal the interrelated relations of domestic subjugation and imperial extraction, each of which produced U.S. discourses of Mexican race that delegitimized Mexico as a nation. Shortly after the protests erupted, claims began to emerge in the U.S. press that Antonio Rodriguez had in fact been born in New Mexico and, as such, was an American citizen. Rather than an investigation to determine the American citizens responsible for the burning, federal authorities were "making every effort to determine" whether Rodriguez was a Mexican or U.S. citizen. Of course, Rodriguez's citizenship was important because the American government was liable to pay indemnities to the families of foreign citizens killed by mob violence. Beyond the issue of indemnity, however, the American press invoked doubt around Rodriguez's citizenship to undermine the moral basis for Mexican protest. "Although the Mexicans have attacked Americans throughout Mexico and started several good-sized riots since the event," the *Washington Herald* observed, "the Mexican government has not yet proved that Rodriguez was a Mexican citizen."[31] "Since any grievance that Mexico has is based on the death of Rodriguez, the state department will endeavor to determine his nationality at once," another report explained. "If Rodriguez is found to be an American, Mexico's cause for anger will be gone."[32] The idea that the true problem with the lynching lay in the Rodriguez's citizenship is at once disingenuous and revealing. The narrow definition of "Mexican" as a citizenship status obscured the subsumption of Mexican nationality into Mexican "race" that Americans made central to social relations along the border. That Mexican racial difference was continually marked and enforced in practice often made the legal issue of Mexican nationality unimportant in the minds of white Texans. As Mae Ngai has observed, in the early twentieth century U.S.-born persons of Mexican ethnicity were treated as "alien citizens," formally American but permanently foreign and unassimilable.[33]

While some Americans insisted on the importance of Rodriguez's nationality to the political meaning of the lynching, others made light of it. In late November, the *Houston Post* reprinted a joke about the Rodriguez fallout, originally printed in a South Carolina paper. "It seems that the so-called Mexican lynched by the Texas mob was a citizen of New Mexico, and no greaser at all. 'Madam,' said the Texas ranger to the widow of the man he had lynched by mistake, 'the joke's on us.'"[34] The "joke" is striking for several reasons. Its narrative moves seamlessly from "the Texas mob" to "the Texas ranger" as the agent of the lynching, without any suggestion that it would be improper for a law enforcement officer to lynch a "greaser." The joke plays upon the difference between a "citizen of New Mexico" and a "greaser" born in Mexico, at once immaterial and legally significant. The mob is disappointed when they learn it was not a "real" Mexican they lynched but this fact was undetectable to them during the act of lynching. Thus, while highlighting the technical distinction between a Mexican born in U.S. territory and one born below the border, the joke also emphasizes the supposedly insubstantial nature of that distinction on the ground.[35]

The reflections of Texas congressman James Slayden on the growing presence of Mexicans in his home state in 1921 offer further insight into American constructions of Mexican race. Slayden suggested that Mexican labor was being courted by planters who were facing an exodus of black labor and desperate for replacements. Sneering at the planters' selfish lack of regard for the well-being of their country, he wrote that they welcomed Mexicans "as they would welcome fresh arrivals from the Congo." Though he noted the marked differences in the legal standing of Mexicans and African Americans, he asserted that the "word Mexican is used to indicate race, not a citizen or subject of that country ... Mexicans ... are 'Mexicans' just as all blacks are Negroes though they may have five generations of American ancestors."[36] This conflation of Mexican race and citizenship makes true American identity impossible for individual Mexicans by marking their permanent racial difference. In making Mexicanness on a par with Negro-ness, a nationless racial status, Slayden also depreciates the meaning of Mexican nationality. Rather than a state of subjecthood comprised of birthright, civic duty, and patriotism, Mexican race is treated as deep and inescapable subnormality.

Just as they cast doubt on Rodriguez's formal Mexican citizenship, Americans also cast doubt on the sincerity of the protestors' nationalist indignation. The U.S. Secretary of State Philander Knox issued a statement regretting that the lynching should have been "made the excuse" for a demonstration of anti-American aggression.[37] American Consul Samuel E. Magill rejected Mexicans' assertions of outrage over Rodriguez's burning, claiming that many rioters "knew little and cared less about it," surmising instead that the riots were caused by "a deep-seated jealousy or hatred of all things and persons American."[38] Michael J. Slatterly, a mine operator who had been living in Guadalajara in 1910, arrived at a similar conclusion in his testimony to a Senate hearing on Mexican "outrages" against American citizens nine years later. "For two days and two nights the mobs just ran riot. Every American house was stoned." When he was asked by a member of the Senate committee whether the Mexicans had any "patriotic pretext" for the rioting, he responded, "Absolutely none at all."[39]

The denigration of Mexican patriotism formed a recurring theme of U.S. interventionist discourse in the period. Some Americans suggested that for Mexicans nationalism was not the sacred and deeply felt attachment that Americans experienced, but opportunism, pretense, and jealousy. Johns Hopkins Professor of Archeology William Gates, who authored a number of widely read articles in the *North American Review* urging U.S. intervention in Mexico, explicitly dismissed the notion of Mexican patriotism. The patriotism of the few upper-class Mexicans who "shriek nonintervention and the Saxon peril," he wrote to Secretary of War Newton Baker, was of the "chip on the shoulder" variety, "which is not patriotism at all." On the other hand, the Indian masses "would welcome us as new and 'trustable' masters. They are not after 'patriotism' and sovereignty, but bread and a chance."[40]

Arguing that the United States should more actively assert its will below the border to protect the considerable economic interests of American capitalists, Roland G. Usher, a professor of history at Washington University, pointed to the nation's previous dealings with Native Americans to highlight the folly of nonintervention. Articulating a notion often repeated by American capitalists and settlers in Mexico, Usher asserted that Mexico was not actually a nation in any way that counted but was rather a fractious collection of "Indian tribes."

> Essentially, the Mexican problem is not an international issue of magnitude, but another phase of the Indian problem we have already met so many times. That inconsiderable proportion of white men must not blind us to the essential facts and allow us to look upon Mexico as a white nation or even as a nation at all.

Through a combined strategy of "peaceful occupation" and extermination when necessary, white men had taken the land they desired. Usher envisioned that America's future in Mexico as the next chapter of what had already happened in Georgia, Oklahoma, Texas, and California, as white men would take ownership of the last of the "red men's" possessions on the American continent. After all, he stated, apparently without irony, "If it is wrong for us to intervene in Mexico, the history of the United States is the record of a deliberate crime without parallel for magnitude in history."[41] Though Usher acknowledged the United States' diplomatic relationship with the Mexican Republic slightly complicated this picture of transcontinental domination, these arguments illustrate the manner in which Americans commonly likened Mexicans to stateless Native Americans in order to disavow Mexican sovereignty.

Just as the status of Mexican nationality was constructed as ideologically and historically illegitimate, ethnic Mexicans in the U.S. were perpetually tied to the imagined barbarism of Mexico. This was vividly illustrated in Rock Springs in the days after the anti-American protests in Mexico City. White residents in the town were filled with apprehension. Reports had been received that armed Mexicans were making their way to Rock Springs, "with the avowed purpose of making an attack on this town and avenging the recent burning." Reminiscent of the reports that white men poured into Palestine from neighboring counties to put down the "rising negros," U.S. papers now told of cowboys and ranchmen from the surrounding vicinity, armed with rifles and revolvers, pouring into Rock Springs in readiness to meet the coming "invasion." Paranoia of Mexican "invasion" was not limited to the town where the lynching occurred. The *Buffalo Evening News* reported that sixty armed Mexicans had crossed the border and were marching toward Marathon, Texas. Reflecting a generalized suspicion of Mexicans, the article noted that Marathon was approximately 100 miles away from where the lynching occurred and "[w]hy the Mexicans should make that town their objective is a mystery." Nevertheless, scouts had been sent out and sentries sat on guard. Despite their readiness, however, the *Baltimore*

Sun reported with a hint of amusement, there was not "a Mexican in sight."[42]

Americans' hostile fears were surely less amusing for ethnic Mexican residents in Texas who became the focus of mobs of angry white Texans who had heard the rumors of Mexican armies. Some reports blamed Mexicans for the violence against them, claiming that fights had broken out because "ignorant Mexican laborers" heard rumors that Americans were trying to take possession of Mexico City. Near Rio Grande City, Mexicans were badly beaten by Anglo men and others fled across the border. In Zapata, Starr, Webb, and Maverick counties, more fights were reported between "citizens" and "Mexicans." Ethnic Mexicans who denied knowing anything about Rodriguez or events in Mexico City were attacked by Anglos.[43] Mexicans in a town called Carrizo Springs were clubbed. The Mexican Embassy reported similar problems in Cristal City, Texas, and elsewhere in the state reports emerged of Mexicans fleeing across the border for fear they would be "killed by cowboys." One Mexican immigrant in Oklahoma wrote to President Díaz requesting funds for transport back to Mexico: "I have no one to complain to except God and you … I hope that you will have the kindness to take me out of this ungrateful land."[44]

Blackness and nationhood in Mexico

For the rest of this chapter, I will examine the different ways in which blackness was invoked by borderlands radicals and protestors in Mexico City in their responses to the Rodriguez lynching and in their framing of Mexican race and nation. If these social actors pointed to Americans' practices of racist terror as evidence of their barbarism, they also employed racist constructions of blackness to bolster their own defense of Mexican race. Both aspects of this discourse, I will suggest, are emergent from historical processes spanning the Americas. While the histories of New World slavery and the racisms it engendered in the United States and Mexico are distinct, they cannot be neatly separated at the border. If the formation of Mexican race, as Lomnitz argues, was driven by the "rise of the United States as an empire," anti-black racism in its stringent and peculiarly American form permeated the logic of U.S. projects of continental expansion and transnational imperialism. Anti-black racism also shaped the often-hostile social landscape Mexicans encountered when they crossed the border.[45] As such, the structures and discourses of U.S. anti-black racism shaped the border dialectics within which Mexicans forged ideologies of race and nation.

At the same time, Mexico's own projects of nation-building and identity-making have demonstrated considerable ambivalence about the country's own demographic and historical legacies of transatlantic slavery. Mónica Moreno Figueroa and Emiko Saldívar Tanaka observe that "[s]ince 1810 Mexico has used its 'kinder' treatment of indigenous people and the early abolition of slavery as a central point of comparison between the racist segregationist culture of the United States and Mexico's 'inclusive and just' mestizaje."[46] However, despite continually differentiating Mexico's social equality from North America's rigid schema of race, the anti-imperialist discourses of Mexican race and national identity that crystalized in the revolutionary era have worked to obscure anti-black racism in Mexico and the presence of black people themselves. It is telling in this regard that national pride about the early abolition of slavery does not commonly include a celebration of the fact that Vicente Guerrero, hero of the War of Independence against Spain and later the second president of Mexico, who signed the 1829 decree abolishing slavery, was himself of African descent.[47] As a further striking example of the ways in which blackness has been made absent from "collective imaginings of the nation," the state has not undertaken any effort to numerate the black population since Mexico's independence.[48]

As scholars of Mexico's diasporic African presence have documented, the ideologies of mestizaje that made Indianness central to Mexican race often relegated blackness to the distant colonial past. Attempting to consolidate a cohesive national identity in the looming presence of the United States and Europe and under continuing threats of foreign intervention, Mexican intellectuals and political leaders sometimes anxiously adhered to dominant streams of scientific racism, even as they rejected U.S. racial doctrines.[49] Where the relationship between Spanish colonizers and indigenous peoples became central to narratives of Mexican peoplehood, slavery and African-descended people were imagined as peripheral to Mexico's history. Marisela Jiménez Ramos observes that prominent nineteenth-century Mexican historians contemplating national identity did not deny a black presence in the nation's history but strictly regulated it. Although the vast majority of people of African descent by the early nineteenth century were free, these historians "make little mention of Blacks outside of the history of slavery and even then it is only to point out that there were few slaves." For such authors, once independent Mexico abolished the colonial institution of slavery, so too was any potential problem of blackness abolished. The "few" black people were imagined to have been completely "absorbed" and thus essentially vanished from contemporary Mexico.[50]

One Mexican scholar to ponder the influence of African ancestry on Mexican people in the twentieth century was the anthropologist Alfonso Toro. In a short but intriguing 1920 essay, he suggested that while physical traces had largely disappeared, it was possible that some moral characteristics had been transmitted that remained evident in the national body. Noting that colonial missionaries had depicted "the blacks as spiteful, hypocritical and always ready to rise up," he suggested that "black blood" might then explain "the indocility of the Mexican people to submit to their rulers and their tendency to revolutionize."[51] Rather than the figure of the "docile black," Toro's conjecture associates blackness with resistance.

The prolific nineteenth-century historian and grandson of Vicente Guerrero, Vicente Riva Palacio, also made this connection in a series of novels and stories based upon his own archival research that explored caste, slavery, and Indian and black rebellion in colonial Mexico. One of Rivas Palacio's stories, *The Thirty-Three Negroes and Other National Episodes*, first published in 1870, offered an account of a slave insurrection, led by an enslaved man named Yanga. Drawn from the records of the Inquisition, Riva Palacio's story tells how three years after colonial authorities signed a treaty with Yanga they executed twenty-nine black men and four black women when rumors emerged that they were planning insurrection and the slaughter of the white population. Given his family history and his efforts to foster a national memory of slave resistance, it becomes all the more conspicuous that, as discussed in Chapter 2, Riva Palacio conceptualized Mexico's national race as Spanish and indigenous. Rather than claiming rebellious slaves as racial forebears of the nation, Ben Vinson suggests that Riva Palacio presented Yanga's struggle against Spanish authority as a means for nineteenth-century Mexicans to think about their own struggles against foreign oppressors. "Embedded distantly in the secure comfort of the early colonial period," the narrative of Yanga's struggle bears inspirational anti-colonial lessons for modern Mexicans but blackness remains ambivalently both part and not part of the nation.[52]

We can see the same pattern of historical recognition and erasure, this time with an even more distinct helping of anti-black racism, in the work of Vasconcelos. Vasconcelos also drew associations between "black blood" and the Latin American racial drive toward liberation. Juliette Hooker notes that in his 1927 essay "Indología" Vasconcelos rebuked Latin Americans ashamed of their nations' African ancestry. "[B]eing a mulatto," he asserted, was "the most illustrious citizenship card in America" (America here being understood in the anti-colonial hemispheric sense, rather than as a misnomer for the United States). Emphasizing the importance of African ancestry in Latin American identity, Vasconcelos lamented that he himself did not have any "black blood" and noted his belief that "even Bolívar was [a mulatto]."[53] However, Vasconcelos reiterated blackness as a unique U.S. problem. Like white Americans themselves, he also placed the source of American racism in black difference: "North Americans have held very firmly to their resolution to maintain a pure stock, the reason being that they are faced with the

Blacks ... We have very few Blacks, and a large part of them is already becoming a mulatto population."[54] In *Cosmic Race*, as Vasconcelos enthused about the new racial type being forged, he noted that alongside the mestizo and the Indian, "even the Black" was superior to the white in a number of spiritual capacities. "The drop put in our blood by the Black, eager for sensual joy, intoxicated with dances and unbridled lust," would be stirred with the "infinite quietude" provided by indigenous blood and the "clear mind of the White."[55] The characterization of black blood as a force of lust and joy, rather than culture or capacity, and the specification of the amount in the new Latin race as a "drop" indicates the highly restricted role that Vasconcelos imagined for African ancestry in the blended race of the future. The "drop of black blood" which would condemn a white person in the U.S. to the wrong side of the color line could enhance and invigorate the new mestizo, but in either case blackness was a problem. Indeed, Vasconcelos's trajectory of counter Anglo-Saxon American race-making asserted its own vision of black extinction: "[I]n a few decades of aesthetic eugenics," he mused, "the Black may disappear, together with the types that a free instinct of beauty may go on signalling as fundamentally recessive and undeserving, for that reason, of perpetuation."[56]

Despite this erasure of blackness from ideologies of Mexican race and nation, across the nineteenth and early twentieth centuries, as will be explored further in Chapter 5, a number of Mexicans and Americans linked African American freedom in various ways with Mexico and/or Mexicans. During the period of the Mexican Revolution, as their fellow countrymen called for the invasion of Mexico, U.S. radicals posited American civilization as wanting in comparison to Mexico's. In 1919, Chandler Owen and A. Phillip Randolph, editors of the radical black magazine the *Messenger*, asserted that "Mexico is the fairest country to the Negro on the American continent" and that "all talk of establishing law and order in Mexico is a sham; for if the United States is really interested in establishing law and order, it has a splendid opportunity to begin at home." They further noted the irony of black soldiers being sent from Texas "supposedly to protect life and property in Mexico when their own life and property are not protected in Texas."[57]

The African American boxing champion Jack Johnson also presented Mexico as a refuge from American violence, but his evaluations were grounded in his own lived experience. Convicted under the federal Mann Act against "white slave trafficking" because he married a white woman, Johnson fled the United States and spent seven years living in exile in Europe and Latin America. During his time in Mexico, he developed a warm relationship with the Carranza regime and publicly expressed his enthusiasm for the opportunities that Mexico offered black people. He took out a number of advertisements in the black press in the United States, as well as in the leftist, English-language magazine *Gale's*, published in Mexico City, urging African Americans to buy homes in the country.

> COLORED PEOPLE: You who are lynched, tortured, mobbed, persecuted, and discriminated against in the boasted "land of Liberty," the United States. Own a home in Mexico where one man is as good as another, and it is not your nationality that counts but simply you. Write for particulars. Jack Johnson Land Co.[58]

In addition to telling the world what Mexico could do for black people, Johnson also offered a vision of what black men might do for Mexico. An American agent spying on the Socialist Party in Mexico reported to Washington that Johnson pledged in a speech before a cheering crowd in Nuevo Laredo that if the "gringos invaded Mexico, American blacks would stand alongside their Mexican brothers."[59]

Johnson's ardent relationship with Mexico was monitored with deep suspicion by U.S. government officials. Throughout the 1910s, New Mexico Senator Albert Fall, deeply embedded with U.S. business interests operating in Mexico, particularly the oil industry, waged a relentless campaign for U.S. intervention in Mexico, culminating in a Senate investigation into Mexican "outrages on citizens of the United States in Mexico."[60] In order to make a compelling case for intervention, Fall cast American colonists as latter-day pioneers savaged by barbarians and neglected by their own government.[61] Among his many contributions to the hearings, Fall entered Johnson's *Gale's* advertisement into the record. A white American witness was also asked to testify about Johnson's confrontation with imported Jim Crow in Sanborn's, a U.S.-owned restaurant in Mexico City. Refused service by the white owner Walter Sanborn, Johnson returned with military officials of the Carranza government. They forced Sanborn to serve Johnson and to apologize to him, informing him that Mexico was not "a white man's country" and that in Mexico he must serve everybody regardless of their color. At this result, the crowd that had gathered outside the restaurant shouted "Viva Johnson!" and "Viva Mexico!", celebrating this subversion of American racism as a victory for both Johnson and the nation. While the incident was also lauded in the black press in the U.S., for the Fall committee it illustrated the illegitimate authority of the Mexican government and its supposedly outrageous violations of the rights of (white) Americans.[62] As I will discuss shortly, Johnson had entered the imagination of Mexicans before he crossed the border, as the students protesting Rodriguez's lynching in 1910 alluded to his feats in the boxing ring. While Johnson's relationship with Mexico illustrates the productive potential of anti-racist, anti-imperialist transborder solidarity, it emerged within a complex historical landscape, a fact laid bare in the protest discourse of 1910.

Lynching, civilization, and "barbarous Mexico"

In his response to the Rodriguez lynching in *Regeneración*, Ricardo Flores Magón used anti-black violence as a benchmark with which to evidence the depth of oppression Mexicans faced in Texas. "Everyone knows the contempt with which [Americans] treat the Mexican people [that live in the United States]; everyone knows that in Texas they treat Mexicans worse than the negroes."[63] There is a discomforting edge to this use of comparison. Tiffany Willoughby-Herald has explored the pitfalls of using slavery and anti-black lynching as a historical analogy through which to measure the oppression of non-black groups. She points out that when scholars and activists seek to demonstrate the subjection of a racialized people by marshaling a comparison with slavery or lynching, the byproduct is often "antipathy for blackness" rather than meaningful solidarity. Claims that a particular group has been exploited or abused "even worse" than African Americans, she argues, rearticulate the demands of white laborers, suffragettes, and others that they must not be "reduced to the status of the unfortunate African."[64] If not all who use blackness as a barometer espouse explicit anti-black racism, the uncritical use of the "even worse" often has the effect of problematizing the "reduction" of the non-black group while naturalizing the "status of the African" as inevitable.

African Americans faced the forms of oppression – exclusion from public spaces and schools, bodily violence, criminalization – that Flores Magón highlights as being forced upon Mexicans. Therefore his assertion that Mexicans are treated "worse than the blacks" implicitly suggests that these forms of exclusion and social violence are somehow less oppressive when applied to African Americans. The English-language *Regeneración* article on the Rodriguez lynching also establishes the depths of anti-Mexican racism with reference to white Americans' violence against African Americans: "Respectable lawbreakers, hardened by decades of negro burnings, have again gratified their lust for blood and contempt of the law by using as the target of their distracted instincts a Mexican, whom in their racial conceit they class even below the negro."[65] While the author clearly rejects the "racial conceit" and "contempt" of white Americans who would classify Mexicans "even below the negro," this does not entail an explicit rejection of "the negro's" position as a figure of social abjection. The rhetorical move of "like blacks" or "even worse than blacks" is an approximation that simultaneously differentiates. The "decades of negro burnings" are invoked merely as a measure of the Mexican's humiliation rather than outrages in their own right. The claim that Mexicans were treated "even worse" than African Americans in Texas belies the ferocity of anti-black violence and apartheid, even as they are used as a baseline for racial degradation.

A group of university students in Mexico City also drew connections between Rodriguez's lynching and U.S. anti-black racism, but in a manner that linked African Americans and Mexicans in their common suffering. In a circular that was later disseminated in the U.S. media as illustrative of "the inflammatory literature" inciting the anti-American outbreaks, the students highlighted the hypocrisy of those who dishonored and disdained Mexico's civilization and yet "bathed [an unarmed man] in petroleum and then [set] fire to him." Rather than "heroes of civilization," Americans had shown themselves to be "followers of Torquemada," the analogy likening supposedly modern Americans with the ancient cruelties of the Spanish Inquisition. Perhaps rather pointedly, Spain was an oppressor that Mexicans had already thrown out. To articulate the discordance between U.S. accusations of Mexican backwardness and its own dismal record of savagery, the students pointed to Americans' treatment of Mexicans and African Americans north of the border:

> Barbarous Mexico, they call our country, they who applied the torch to the clothes of Rodriguez; barbarous Mexico, they defied and outraged the law, snatching from it a man whose life ought to have been sacred because it was under society's protection; barbarous Mexico, they, those organized assassins of defenseless strangers and opprest [sic.] negroes; barbarous Mexico, they, those idealizers of the dethroned king of the prize-ring, Jim Jeffries![66]

The students, then, highlight the common vulnerability of "defenseless strangers" – in other words Mexican immigrants – and "opprest negroes" to the voracious racism and violence of white Americans. Here migrants' status as strangers in an unfriendly land poignantly resonates with the oppression of African Americans.

The striking description of Americans as "idealizers" of Jim Jeffries, an epithet apparently on a par with "organized assassins", further connects white Americans' savage disposition against unfortunate Mexicans who have crossed the Rio Grande to their subjugation of black U.S. citizens. Four months before the Texas mob tied Rodriguez to the stake, the dethroned Jeffries, a former heavyweight champion, had come out of retirement to fight Jack Johnson, then the current champion. Newspapers around the country pleaded with Jeffries, dubbed the "Hope of the White Race," to win the title back from Johnson. "For the sole purpose of proving that a white man is better than a negro," as he put it, Jeffries eventually agreed to the fight. After he was trounced by Johnson for fifteen rounds, riots erupted throughout the country, in most cases provoked by enraged white men assaulting black men, in some instances fatally. The coverage of the riots in the *Los Angeles Herald* suggests that black jubilation was also met with the brunt of state violence. In its round-up of the violence, it reports that "police beat negroes in Pittsburg and clubbed [them] into submission in St. Louis."[67] In referring to Jeffries as the "dethroned king" in their circular, the Mexican students exposed the pretensions of white American men's claim to superiority, drawing attention to both their race prejudice and the wound to race pride that came with the defeat of their champion at the fists of a black man. The students ended their statement by "[crying out] in the name of our national civilization" against the "assassins of Rock Springs," having noted that their national civilization was one in which "murderers are not burned alive."[68]

The students' denunciation of American barbarism found a "theatrical counterpart," as Lomnitz puts it, in their street demonstration when they happened to encounter an African American man. According to *El Diario*, the man was "lifted onto the shoulders of the crowd and hailed as a representative of a race execrated by the whites of the Union of the North."[69] Though ostensibly an act of solidarity, the hailing and hoisting up of the black man to display his blackness as a symbol of American oppression – a kind of counterpart to the tearing down of the American flag – has a distinctly objectifying quality to it.

The blood of Cuauhtémoc

As well as their schemas of segregated labor and white superiority, American colonists also brought their constructions of the "negro rape fiend" with them to Mexico. The *Mexican Herald*, delivered to every American household in Mexico, was also widely read by Mexican political officials.[70] Stories of criminal "negroes" regularly appeared on the pages of the *Herald*, which covered U.S. as well as Mexican news items. During the unrest, the *Herald* also printed a "History of Lynch Law" to give the weight of historical evidence to its claims that the Rodriguez lynching should not be interpreted as a racial insult to Mexico. Faced with millions of emancipated black people from "the interior of Africa," the article explained, American men had been forced to develop lynching as a practice of social control. Rodriquez's fate had nothing to do with his Mexican race and everything to do with Americans' intense preoccupation with the safety and sanctity of womanhood. Any man who had murdered a woman would have been dealt with in the same fashion. Of course, even this disavowal of lynching as a racializing practice confirms racist claims of black savagery: if lynch law were applied equally to all men, black men's preponderance among those subject to it could only mean that they raped more than others.[71]

Two Mexico City editorials that Henry Lane Wilson forwarded to the secretary of state because of their caustic denunciations of the United States make striking use of anti-black imagery. Though surely familiar with U.S. narratives of lynching and the "fact" of black rape as constructed in those narratives, these authors did not employ notions of black criminality in their critiques of the lynching. Rather, they invoked the construction of blackness as abject and natally alienated in order to outline the heroic proportions of Mexican race and nation. As part of a tirade against American claims to civilization, one of the editorials, printed in *Diario del Hogar*, points to the lynching of black people to highlight the savagery of North American men but also to diminish white manhood: "Go on if you wish in your task of extermination with the valient [sic.] and indomitable negro race, but do not get mixed up with the race of Cuauhtemoc [sic.]."[72] The sarcastic reference to the "valient and indomitable negro race" denigrates African Americans in standard anti-black racist tradition as emasculated and submissive.

Whereas in U.S. lynching narratives the figure of the pleading, terrified black lynching victim magnified the masculine power of white men as the ruthless executors of racial discipline, the Mexican editorial's sneering reference to U.S. anti-black violence seeks to expose Americans' empty pretensions of racial strength and superiority. Employing a similar logic to that present in U.S. myths of frontier warfare, in which violent confrontation with a fierce enemy made men manly, here, Americans' "extermination" of an infirm, inferior race demonstrated their own racial depravity rather than honor or manliness. Cuauhtémoc was the last emperor of the Aztecs, killed by Hernán Cortés in 1525. From the nineteenth century he had been taken up as a symbol of Mexican national identity and the progenitor of later heroes of national struggle.[73] The designation of Mexicans as "the race of Cuauhtémoc" distinguishes them from both the utterly domitable "negro race" and the vile American pretenders.

The second editorial Wilson sent to the secretary of state addressed anti-black violence as a defining feature of U.S. civilization through a discourse itself saturated in anti-black racism. Printed in *El Debate*, the editorial railed at the insulting racial affiliations that lynching drew between Mexicans and African Americans: "The iron hoof of the Texas 'Yankee,' in his barbarous and savage sentiments of race-hatred, is now not trampling upon the negro; but the rottenness of its core has spread out so as to wound and even kill a Mexican, by the iniquitous method of lynching." Noting that "the blond Yankee" only lynched those whom he deemed to be his racial inferior, the editorial's author articulated the conclusion that inevitably had to be drawn from the mob's murder of Rodriguez: "When a Mexican is immolated, it is to be inferred that the social conscience of the state of Texas, in her loathsome scorn, compares the sons of Negroland with the descendants of Cuauhtémoc. Our race is in no way inferior to the Anglo Saxon."[74] The author's use of "Negroland," a purely racial construction dislodged from history and geography, as the imagined native land of black men emphasizes the supposedly incommensurable distance between Mexicans and Negroes and between Mexican nation and black no-nation.

The primary focus of the article is to assert Mexican racial superiority to white Americans, vividly described as "gentlemen pigs," "blond animals," and "the pig-stickers of Dollarland." However, the author's division between Mexican race, sprung from noble and resistant ancestors, and the "trampled upon" race of "Negroland" reasserts well-worn racist constructions of blackness as perpetual primitivity, outside of history and the bounds of moral social ties. Later in the article, to further establish the savagery of U.S. civilization, the editorial asserted that "the land of the DOLLAR ... according to its moral latitude, is situated in the center of Africa."[75] *Diario del Hogar*'s repeated description of Americans as "pigmies" also works to ridicule Americans' racial arrogance by likening them to "primitive" Africans, whose small stature evinces a humiliating unmanliness. Despite their economic strength, as "pigmies of culture" or "pigmies of human understanding," the rhetoric suggests, North Americans were culturally equivalent to the primitive blacks they tortured. Mexicans, the "sons of Anahuac," the center of Aztec civilization, "are proud gentlemen, impoverished aristocrats."[76] Despite their present dispossession and humiliation at the hands of savage North Americans, their history demonstrates their inherent racial and cultural superiority and thus the injustice of their present treatment. The killing of Rodriguez by an "iniquitous" method used for killing the natally alienated degrades the nation as it denies their history, treating the Mexican like a being "without a country."

The depiction of "negroes" and "Sons of Cuauhtémoc" as mutually exclusive captures the manner in which people of African descent in Mexico and their particular contributions to national independence were elided in the production of national memory. Historian Ted Vincent has argued that large proportions of people of African descent were engaged in Mexico's War of Independence from Spain because of the insurgency's promise of social equality and also because the area in which much of the struggle was waged was heavily populated by people of African descent.[77] Long before the war, Africans in New Spain, as in British North America, were viewed as dangerous to the colonial project. In a 1590 economic survey of the Mexican colony, a Spanish writer observed of the enslaved population, "They are well known to be our enemies." Yanga's struggle against colonial authorities in Vera Cruz, which, as noted above, was memorialized by Mexican historian Riva Palacio, was the first successful slave rebellion on the continent. During the course of the uprising, enslaved people freed themselves and built a maroon settlement in the mountains, eventually negotiating territorial autonomy from the Spanish authorities. Their settlement was officially established as a town, today known as Yanga.[78] The exclusion of such struggles from the dominant narratives of Mexican nation reverberates in the imagery of blackness deployed in the Rodriguez discourse. Clearly the authors of these editorials used African Americans, seen through the prism of U.S. anti-black discourse, as their reference, yet the positioning of the abject, nationless "negro" as the antithesis of Mexican peoplehood also reflects Mexico's own history of slavery and its conspicuous inattention to its African-descended population.

A stoic death

In this final section of the chapter, I will examine how the familiar themes of resistance and manly death emerged in the Rodriguez protest discourse. Though Rodriguez's killers, as Mexican and American observers pointed out, used methods that many of their white countrymen had exacted upon African Americans, printed accounts of the killing often differed from the standard narratives of anti-black lynching. A few papers told the story of Rodriguez's death using the macabre conventions of the lynching genre forged in the telling of anti-black terrorism. Several papers used an identical subheadline, "Texas Mob Makes Short Work of Confessed Murderer," to that used in reports of a black man named Leonard Johnson lynched five months earlier in Rusk, Texas. In this version of the lynching, in the typical ghoulish style of the anti-black lynching narrative, Rodriguez "cuddles in one corner of his cell" when the mob comes for him; he is described as "trembling and begging for mercy" when they drag him to the pyre. The accounts note his "groan of agony" as the "flames leap around his body."[79] Yet other accounts of the burning made explicit reference to Rodriguez's composure during the ordeal. The *El Paso Herald*, for example, commented that he met his death "without emotion." The *Houston Post* reported that Rodriguez struggled "but never whimpered." On November 4, the *St. Louis Star and Times* reported that Rodriguez "showed no emotion when tied to the stake and died without a plea for mercy."[80]

Interestingly, within the flurry of discourse of Mexican rage, political tension between the two nations, and murmurs of potential war, in several papers a new version of Rodriguez's burning emerged. In some cases, this new version was recounted in exactly the same article that assured readers that the "alleged uprising" of Mexicans heading toward Texas was a fantasy, and that "everything [was] quiet along the border." Appearing next to notices of political meetings in Guadalajara, Mexico, in which Mexican men pledged their services to fight Americans in the case of war, or evaluations of the current diplomatic situation between the two nations, the telling of Rodriguez's lynching in these stories differed markedly from earlier accounts. In contrast to earlier stories stating that Texans had made "short work" of the alleged murderer, the new telling emphasized that "many Mexicans" had taken part in the lynching. In fact, they specified, the "Americans were for hanging the man but the Mexicans cried, "Burn him, burn him."[81] In addition to the claim that it was Mexicans who insisted upon death by fire, these new accounts of Rodriguez's lynching printed after the rumored march of Mexicans on Texas offered a selection of other "facts" seemingly designed to illustrate its moral legitimacy: "No ill feeling was displayed" before or after the event; Mexicans had joined in the posse that searched for Rodriguez. Included in these lustrating details is an embellished account of the moment of his death:

> So he was tied to a mesquite tree, other wood piled around him, oil poured on and the mass set on fire. The man's body was burned to a cinder. Rodriguez displayed not a bit of nervousness. All the while the flames were lashing his body he jeered at the crowd.[82]

On the one hand, Rodriguez's demeanor in death might be read as further evidence of his guilt. He is unrepentant of his terrible crimes and jeers at those who bring justice. On the other hand, the assertion that he "displayed not a bit of nervousness," and the description of his death as "stoic" which appeared in some versions of the story, are starkly divergent from the image of Rodriquez "trembling and begging" his captors for mercy, a recurring trope in the "folk pornography" of anti-black lynching.[83] Just as his recalcitrance in death works to legitimize his fate by establishing his continued threat, it also does so by granting Rodriguez a kind of masculine, if sinister, agency. He remains defiant, even as the flames are "lashing his body," never disintegrating into abject, pleading submission to his captors. Though a murderer (a "bad Mexican," as one of the articles put it), Rodriguez nonetheless died a masculine death. Like the more conspicuous articulation of the participation of Mexican men in the hunting and burning, the retelling of Rodriguez's "stoic death" seems to insinuate that the burning was not a racial insult but an act of brutal but righteous justice, undertaken by Mexican and American men upon a criminal among them.

The two Mexico City editorials sent by Henry Lane Wilson to the secretary of state cited Rodriguez's supposedly staunch demeanor as he was murdered and envisioned this as part of Mexicans' proud racial heritage of resistance. One noted that this "unfortunate compatriot met his death with the imperturbable calmness of his heroic race."[84] The other, directing itself to the United States, asserted not only that the blood of Cuauhtémoc showed itself in Rodriguez's manly death, but also that his martyrdom bore ill tides for the nation that murdered him.

> You have saciated [sic.] your barbarous appetite, by burning alive Antonio Rodriguez, in whose veins flows the blood of Cuauhtémoc, but he, without a complaint or gesture [in] the face of his martyrdom cast upon you the eternal curse which you bear stamped on your foreheads.[85]

The phrases used to describe Rodriguez's death – "without complaint or gesture," "imperturbable calmness" – are markedly similar to the early accounts of the lynching in the American press, noted above, that Rodriguez died "without emotion" or "plea for mercy." In the Mexican protest discourse, U.S. reports of Rodriguez's implied strength in the face of torture and fire were imbued with a deep nationalist meaning.

Heroic and violent death, as I will explore further in the next chapter, has often been a potent resource in narratives of manhood and nation. As a hero of national history, Cuauhtémoc was significant not for victory in arms over his enemies but for enduring his enemies' torments without submitting – an imagery that clearly created potent grounds for imagining Rodriguez as a figure of national defiance. In 1887 the Díaz regime completed a massive neoclassical monument to Cuauhtémoc on the Paseo de la Reforma, the main thoroughfare in Mexico City. An observer of the monument's dedication eulogized its emotional meaning for modern Mexicans as follows:

> In Cuauhtémoc we do not see the last descendant of the Aztec kings ... [instead] we view in him the hero of the fatherland ... Cuauhtémoc conquered, Cuauhtémoc imprisoned and enchained, Cuauhtémoc powerless to defend his throne by means of arms, defended it suffering valiantly the wicked and terrible torments ... [providing] with such heroic sacrifice [a] most solemn protest against usurpation which later should produce its greatest and most precious fruits.[86]

As Lyman Johnson points out, in multiple instances within Latin American national mythologies, the death of a martyr at the hands of cruel enemies, and often preceded by torment and bodily suffering, has been represented as giving life to a people and a nation.[87] Cuauhtémoc's defeat fulfills the sacred manly imperative to choose death before submission. The vulnerability of his body to his Spanish tormentors is honorable, evidence of virility rather than abjection, making possible "the precious fruits" of nationhood. The visual narrative around the monument pedestal is striking. Cuauhtémoc gestures to Cortés's knife, suggesting that he would rather be killed than live as a captive. The next panel shows Cuauhtémoc and a kinsman being tortured by Cortés in an attempt to force them to reveal the whereabouts of hidden treasure. With obvious resonance for the Rodriguez lynching,

Cuauhtémoc's feet are coated in oil and burned in fire, yet he remains calm, rather than indulging the pain.

The suggestive parallel between the immolating fire of U.S. barbarians and Spanish conquerors is drawn out in the students' statement, which also emphasized the noble nature of Rodriguez's death. "With his foot in the furnace," it read, "Rodriguez died for the country he loved."[88] Mexicans, disadvantaged by poverty, might be subject to insult from the "blond beasts," but remained "the sons of a proud and noble race" in their endurance.[89] Even in the face of material domination, an internal masculine autonomy could be maintained. Acknowledging the vulnerability of Mexicans to American power, the *Debate* editorial insisted: "If … we find ourselves compelled on some occasions to submit to the kicks of the 'Yankee' hoof, it does not mean that we acknowledge any superiority, either ethnical or individual, in the shopkeepers that shed the blood of the Spanish lion."[90] Unlike the "negro race," trampled under Yankee hooves, Mexicans were truly "valient [sic.]" and "indomitable." Their "ethnical" and national honor, forged through a history of resistance, elevated their suffering above the violation of their bodies.

In their contemplations of relations between Mexico and the United States, for the Mexican writers considered here the violent subjection of black people was presented as a defining practice of American civilization, one which endangered Mexican migrants but which also demonstrated the moral and cultural superiority of the Mexican nation. In the protest discourse that emerged in response to the lynching, the imagined relationship between Mexicans and blackness fluctuates considerably across texts. The students' statement drew a connection of common vulnerability between "opprest negroes" and "defenseless strangers," as such emphasizing the migrant's distance from homeland rather than his national superiority. In contrast, the construction of Mexicans as "sons of Cuauhtémoc" insisted upon their elevated place within the family of nations and the civilizational pedigree of their blood, using anti-black imagery to deny "defenselessness" and unmanly vulnerability.

White Americans' imperialist arguments tied Mexicans' indigenous ancestry to lack of civilizational achievement and to a dysfunctional, stilted, and therefore violable nationhood. As they denied Americans' right to lynch Mexicans because of their historical and ancestral qualifications, Mexicans challenged the content of American race claims but nevertheless rearticulated the underlying logic that linked constructions of national civilization and racial worth. While necessarily distinct and yet not entirely separate from U.S. imaginaries of "savage tribes," "faithful slaves," and "black rapists," the exclusion of blackness from Mexican national identity and the celebration of ancestral Aztec resistance in some Mexican expressions of anti-U.S. protest after the Rodriguez lynching reflect the imbricated transborder processes of race-making in the Americas.

Notes

1. Note from Mexican Embassy to President Taft, November 13, 1910, Records of the Department of State Relating to Internal Affairs of Mexico 1910–1929, NARA 812.00/380, Cambridge University Library.
2. Telegram from Ambassador Wilson to Secretary of State, November 14, 1910, regarding interview with President Díaz, NARA 812.00/379. Wary that, if achieved, the lynching would further strain relations with Mexico, the State Department sent a telegram to the governor of Oklahoma urging that local authorities prevent such an occurrence at all costs. "Diaz Again Demands Action on Lynching," November 14, 1910, *New York Times*, 4.
3. Letter from Henry Lane Wilson to Secretary of State, November 10, 1910, NARA 812.00/385, pp. 2–4.
4. Telegram from Taft to Knox, November 11, 1910, NARA 812.00/362.
5. "Americans Victims of Mobs in Mexico," November 10, 1910, *Los Angeles Times*, 1, 15; "U.S. Flag Ripped up by Mexican Mob," November 10, 1910, *York Daily* (York, PA), 1; "Rioting in Mexico against Americans," November 10, 1910, *New York Times*, 1; "Mobs Raged in the Streets of Mexico," November 10, 1910, *Houston Post*, 1.
6. Cited in Rice, "The Lynching of Antonio Rodriguez," 28–29.
7. "Comments of the Local Press on the Lynching and Demonstrations," November 11, 1910, *Mexican Herald*, 5.
8. Carrigan and Webb, *Forgotten Dead*, 157–58.
9. "Mexico," November 24, 1910, *New York Age*, 4.
10. William D. Carrigan and Clive Webb, "*Muerto por Unos Desconocidos* (Killed by Persons Unknown): Mob Violence against Blacks and Mexicans," in *Beyond Black and White: Race, Ethnicity, and Gender in the U.S. South and Southwest*, ed. Stephanie Cole and Alison M. Parker (College Station: Texas A&M University Press, 2004), 36–37. Equal Justice Initiative, "Lynching in America: Confronting the Legacy of Racial Terror," report (Montgomery, AL: Equal Justice Initiative 2017).
11. Carrigan and Webb, *Forgotten Dead*, 83. Carrigan and Webb note that in nineteenth-century California, large crowds often gathered to witness and/or participate in the killing. A Mexican woman named Juanita, for example, was hung before a mob of hundreds in 1851. *Forgotten Dead*, 81, 69–70. For an analysis of the Juanita lynching, see Nicole Marie Guidotti-Hernández, *Unspeakable Violence: Remapping U.S. and Mexican National Imaginaries* (Durham, NC: Duke University Press, 2011).
12. Texas State Legislature, *Proceedings of the Joint Committee of the Senate and the House in the Investigation of the Texas State Ranger Force*, 36th

Texas Legislature, Regular Session (Austin, 1919), vol. 1, 27–28. Ribb, "*La Rinchada*," 68.

13 David Garland, "Penal Excess and Surplus Meaning: Public Torture Lynchings in Twentieth-Century America," *Law & Society Review* 39, no. 4 (2005): 798, 803.
14 Carrigan and Webb, *Forgotten Dead*, 83.
15 Patterson, *Rituals of Blood*, 191–92.
16 Garland, "Penal Excess and Surplus Meaning," 813–14. Stuart Banner, *The Death Penalty: An American History* (Cambridge, MA, and London: Harvard University Press, 2002), 71.
17 Friend, "'The Crushing of Southern Manhood,'" 26. Eric Foner, "The Meaning of Freedom in the Age of Emancipation," *Journal of American History* 81, no. 2 (1994): 449.
18 Patterson, *Slavery and Social Death*, 5.
19 Litwack, *Been in the Storm so Long*, 238.
20 Patterson, *Slavery and Social Death*, 7.
21 W.E.B. Du Bois, *The World and Africa: An Inquiry into the Part which African Has Played in World History* (New York: International Publishers, 1992), 34, 20.
22 Jared Sexton, "People-of-Color-Blindness: Notes on the Afterlife of Slavery," *Social Text* 28, no. 2 (2010): 41.
23 Lomnitz, "Los Orígenes de Nuestra Supuesta Homogeneidad," 36.
24 Juliet Hooker, *Theorizing Race in the Americas: Douglass, Sarmiento, Du Bois, and Vasconcelos* (New York: Oxford University Press, 2017), 184. For an interesting account of Vasconcelos's childhood see Luis A. Marentes, *José Vasconcelos and the Writing of the Mexican Revolution* (New York: Twayne Publishers, 2000). 39–47.
25 Hart, *Empire and Revolution*, 167, 260, 272. And more generally, 71–135.
26 Lomnitz, "Los Orígenes de Nuestra Supuesta Homogeneidad," 30. Hart, *Empire and Revolution*, 230, 260–61.
27 Hart, *Empire and Revolution*, 271, 260–61. Lomnitz, "Los Orígenes de Nuestra Supuesta Homogeneidad," 30.
28 "Reaping the Whirlwind," November 12, 1910, *Regeneración*, 4.
29 "Yankilandia," November 7, 1910, *El Diario del Hogar*. Enclosure in letter to Secretary of State from Henry Lane Wilson, November 10, 1910, NARA 812.00/385. Anuahac is a Nahuatl name, meaning "By the Water," for Mexico.
30 "U.S. Flag Ripped up by Mexican Mob," November 10, 1910, *York Daily* (York, PA), 1. "Mexican Hostility," November 26, 1910, *Literary Digest*, 41, no. 22 (1910): 965.
31 "Try to Spread Anti-American Feeling," November 17, 1910, *Montrose Democrat* (Montrose, PA), 4. "Another Mexican Killed in Texas," November 15, 1910, *Washington Herald*, 1.
32 "Try to Spread Anti-American Feeling," November 17, 1910, *Montrose Democrat*, 4; "A Question of Nativity," November 14, 1910, *Daily Republican* (Rushville, IN), 7.

33 Mae M. Ngai, *Impossible Subjects: Illegal Aliens and the Making of Modern America* (Princeton: Princeton University Press, 2004), 8.
34 "Texas in the Limelight," November 23, 1910, *Houston Post*, 6.
35 New Mexico was not admitted to statehood until 1912. From annexation after the Mexican–American War it was administered as an incorporated territory of the United States.
36 James L. Slayden, "Some Observations on Mexican Immigration," *Annals of the American Academy of Political and Social Science* 93, no. 1 (1921): 125.
37 "Mexico Prevents Further Rioting," November 11, 1910, *New York Times*, 1.
38 Frederick C. Turner, "Anti-Americanism in Mexico, 1910–1913," *Hispanic American Historical Review* 47, no. 4 (1967): 506.
39 Rice, "The Lynching of Antonio Rodriguez," 23–24. Committee on Foreign Relations, "Investigation of Mexican Affairs," 2003.
40 Ibid., 312.
41 Roland G. Usher, "The Real Mexican Problem," *North American Review* 200, no. 704 (1914): 46–47, 51.
42 "Texans Arm in Anticipation of Invasion," November 16, 1910, *San Francisco Call*, 2; "Fear Trouble," November 15, 1910, *Houston Post*, 8.; "Armed Mexicans Said to Have Crossed the Border," November 18, 1910, *Buffalo Evening News*, 1. "Texans Ready to Fight," November 16, 1910, *Baltimore Sun*, 2.
43 "Strong Measure to Suppress Rioters," November 11, 1910, *Buffalo Evening News*, 10; "Americans Will Be Protected," November 11, 1910, *Warren Times Mirror* (Warren, PA), 7.
44 Rosales, *"Pobre Raza!": Violence, Justice, and Mobilization among Mexico Lindo Immigrants, 1900–1936*, 111. Rice, "The Lynching of Antonio Rodriguez," 47–48.
45 Lomnitz, "Los Orígenes de Nuestra Supuesta Homogeneidad," 36. On Mexicans in Texas and anti-black racism, see, Neil Foley, "Partly Colored or Other White: Mexican Americans and Their Problem with the Color Line," in *Beyond Black and White: Race, Ethnicity, and Gender in the U.S. South and Southwest*, ed. Stephanie Cole, Alison M. Parker, and Laura F. Edwards (College Station: Texas A&M University Press, 2004); Neil Foley, *The White Scourge: Mexicans, Blacks, and Poor Whites in Texas Cotton Culture* (Berkeley: University of California Press, 1997).
46 Mónica G. Morena Figueroa and Emiko Tanaka Saldívar, "'We Are Not Racists, We Are Mexicans': Privilege, Nationalism and Post-Race Ideology in Mexico," *Critical Sociology* 42, no. 4–5 (2016): 522.
47 Christina A. Sue, *Land of the Cosmic Race: Race Mixture, Racism, and Blackness in Mexico* (New York: Oxford University Press, 2013), 114–15. Ted Vincent, "The Blacks who Freed Mexico," *Journal of Negro History* 79, no. 3 (1994): 153.
48 Sue, *Land of the Cosmic Race*, 16–17.
49 María Elisa Velázquez, "Africanos y Afrodescendientes en México: Premisas Que Obstaculizan Entender su Pasado y Presente," *Cuicuilco* 18 (2011): 17. Ben Vinson III, "Fading from Memory: Historiographical Reflections on

the Afro-Mexican Presence," *Review of Black Political Economy* 33, no. 1 (2005): 67.
50 Maricela Jiménez Ramos, "Black Mexico: Nineteenth Century of Race and Nation," Ph.D. dissertation (Brown University, 2009), 95–96. See also Sue, *Land of the Cosmic Race*. Vinson III, "Fading from Memory." Bobby Vaughn, "México Negro: From the Shadows of Nationalist Mestizaje to New Possibilities in Afro-Mexican Identity," *Journal of Pan African Studies* 16, no. 1 (2013).
51 Alfonso Toro, "Influencia de la Raza Negra en la Formación del Pueblo Mexicano," *Ethnos* 8–12 (1920–1921): 218.
52 Theodore G. Vincent, "The Contributions of Mexico's First Black President, Vicente Guerrero," *Journal of Negro History* 86, no. 2 (2001): 154. Ben Vinson III, "Afro-Mexican History: Trends and Directions in Scholarship," *History Compass* 3, no. LA 156 (2005): 2. Jiménez Ramos, "Black Mexico," 209.
53 Hooker, *Theorizing Race in the Americas*, 175.
54 Vasconcelos, *The Cosmic Race*, 26.
55 Ibid., 32, 22.
56 Ibid., 26.
57 "Mexican Intervention," *Messenger*, 2, no. 11 (1919): 17–18.
58 Gerald Horne, *Black and Brown: African Americans and the Mexican Revolution, 1910–1920* (New York: New York University Press, 2005), 34. Committee on Foreign Relations, "Investigation of Mexican Affairs," 1113–14.

For more on Jack Johnson, see: Theresa Runstedtler, *Jack Johnson, Rebel Sojourner: Boxing in the Shadow of the Global Color Line* (Berkeley: University of California Press, 2012).
59 Horne, *Black and Brown*, 35.
60 Linda B. Hall, *Oil, Banks and Politics: The United States and Postrevolutionary Mexico, 1917–1924* (Austin: University of Texas Press, 1995), ch. 3: "Albert Fall and Mexican Oil."
61 Ribb, "*La Rinchada*," 88–89.
62 Horne, *Black and Brown*, 34. Committee on Foreign Relations, "Investigation of Mexican Affairs," 1113–14.
63 "La Repercusion de un Linchamiento," November 12, 1910, *Regeneración*, 1.
64 Tiffany Willoughby-Herard, "More Expendable than Slaves? Racial Justice and the After-Life of Slavery," *Politics, Groups, and Identities* 2, no. 3 (2014): 516, 514.
65 "Reaping the Whirlwind," November 12, 1910. *Regeneración*, 4.
66 "Mexican Hostility," *Literary Digest*, 966.
67 Bederman, *Manliness and Civilization*, 1–3. In Uvalia, Georgia, for instance, white rioters killed three black men. Bederman writes that there were also instances in which black men attacked white men making derogatory comments about the champion. "Fight News is Followed by Race Riots in Many Parts of the Country," July 5, 1910, *Los Angeles Herald*, 1.
68 "Mexican Hostility", *Literary Digest*, 966.
69 Lomnitz, "Los Orígenes de Nuestra Supuesta Homogeneidad," 34. Rice, "The Lynching of Antonio Rodriguez", 35.

70 Jerry W. Knudson, "The *Mexican Herald*: Outpost of Empire, 1895–1915," *Gazette* 63, no. 5 (2001): 389.
71 "The History of Lynch Law in the United States," November 13, 1910, *Mexican Herald*, 1.
72 "Yankilandia", *El Diario del Hogar.*
73 Lyman L. Johnson, *Death, Dismemberment, and Memory: Body Politics in Latin America* (Albuquerque: University of New Mexico Press, 2004), 213.
74 "La Pezuna de Dollaria" (translated as "The Cloven Feet of the Counting-House Nobility" in English-language enclosure), November 5, 1910, *El Debate*, Enclosure no. 1 in Letter to Secretary of State from American Ambassador Wilson, November 10, 1910, NARA 812.00/385.
75 "Yankilandia", *El Diario del Hogar.*
76 Ibid.
77 Vinson III, "Fading from Memory"; Vincent, "The Blacks who Freed Mexico," 260. Vincent suggests that part of the reason that "the Afro-Mexican role in the war is obscured [is] because insurgent politics were aimed at minimizing race to maximize unity."
78 Vinson III, "Fading from Memory," 60, 59. Sue, *Land of the Cosmic Race*, 118. Sue notes that Yanga bears a banner at its entrance that reads "Welcome to Yanga – the first free town of America." A statute depicting Yanga with machete in hand stands in the town. However, the town's story has been "relegated to the extreme margins of Mexican national narratives."
79 "Negro Burned to Stake," June 25, 1910, *Indiana Gazette*, 3; "Negro Burned to Stake", June 25, 1910, *Record-Argus* (Greenville, PA), 1. In these articles, Johnson is referred to as "the frightened negro" and described as "pleading for his life." "Mexican Burned at Stake by Mob," November 7, 1910, *Sheboygan Press* (Sheboygan, WI), 5; "Mexican Burned at Stake by Mob," November 5, 1910, *Dixon Evening Telegraph*, 7.
80 "Texans Burn Mexican Citizen of Mexico who Killed Woman," November 4, 1910, *El Paso Herald*, 1. "Burned at Stake", November 4, 1910, *Houston Post*, 4. "Murderer Burns at Stake," November 4, 1910, *St. Louis Star and Times*, 4. A similar account appears in "Mexican Burned at Stake," November 5, 1910, *Baltimore Sun*, 1. A Shreveport paper described Rodriguez as "[meeting] his doom calmly." "Burned at Stake Fate of Mexican," November 10, 1910, *Caucasian* (Shreveport, LA), 2. In its reporting of the incident, which was in the context of the diplomatic issues that it had caused, the *New York Times* also described Rodriguez as "offering little resistance." "Why Rodriguez Was Burned," November 11, 1910, *New York Times*, 2.
81 This version of the story appeared in: "Armed Mexicans May Come," November 16, 1910, *Morning Star* (Wilmington, NC), 1; "A Use of Mexican Troubles," November 16, 1910, *Times-Mercury* (Hickory, NC) 2. "Rock Springs in No Danger," November 16, 1910, *Times* (Shreveport, LA), 1; "Rock Springs Safe," November 17, 1910, *Town Talk* (Alexandria, LA), 3.
82 Ibid. In the version in the North Carolina papers, instead of "display[ing] not a bit of nervousness," Rodriguez is described as dying a "stoic death."

83 Patricia Bernstein, "An 'Exciting Occurrence': The Lynching," in *Anti-Black Violence in Twentieth-Century Texas*, ed. Bruce A. Glasrud (College Station: Texas A&M University Press, 2015), 54. Hall, *Revolt against Chivalry*, 150.
84 "La Pezuna de Dollaria," November 5, 1910, *El Debate*.
85 "Yankilandia," *El Diario del Hogar*.
86 Johnson, *Death, Dismemberment, and Memory*, 214–16.
87 Ibid.
88 "Mexican Hostility", *Literary Digest*, 966.
89 "La Pezuna de Dollaria," *El Debate*.
90 Ibid.

4

Without a tremor

On December 10, 1917, a company of engineers from Fort Sam Houston near San Antonio worked through the night by the light of bonfires to build a scaffold in a clearing of mesquite trees. The fires were still burning in the dark of the early morning of the 11th when the trucks arrived carrying thirteen members of the Third Battalion of the Twenty-Fourth U.S. Infantry. After the men were hanged, Mexican laborers removed the hangman's knots then put the bodies in wooden coffins. Each man was buried with a soda water bottle containing a slip of paper on which his name and rank were typewritten, as well as a note which read, "Died December 11, 1917 at Fort Sam Houston." The laborers buried the coffins in makeshift graves marked with tin plates numbered 1 to 13. Before the army issued a formal announcement of their execution, which had been carried out in secret, the scaffold was taken apart and the timber burned. "One might tramp for hours over the hundreds of brush-covered acres of the military reservation," the readers of the *New York Times* were told on December 12, "without finding either execution site or burial ground."[1] The execution was at once a carefully orchestrated military spectacle and an act of obliteration.

The dead men had been convicted of willfully disobeying the lawful commands of their superior officer, mutiny, murder, and felonious assault. After weeks stationed near a city where policemen and civilians assaulted and abused them, on the night of August 23, approximately 100 men of the Twenty-Fourth Infantry armed themselves and left their camp, defying the orders of their white officers. They marched on the city of Houston in "semi-military formation" to seek out the policemen who had beaten, arrested, and shot at two of their comrades. Though their intended target had been the city's police, in addition to five officers, four killed at the scene and another who died later from his wounds, their victims included two white soldiers and eight civilians. Among the dead killed in the Twenty-Fourth's hail of bullets was a Mexican American man who had been sleeping on a bench in the backyard of the boarding house where he roomed.[2] After the nation's largest-ever court martial of sixty-three men, thirteen of them were sentenced to death without the chance to appeal, while a further forty-one were sentenced to terms of life-imprisonment at Leavenworth Federal Penitentiary. Two subsequent courts martial sentenced sixteen more men to hang and twelve to life terms.[3]

Less than two months before the soldiers of the Twenty-Fourth marched on Houston's white policemen, a mob of white civilians, facilitated by the indifference, incompetence, or direct assistance of police and national guardsmen, murdered perhaps hundreds of black people on the streets of East St. Louis.[4] As in the explanations of lynching that understood white people's resort to barbarism as an exasperated response to incomprehensible black deviance, coverage of East St. Louis in white newspapers decried the cruelty of the mob while also highlighting the polluting effects of the city's deluge of black migrants. Though distancing himself from the violence of "raw country yaps" and "undisciplined boys," one "prominent" white man told a reporter that black migrants from the South "were intoxicated with the new freedom they found ... and flaunted themselves in a manner that would have been intolerable even in a white man." In the days that followed, the savagery of the mob's punishment and the suffering of the black populace were described in graphic detail in newspapers across the country. The subheadline for reporter Carlos Hurd's first-person account in the *St. Louis Post Dispatch* promised a "Vivid Description of Massacring of Negroes." The graphic depictions of black people's death and torture in U.S. newspapers, which told of scores of victims wretched, exposed, and undifferentiated by "age or sex, innocence or guilt," as one account put it, indulged tropes of black vulnerability, criminality, and decay.[5]

In responding to the mutiny in Houston and the execution of the men condemned for it, the print media produced an imagery that alternately radically subverted and rearticulated the usual tropes of anti-black violence. "It is difficult for one of Negro blood to write of Houston," W.E.B. Du Bois wrote after the men of the Twenty-Fourth marched.

> Is not the ink within the very wells crimsoned with the blood of martyrs? Do they not cry unavenged, saying: Always WE pay, always WE die; always, whether right or wrong, it is SO MANY NEGROES killed, so many NEGROES wounded. But here, at last, at Houston is a change. Here, at last, white folk died.[6]

Du Bois found no cause for exultation in the death of white folk; "we did not have to have Houston," he concluded, "in order to know that black men will not always be mere victims." Du Bois asserted that the men had to be punished for their actions, which he described as "another injustice." Other black writers framed the mutiny in different terms. An untitled editorial clipped by military intelligence asserted, "Of course it was a crime for them to go out and kill citizens of Houston; so is it a crime for revolutionists to rise up and chop off the heads of their overlords."[7] Both this unnamed author and Du Bois were agreed upon the soldierly valor of the men of the Twenty-Fourth. Rather than a lack of discipline, their terrible actions were the result of upright manhood tormented by intolerable conditions. "[These men] were not young recruits," Du Bois wrote, "they were not wild and drunken wastrels; they were disciplined men who said 'This is enough; we'll stand no more!'"[8] African American leaders and civilians articulating a range of political values, from those insisting on black patriotism as well as those who questioned whether black men should fight for a democracy that excluded them, reasserted the manliness and martial worth of the Twenty-Fourth Infantry. The socialist editors of the *Messenger*, for example, referred to the hanged men as "some of the bravest, most patriotic soldiers which the United States has ever had."[9]

Exploring the rich symbolic relationship between manhood, violence, and death produced in nationalist discourses of war and patriotism as well as black authors' indictment of American racial order, in this chapter I will trace the conditions from which the Houston Mutiny erupted and examine the ways in which a range of observers sought to give meaning to the state's hanging of the thirteen men. The state's execution of the men catalyzed a multivalent gendered discourse of self-sacrifice and heroism that, depending on the telling, could be read to demonstrate the men's affinity to or rejection of the nation. I will argue that just as a number of African American writers invoked the soldiers' manly death to denounce the racial order against which they had struck, the same imagery was used by the white press to subtly legitimize their punishment and obscure the intelligibility of black dissent. In such accounts the killing and dying of the men of the Twenty-Fourth diverge from the familiar tropes of violent black subjection, but nevertheless reconstitute black difference.

"As he does not cherish life"

Colonel George O. Cress, who investigated the mutiny in Houston, concluded in his report for the Southern Department of the Inspector General of the U.S. Army that there was a fundamental "incompatibility between the handling of the negro by the civil authorities of Houston, and the training of the negro soldiers as pursued in the service, where effort is made to increase his self-respect, his respect for the uniform and for the authority of the government."[10] While explicitly identifying the city's treatment of "the negro race," the resentment of the men at Jim Crow laws and the brutality of the police as causative factors in the mutiny, Cress concluded that "the tendency of the negro soldier, with fire arms in his possession, unless he is properly handled by officers who know his racial characteristics, is to become arrogant, overbearing, and abusive, and a menace to the community in which he happens to be stationed."[11]

Like Colonel Cress, the Jamaican-born Harlem radical Hubert Harrison also drew links between the mutiny and anti-black violence and also identified black soldiers as an inevitable "menace" but he did not couch his reasoning in vague racial terms about the Negro's "tendencies." He compared the acts of the black soldiers to the 1916 lynching of black teenager Jesse Washington in Waco, Texas, which had been watched by a crowd of ten to fifteen thousand. "Both killings were illegal," Harrison wrote. "But every fool knows that the spirit of lawlessness, mob-violence and race hatred which found expression in the first was the thing which called forth the second." His conclusion summarized explicitly what was implicit in federal, local, and military authorities' responses to black soldiers: "Negro soldiers (disguise it how we will) must always be a menace to any state which lynches Negro civilians."[12] Both Harrison's and Cress's pessimistic assessments of the volatile situation presented by the black soldier reflect the broader tensions inherent in the nation's regulation of racial domination at a time of war.

In the wartime atmosphere of hyper-nationalist vigilance against subversion, deeply rooted suspicion of African Americans as a lurking internal force of disorder intensified. After East St. Louis, rather than seek to ameliorate the violent subordination that essentially undergirded fears of black subversion, many white Americans and the government responded with further repression. As part of a broader repression of radicalism and dissent, the government initiated an extensive surveillance project on black civilians, soldiers, leaders, and press.[13] There was particular concern, investigated vigorously by the Bureau of Investigation, that German agents would seduce African Americans, an anxiety rearticulating the positioning of black people as an internal enemy, to be manipulated by external foes. Reflecting the voracious violence to which black people were subject and the perceived threat of black men in uniform, at least nineteen black soldiers were lynched during the war years.[14]

The relationship of black men to the state and to the gun, as Adriane Lentz-Smith has observed, was profoundly reshaped during the Great War: "In peacetime, white people could write off black resistance and rebellion as criminality, pathology, or isolated occurrences ... However, the world war required that tens of thousands of African Americans harness violence against white men in the service of a segregated state and contested nation."[15] Given the invigorated symbolic importance of violence in national discourses of war and nation, as well as, of course, the deadly mob violence to which African Americans were increasingly vulnerable during the war years, ideologies of armed self-defense gained greater acceptance among black middle classes.[16] While in 1917, some black newspaper editors and political leaders sought to emphasize the loyalty of the black population, and particularly black soldiers, to the nation and the war effort, many African Americans were decidedly ambivalent to the war, "unimpressed or repulsed by the home-front propaganda," as Mark Ellis puts it, and increasingly militant in their rejection of racist subordination.[17] Black writers and activists describing themselves as New Negroes struck a militant stance against both domestic racism and broader global relations of colonialism. While they rejected the racist humiliations of American social order, as well as the notion that black men should die to defend it in a segregated military, as Matthew Guterl notes, they celebrated the manly qualities of the black soldier, "link[ing] black male experience in battle with racial self-determination."[18] Thus the black soldier could be linked to discourses of nationalist patriotism as well as black self-defense.

Integral to discourses of black men's determination to defend their manhood and people was the assertion of their readiness to die. In 1919 riots tore through cities across the United States, in which black communities met white attackers with armed resistance, often with black veterans in the vanguard. An editorial printed in the black publication the *Veteran*, and subsequently flagged by the Bureau of Investigation, asserted that these smoldering sites of violence demonstrated that "Uncle Tom is dead and that a new Negro rises in his tracks, a Negro who values liberty as he does not cherish life."[19] Guterl writes that a varied range of black leaders, from Du Bois to more militant radicals like Cyril Briggs, "were united in their respect for the symbolic importance of male death in the service of race-patriotism."[20] The black man armed and ready to die for his freedom disrupted the constructions of black abnormality and death, including the degenerating race lingering in immorality and disease in social science and the exposed and abject victims of white fury that proliferated in the white press. As I will discuss in more detail below, in keeping with the modern linkage between sacrifice, manhood, and nation, it was the perceived willingness of the men of the Twenty-Fourth to die for true democracy that many black observers highlighted as meaningful rather than merely their armed retaliation against the white men who abused them.

Black readiness for self-sacrificial death was also among the themes that alarmed and offended agents of the state. When Attorney General A. Mitchell Palmer submitted a report to the Senate compiling the Bureau of Investigation's surveillance against "persons advising anarchy, sedition and the forcible overthrow of the government," it included a twenty-seven-page section titled, "Radicalism and Sedition among Negroes as Reflected in their Publications." "Among the more salient points to be noted in the present attitude of the Negro leaders," the report read, summarizing the key areas of trouble, "are first, the ill-governed reaction toward race rioting; second, the threat of retaliatory measures in connection with lynching."[21] In other words, it was resistance to lynching and mob violence, rather than lynching and mob violence themselves, that were deemed to endanger the government and social order. Adherence to Soviet doctrines only came fourth on the list.

The Bureau of Investigation was particularly rankled by the *Messenger*, "the most able and dangerous of all the Negro publications." An editorial from the September 1919 issue, described as "more insolently offensive than any of its other issues," does not extol the virtues of socialist revolution but the New Negroes' commitment to self-defense: "The demand is uncompromisingly made for either liberty or death, and since death is likely to be a two-edged sword it will be to the advantage of those in a position to do so to give the race its long-denied liberty." "The new Negro," the editorial concludes, "has arrived with stiffened backbone, dauntless manhood, defiant eye, steady hand, and a will of iron."[22] As Arthur Waskow writes, in the Bureau of Investigation's analysis, "a challenge to white supremacy was not only 'insolent' but a 'radical opposition to the Government' ... equivalent to an attack on law, order, and Americanism."[23] From such a perspective, the mutiny in Houston, where black men turned their guns on white people, surely confirmed the danger to America suspected to inhere in black men's declarations of "liberty or death." And yet as the soldiers were punished, as I will discuss below, the imagery of death and manhood proved to be remarkably flexible.

The mutiny

When the men of the Twenty-Fourth Infantry arrived in Houston at the end of July to guard the construction of a cantonment at Camp Logan on the outskirts of the city, the city's official reaction was one of muted optimism. Despite considerable apprehension on behalf of the white citizenry, the Houston Chamber of Commerce, eager to secure lucrative federal contracts, agreed to the temporary presence of the Twenty-Fourth in the city after being informed by the War Department that black troops were the only ones available. In anticipation of their arrival, local press printed positive stories of the men, citing their officers' comments that the men were disciplined and "bear-cats" of fighters, drawn from the "best and most intelligent

Negroes" in the country. The *Houston Chronicle* highlighted their record as veterans of the Pershing expedition into Mexico.²⁴

However, despite this veneer of optimism, it soon became clear that the city's deeply rooted structural racism and history of racialized police brutality made the presence of black men, armed, uniformed, and vested with the authority of the U.S. Army, inherently problematic. In contrast to the paradigmatic fears about "white womanhood," in Houston it was interactions between the soldiers and male streetcar conductors, laborers at the cantonment, and, above all, policemen that became flashpoints during the month that the Twenty-Fourth were stationed there. Streetcar conductors reported that on a number of occasions the soldiers took seats in the white section or removed the segregation signs, throwing them out of the window or keeping them as souvenirs. During the proceedings of the Houston Board of Inquiry into the causes of the mutiny, one member of the Board was particularly incensed at stories of parties in which black soldiers danced "with Jim Crow signs pinned on them as badges."²⁵ The soldiers of the Twenty-Fourth also resisted segregation at the construction camp they were charged with guarding. Separate drinking water was provided for each group of men, labeled "white" and "colored." As the men of the Twenty-Fourth refused to drink from the "colored" containers, they were eventually provided with new containers labeled "Guard."

The depth of hostility the soldiers experienced is captured in the comment of one of the workmen at the construction site the Twenty-Fourth guarded who was overheard suggesting that the black guards would "look good with coils around their necks."²⁶ The white commanding officers were ineffectual in protecting the men from abuse. When sixteen provost guards from among the men were chosen to help patrol black neighborhoods frequented by the soldiers and thus to maintain order, military officials agreed that the men would not be armed, a decision that was made without precedent to defer to local white people's opposition to the arming of black men.²⁷

While there were thus multiple layers of grievance, "[t]he primary cause of the Houston riot," the NAACP asserted, "was the habitual brutality of the white police officers of Houston in their treatment of colored people."²⁸ The incident that sparked the mutiny began on the afternoon of August 23. Two white police officers, Lee Sparks and Rufe Daniels, entered the home of a black woman, Sarah Travers, in pursuit of a black civilian man. Sparks was already well known for his brutality against black people and was frank about his tactics when he spoke to the Houston Board of Inquiry. He testified that he "thought it necessary to use more force than was legally or morally necessary" when making arrests "in thickly populated negro sections where the most vicious elements of the negroes congregate ... in order to keep the other negroes from running away with him." Indeed, the Sunday after the soldiers' march on Houston, Sparks shot and killed a black civilian man.[29] In her interaction with him, Travers later told NAACP investigators that Sparks slapped her and both officers verbally abused her. They then forced her outside barefoot, wearing only an "old dress-skirt and a pair of panties and a ol' raggedy waist." When she asked to be allowed to put some clothes on, Sparks told her, "No, we'll take you just as you are. If you was naked we'd take you." A black soldier named Alonzo Edwards approached Sparks and asked if Travers could be allowed to dress herself. Sparks responded by beating and arresting him for interfering in Travers' arrest. Later in the day, another soldier, Corporal Charles Baltimore, one of the unarmed provost guards and also one the thirteen men who would be executed in December, approached Sparks to enquire after Edwards. Incensed that Baltimore presumed to question him, Sparks pistol-whipped him and fired shots at him as he fled. Baltimore was then also arrested. When he did not return to camp, a rumor spread among the men that the police had killed him.[30]

Eugenia Draper, a local black woman who was the girlfriend and later wife of a private in the regiment, was present in the camp on the night of the mutiny. As she later testified before the court martial that tried the second round of accused mutineers, the camp was deluged by rain when news came that Baltimore had been killed by the police. As she waited out the rain in a tent with her boyfriend, she listened to the tense conversations of the groups of soldiers passing by. "I could hear some of them saying that he was a good man, and they felt that he must have been mistreated, and they didn't feel that they would be doing right to not go out and take it up."[31] When Baltimore returned to the camp alive, the tension did not ease. One of the white commanding officers witnessed men taking ammunition and issued an order for the entire camp to disarm. A number of men resisted handing over their rifles, while others did so reluctantly. The rage and sorrow that had been building for a month came to a breaking point. One man later testified before the court martial that one of the mutineers wept as he resolved to shoot up "the God damn town because he was tired of seeing soldiers come in there with their heads all beat up."[32] And then a cry rang out through the camp, "Get your guns men! The white mob is coming!" In his report, Cress suggested this alarm was falsely raised by the leaders of the mutiny, to push the others into falling in. Historians disagree about whether a white mob fired on the camp. Certainly, in the wake of the pogrom at East St. Louis and the more general tide of anti-black violence, the threat would have been all too credible. Whatever the origin of the call, approximately 100 men did get their guns and set out, the largest group of them led by Vida Henry, a thirteen-year veteran, who threatened to shoot deserters. Before they set out on the march, one man later testified, Vida Henry had told the men to "Get plenty of ammunition and save one for yourself."[33]

The raid on Houston lasted approximately two hours. For the white people of Houston, the sight of black soldiers "marching all in a line," four abreast, was electrifying. "The negroes deliberately shot down every white man in sight. Then they came on up the street toward us," one white witness told the Houston Board of Inquiry. "They were walking and shooting coolly and with deliberation, halting to take aim."[34] Robert Haynes suggests white witnesses exaggerated the attack's precision to demonstrate that it was premeditated. Nevertheless, when civilians with no fighting experience encountered combat veterans armed with Springfield rifles, the most powerful weapon of the day, the results produced "paroxysms" of panic in the white population.[35]

Colonel Cress's assertion in his investigative report that the men had "the evident intent of murdering every white person they saw" is belied by the relatively limited number of casualties. In contrast to the white mob's unrestrained violence against all black people in East St. Louis, the primary object of the mutinous soldiers was to punish the police who had brutalized them, and they set out to attack the police station.[36] In the course of their march, they found and killed the police officer Rufus Daniels, who had been involved in the altercation with Edwards and Baltimore. Their plan to march on the police station, however, became derailed when the men killed two national guardsmen they mistook for policemen, a fact that the men worried would have grave consequences. A number of the men, some of whom had joined the march under duress, had already looked for opportunities to desert. Their numbers depleted, several of them wounded and others reporting having seen carloads of militia coming for them, the majority of the men decided that it was time to end the raid and return to camp before it was too late.[37]

The men who had stayed behind set up a firing line around the perimeter of the camp to protect themselves from potential attacks by a white mob or by the leaders of the mutineers, who had threated to come back and shoot those who did not join them. Eugenia Draper testified that she and her future husband waited all night on the firing line. Around 2 a.m., Charles Baltimore and some of the other men returned to the camp. Baltimore, rifle in hand, lay down next to Eugenia and her boyfriend and recounted the events of the march. He "got the partner of this fellow that hit him," he reported, but had not found Sparks. She relayed Baltimore's account of Vida Henry's fate to the court martial. "He said [Henry] was shot and was asking some man to kill him, but none of them would kill him … he said he was a soldier – his father was a soldier and he was a soldier, and he didn't leave camp with the intention of coming back." Henry agreed to wait until the men were gone before taking his own life. As the others took their leave of him, he shook each man's hand in turn, bidding them farewell.[38]

The morning after the mutiny, the *Houston Post* reported that in the district of the city that the soldiers had passed through nearly every house had been penetrated by bullets. It noted that the holes were mostly high enough to pass over a person lying on the floor, indicating that this is how many of the residents would have spent the night. It was noted that efforts were not made to get to the riot district until "almost two hours after the first shots were heard." When help finally reached the area, the "neighborhood was as quiet as a forest and as dark." The terror of the people inside the bullet-riddled houses is made evident:

> The belief was general that the blacks had taken charge of the city and that police officers and white troops were helpless. When anyone would be aroused at these places, the first question was "where are the negroes." After that it often took several minutes to convince those of the neighborhood that the trouble had passed. Often it was impossible to coax citizens to their doors.[39]

In the days after the mutiny, the National Guard searched homes of black people and confiscated their weapons, while police distributed guns to white civilians.[40] Unfounded rumors that black civilians and the black soldiers of the Eighth Infantry, still stationed in Houston, were plotting to rise up were apparently so fervent in the aftermath of the mutiny that Major General George Bell and J.C. Hutcheson, the mayor of Houston, found it necessary to address the public through notices published on the front page of the *Post*. "There is abundant evidence," Bell admonished, "to show that many people in Houston have worked themselves up into a state of frenzy bordering on hysteria on the subject of these colored troops."[41]

However, the lingering fears and vulnerability of the white population was frequently dissimulated in the national press. Four black men died as a result of the mutiny but none of them was killed by white men. Apart from Henry, two soldiers were accidentally shot by their own men and another who had been wounded during the mutiny died from gangrene that resulted from medical neglect in custody. That white men did not kill "negroes" seemed to be difficult for members of the press to comprehend. After cataloging the white casualties of the "outbreak of negro soldiers," both the *Los Angeles Times* and the *New York Times* reported that "[i]t is not known how many negroes are dead," leaving open the possibility that the imbalance of death may yet be righted.[42] Fictitious details of white men acting to bring "the negroes ... under control" figured in numerous early accounts of the mutiny. The *Washington Times*, which titled its story on the riots, "Bayonets Bring 100 Negroes to Yield," offered a fantasy of black surrender: "About one hundred of the negro soldiers ... threw down their Springfield rifles and surrendered this afternoon when white soldiers, who had them surrounded for several hours, closed in with fixed bayonets." The *Times* also claimed that Henry's head had been shot off with a shotgun, "indicating he had been killed by a civilian."[43]

As the expected black casualties did not materialize, the coverage of subsequent days stopped speculating on how many black men might be dead. However, the difficulty some had in accepting the casualty count was again apparent seven years after the mutiny. When five members of the Twenty-Fourth who had been convicted of participating in the mutiny were paroled from the federal penitentiary at Leavenworth, a short article in the *Courier-Gazette* of McKinney, Texas, reminded its readers of the now-distant events of the mutiny. After falsely asserting that white men, women, and children were killed by the "rioting negroes, many of them drunk, as they invaded the city," it invented an alternative conclusion to the drama that would be more in keeping with its readers' sensibilities: "A hastily organized force of 500 citizens stopped the negroes before they were well into the city and a night of sanguinary shooting followed in which many of the negroes were slain."[44]

The apparently confounding lack of black deaths in the mutiny were also made comprehensible through a discourse of white "restraint." Newton Baker, the secretary of war, wrote to President Wilson that the people of Houston should be commended for their restraint and deserved credit for not attacking the "colored people of their own community and generally not to have permitted an East St. Louis riot to arise out of a very provoking and tragic situation."[45] His comment suggests that white wrath would naturally exert itself in violence as it also hints that the pogrom in East St. Louis was provoked by black wrongdoing. When the men of the Twenty-Fourth were officially disarmed and removed to Columbus, New Mexico, a few papers around the country dramatized the story in a manner that clearly fit within established racial logic. Describing the scene in which the soldiers relinquished their guns and boarded trains for New Mexico under guard, these papers described the men as being "spirited away" from Houston by military authorities "for fear that the wrath of the white citizens of Texas would result in a wholesale massacre."[46]

Constructions of death and manhood

In his study of the emergence of modern masculinity and European nationalism, George Mosse identifies the importance of rituals and figurations of death as a means of symbolically reinforcing the separation of the outsider (in Mosse's study, the homosexual and the Jew) from society. As the modern ideals of manhood were wrought in a context of war and revolution, "[h]eroism, death and sacrifice became associated with manliness." "Commitment to an impersonal cause sanctified the life and death of the individual," Mosse writes, "it was the prerequisite for heroic manhood."[47] Whereas the beauty of the idealized male body was made more vivid in its encounter with sacrificial death in nationalist art and sculpture, the lingering death that hung around the "abnormal" in cultural discourse signaled their necessary exclusion:

> The death of the outsider was never far from the imagination of those inside society. The young masturbator in agony in Bertrand's museum demonstrated the wages of sin, while a fixed and deathlike gloom was said to dominate the facial expressions of the insane. All seemed close to death – the Jews prematurely old, the homosexual burned out, exhausted, and the insane steeped in gloom. Just as their life had differed from that of the respectable bourgeois, so their death had to be different.

The lonely, painful, and abject death of the outsider dramatized his alienation from bourgeois society and the normative moral life of the nation.[48] Mosse notes that from the eighteenth century, the claim that Jews were "incapable of martyrdom" formed a thread in the tapestry of Jewish abnormality: "In the face of death they screamed, cursed and defended themselves."[49] The inability to die well demonstrates the Jew's unfitness for manhood.

Like the outsiders that Mosse describes, in the early twentieth century U.S. popular and scientific discourses generated an imagery of black soldiers as "close to death." Among the avid investigators of black degeneration after emancipation, military officials and medical practitioners helped to elaborate the black man's body as abnormal and as inherently incompatible with military duty. From the Civil War, interpretations of "excessive morbidity and mortality" among black enlistees became central to pessimistic assessments of the potential of African Americans to become fit, vigorous soldiers and, by extension, men.[50] In 1918 in a memo on the "Disposal of the colored draft," one high-ranking official described the bulk of black soldiers as a "class of physically inferior men."[51] This inferiority was widely understood in explicitly racial terms. In 1916 a study published in the *Military Surgeon*, for example, argued that elevated rates of black mortality and disease reflected "a purely racial difference" being due "largely to race degeneration" rather than sanitation.[52] Here the excessive, and ignominious, dying of black soldiers in hospital beds riddled with tuberculosis, heart disease, nephritis, and syphilis, rather than on the battlefield in glory, evidences their moral and physical degeneracy and their subnormality as a race of men.

Cultural narratives in this period also drew powerful racial connections between black soldiers, degeneracy, and painful death. In her 1906 memoir of Reconstruction, the Southern writer and journalist Myrta Lockett Avary reflected on the emergence of the black rapist. "The rapist is a product of the reconstruction period," she wrote. "His chrysalis was a uniform ... He came into life in the abnormal atmosphere of a time rife with discussions of social equality theories, contentions for coeducation and intermarriage."[53] Avary's figuring of the soldier's uniform as a rapist's chrysalis captures the manner in which early twentieth-century lynching narratives imagined black assertions of social, economic, and political power as sexual perversion. The release of D.W. Griffith's *Birth of a Nation* in 1915, five years after the murders in Slocum and two years before the Houston Mutiny, offered a sweeping cinematic staging of lynching as nation-building that centered on the destruction of the black soldier-turned-rapist. It was seen by millions more people than any other previous film, or any film to follow for the next half-century, and acclaimed by critics, historians, union leaders, and politicians, famously including then President Woodrow Wilson, whose historical work was used by Griffith as reference material.[54] Miriam Bratu Hansen observes that the film was remarkable in its "unprecedented claim to the construction of national history." Griffith placed the emergence of the United States as a "real nation" with the emergence of the Ku Klux Klan's suppression of black sexual and political disorder.[55]

The film presents Reconstruction as the North's disastrous attempt to give black men equality and "[t]he agony that the South endured so that a nation might be born." It tells a story not just of the travails and eventual triumph of the South but the emergence of the American nation – a "birth" that is delivered through the unification of white men, as one of the film's intertitles puts it, "in common defense of their Aryan birthright" and through the death, physical and political, of freed black people.[56] In one of the film's climactic scenes, the Klan defeats a horde black soldiers besieging a white family's cabin, presumably to get to the white woman and girl inside. They then disarm the remaining black militia, who flee in terror, followed by the town's black populace. The film cuts to "the Next Election." Here Klan members on horseback line up in the street and when several black men emerge with a swagger they see the Klan and run away. "The negroes dare not vote," explains the synopsis of the film submitted to the U.S. Copyright Office, "and the threat of a black empire is dissolved."[57] It is made clear that the newborn nation that arose from the ashes of "black rule" required, if not the physical excision of black people, their political excision.

The renewed subjugation of the black population is prefigured by the violent death of Gus, a monstrous black freedman and soldier, who attempts to rape Flora, the angelic youngest daughter of a genteel Southern family. Played by white actor in blackface with cringing movements and rolling eyes, Gus creeps up on Flora, in his soldier's uniform, and expresses his desire to "marry" her. Flora throws herself off a cliff rather than submit to the rape. A terrified Gus is subsequently dragged away by Flora's brother and the Klan brotherhood he has established to be lynched offscreen.[58]

In Thomas Dixon's novel *The Clansman*, the novel upon which the film is based, the text repeatedly draws attention to Gus's uniform. In one scene, as he drills the black militia, Dixon writes that the "full-dress officer's uniform ... only accentuated the coarse bestiality of Gus. His huge jaws seemed to hide completely the gold braid on his collar." When the white-robed men of the Klan lynch him and then dump his body on the lawn of the hated "mulatto" lieutenant governor – another embodiment of the anti-civilization Reconstruction regime – it is noted that he is in "full uniform."[59] Gus's corpse in its uniform is grim evidence of the perverse impossibility of black manhood and citizenship.

In the aftermath of the soldiers' attack on Houston, many white commentators denounced their attack with imagery resonant with that used by Griffith. For some the attack was an impudent attempt to enforce social equality, read access to white women, for others, a "black tide of sweeping death."[60] As we will see, however, the narratives of the execution of the black soldiers of the Twenty-Fourth that circulated in the white print media and official state discourse diverged markedly from the feverish anti-black theatrics of *Birth of a Nation*, though, nonetheless, they made their own links between abnormal death and abnormal race.

A military lynching

Because the country was at war, the executions of the soldiers could be carried out without approval of the president. The preparations were apparently unknown to all but a few of the highest officials in the War Department.[61] The circumstances of the executions speak to the volatility of the situation – the date had been kept secret, the press and public were barred from attendance, and the sentence was carried out without opportunity for appeal. The editors of the *Messenger* highlighted the suspect nature of the proceedings. The soldiers were "tried ... denied the right of appeal, and in medieval fashion, were hustled off to the scaffold." They wrote that military authorities killed the men with such speed, an "Inquisition reaction," because they knew that "every self-respecting Negro and numbers of just, fair and truly patriotic whites would have flooded the White House with telegrams."[62] Giving credence to their claim, several weeks after the executions, President

Wilson issued an order prohibiting the execution of any more American soldiers, except for those serving abroad, before their sentences were reviewed in Washington.[63]

Military officials were also concerned about further unrest among the black troops. Less than two weeks before the execution, a military intelligence officer in New Mexico sent a telegram to Washington, D.C., that a "negro restaurant keeper" in Columbus, where the Twenty-Fourth was now stationed and also the site of Pancho Villa's infamous 1916 raid on U.S. territory, had told a white person there that if the mutineers were punished, the Negro troops would "tear [the] town up." Reflecting the deeply rooted ideological linkage between Mexico and black insurrection, discussed further in the next chapter, the report also claimed that the men would seize machine guns to take across the border and "all would join Villa's" army. Despite the fact that the commanders of the Twenty-Fourth reported that their behavior in New Mexico had been orderly, these rumors were seriously investigated, alongside the local postmaster's alarmed report he had found an NAACP leaflet in the street.[64]

On the Sunday after the executions, George Miller, reverend at St. Augustine's Protestant Episcopal Church in Brooklyn, told his parishioners that though the hangings were legal by the strictures of military law, they amounted to a "military lynching" aimed at "appeasing the people of the South, who had to be avenged."[65] The men themselves had requested to be killed by firing squad, Haynes notes, as they wanted to avoid "suffer[ing] the army's most ignominious punishment – death by hanging."[66] Perhaps reflecting the uncomfortable resonance with lynching as well as the contentious and potentially explosive circumstances, there is a remarkable uniformity to coverage of the execution. The press had been barred from the event and the narratives that circulated in many papers seem to be based on the account given by a C.E. Butzer, a local white man stationed at Fort Houston, where the execution took place. The story of the army hanging of black men was made distinct from the stories of the hanging of black people by white mobs.

To appreciate this fact, a brief examination of the press coverage of the pogrom in East St. Louis enacted six weeks before the Houston Mutiny is instructive. While the nation's newspapers abhorred the cruelty of the white mob in East St. Louis, they provided an unflinching gaze upon its work. A particularly revealing passage appeared in the *St. Louis Post Dispatch*:

> The bodies of 21 negroes, beaten, shot, clubbed and stoned to death, one of them a 2-year-old girl, were in two undertaking establishments, while three other negroes' bodies, partly burned, were still in the streets. Three white men were killed during the evening, James Moore of 423 South Fourth street, Charles Boyle of 442 North Fifth street and Joseph Coleman of 1613 John

street. It seemed that additional bodies of negroes might be found in the burned homes in two districts where incendiary fires were set to drive the negroes out.

Here none of the black dead are named, nor are they distinguished by gender or age, except for the two-year-old girl, in contrast to the three white dead, identified by gender, name, and even address. The unrelenting use of the word "negroes" – "bodies of negroes," "three other negroes' bodies," "additional bodies of negroes," "fires set to drive the negroes out" – configure victims as an ungendered violated mass rather than individual persons.

As in Slocum seven years earlier, the killing was frequently described as an impassioned white fury. "The white blood grows very cruel when aroused," aging South Carolina populist Ben Tillman commented after the riots. In contrast to Slocum, in East St. Louis, white women and youth were also engaged in the bloodshed. Asserting that the "strength of the whites" ranged between three and ten thousand, the *Washington Times* described a scene of anarchic terror: "Women and girls and young boys aided and encouraged maddened white men in the work of wholesale devastation and destruction of life. Men, women, and children stood by and cheered today as negro bodies were recovered from the ruins of homes and the nearby creek."[67] Black people's deaths were again treated as unquantifiable: "No one will ever know the exact toll the riot has taken," the *Washington Herald* commented. "All day long black bodies were lifted from catch basins and sewers."[68] Other national newspapers also offered images of lifeless black victims in spaces of filth and refuse. The *New York Times* noted, "Negroes are lying in the gutters every few feet in some places." Black people's death is obscenely exposed to voyeuristic white crowds. The day after the killing subsided, the *Chicago Tribune* noted that crowds of white people slid down the "precarious sand slopes which led into 'Black Valley'" to look at the bodily remains of black victims among the ruins of their homes. "Officials made no move to take [their remains] away," the *Chicago Tribune* reported.[69]

In contrast to these orgiastic scenes of violence and voyeurism, the published description of the early-morning execution scene of the soldiers of the Twenty-Fourth emphasized silence, solitude, and anonymity. Civilian spectators and press were barred. And yet there is also a macabre theatricality in the reports of the execution. The more extended version of the story printed in a number of papers, often alongside the army's official statement giving a list of those men that hanged, those sentenced to prison, and the few acquitted, offers an eerie visual of the military's terrible power over life and death: "The bonfire illumination for the hanging, the new timbers of the rough scaffold, and the khaki-clad military guard all made an unforgettable picture."[70] The image at once differs from more familiar scenes of killing and recalls them. Compare this "unforgettable picture" of the hanging with the following imagery from the East St. Louis pogrom produced by the *Washington Herald*:

> When fire runs through five city blocks, when there is no light except the reflection of incendiary flames, when the flash and bark of guns and pistols is seen and heard the swish of the lynchers' rope is added to the thousand noises and cries of a mob "hell bent," the negro becomes more or less a frightened animal – and there were thousands of them who screamed their fears as they were pursued here last night.[71]

The images are linked by the morbid elements of fire and rope. In contrast to the primal fury of the mob, however, the military's power at the execution site exudes the ordered regimental authority of the state. A detailed description of the highly choreographed execution procession is offered in some stories, seemingly antithetical to the passionate frenzy of the mob, with its knives and gasoline.

> A floodlight had been arranged to give light for those undertaking the work of preparing the nooses and adjusting them to the necks of the condemned men. The cavalry and infantry guard assembled in hollow square formation around the scaffold and the prisoners were given the order to march upon the death traps.

In contrast to the descriptions of black people's suffering and white people's passion, accounts of the execution emphasize efficiency.

> At 7:17 the major in charge of the execution gave the order to spring the traps. The triggers had been arranged, one for each drop, and six men were assigned to each one. At the word of the command they pulled on the triggers and the thirteen negroes dropped to their death. Eleven of them died almost instantly, the other two quivering a moment or two after the rope became taut.[72]

Though the articulation of the exact moment that the traps were sprung gives an administrative air to the proceedings, the description of the "quivering" bodies of the dying men reveals a lingering carnal fascination with black punishment. The final "obliteration," as several reports put it, of any signs of the graves or execution site, and thus the total disappearance of men's bodies from the world, seems the inverse of the brutalized bodies on display before jeering crowds in East St. Louis. Yet both acts work to extricate the dead from the fold of civilization.

Somebody must die

Where the account of the men's execution made its most striking departure from the rife anti-black imagery in the standard genre of lynching and mob violence is in the description of the men's bearing as they faced death. Despite headlines telling of "Negroes [Dying] on the Scaffold," of "Negro Rioters" being "Disposed of," entirely in keeping with standard lynching headlines, the account of the men's moment of death was strikingly opposed to the usual abjection invested in "terrorized negros" falling prey to white fury. The following description of the men's final moments is taken from an Associated Press report that was printed widely in publications across every region of the nation, black publications as well as white, with only minor variations.

> Without a tremor, they stepped out in soldierly tread and singing a hymn they walked to their places. Prayers were said by a negro minister and by two army chaplains and the men were ordered to stand on the traps. Resuming their song they stood erect and displayed the greatest fortitude while the ropes were adjusted.[73]

As with the reports of Antonio Rodriguez's "stoic" death in Mexico, this narrative of dignity and discipline offered by the mainstream press was given passionate meaning by the black press. Even as the executions were denounced as illegitimate, the excellence of the soldiers in death was treated as evidence of their exemplary manhood. Grief, anger, and disillusionment were intertwined with reverence for the soldiers' sacrifice.

In the following month, the themes of righteousness, suffering, and sacrifice were given a religious framing in the *Crisis*. African American poet Lucian B. Watkins commended the men to God as martyrs in a poem whose stanzas were formed from the Associated Press report of the men's death:

> 7:17, A.M., December 11, 1917.
> Lord, these are Thine! "With soldierly tread –"
> "Without a tremor –" they go their way –
> "Singing a hymn –" they march ahead –
>
> "Singing a song –" of peace today!
> Lord, these are Thine who pay their price
> For what a freeman's soul is worth –
> That what they love may live on earth!
> Lord, these are Thine![74]

As Watkins reimagines the executed men as transcending the earthly domain, the heavenly imagery softens but cannot entirely silence the whisper of a more subversive message. If the men paid the price for a freeman's soul through their own deaths, they initiated that process through killing white men.

William Jordan notes that many editors of black newspapers treated the mutiny "gingerly," offering "obligatory condemnations" of the violence, while also elaborating "explanations of why the soldiers rebelled" and attempting to reconcile with their insistence on African American loyalty to the nation and the war effort.[75] However, some black citizens made no attempt at conciliation. On January 23, 1918, the Bureau of Investigation received a letter forwarded from the United States district attorney at Des Moines. It was filed under "In Re: Lillian Smith, negress. Disloyalty matter." Smith's offending letter had originally been sent to the editor of the *Chieftain*, a paper in Pueblo, Colorado, to upbraid him for printing a story that suggested the men of the Twenty-Fourth had been under the influence of alcohol when they marched on Houston.

The letter was never printed and the presumably alarmed editor forwarded it to the authorities. Smith was clearly a *Crisis* reader. Just as the same phrases of wire reports echoed through newspapers across the country, fragments of Du Bois's somber October 1917 editorial, cited early in this chapter, resurface through Smith's letter, infused, however, with her own undiluted fury. Smith's militantly unapologetic defense of the Twenty-Fourth begins in the same fashion as Du Bois's editorial, but with some embellishment. "It is hard for one of the negro extraction to [write] of Houston," she wrote, adding, "or any of the other southern hell holes." Continuing to refashion Du Bois's original ruminations on the Twenty-Fourth, she wrote, "Those men were not young recruits, they were disciplined men and had stood the insults of those ruffian police and other southern Huns, until they said 'that is enough', we will stand no more, and they stole their arms and fought." Notably she likens Southern white men to the nation's German enemy, who were commonly referred to as Huns.

In the *Crisis*, Du Bois and fellow NAACP author Martha Gruening created a portrait of desperate and rightfully angry men, "whose endurance of wrong and injustice had been strained to breaking point, and who in their turn committed injustices" – injustices that would have to be punished. In contrast, despite borrowing some of the magazine's words, Smith saw a true and righteous manhood manifested in the actions of the Twenty-Fourth, actions that were deliberate, political, and which, above all, could and should be repeated. "[W]hen you said they were under the influence of liquor," she seethed at the *Chieftain*'s editor, "you simply lied. They fought because beneath that black skin flowed a wealth of good red blood, and if those southern Huns keep up their tactics there will be many Houstons." While the *Crisis* report regretted the ends to which the men were driven, Smith was wholly defiant.

> All I am sorry is that their leader was seriously wounded. Otherwise they would have got old Sparks – that bully white ruffian, who, has entered colored women's homes when they have been in their bath and killed two or three negroes, for nothing and is still going unpunished. The other policeman, Rufe Daniels is dead and in hell thank God. He won't beat up any more negroes. There is no love in our hearts for the American white man.[76]

No doubt even more alarming to the *Chieftain*'s editor and the federal authorities than her refusal to condemn any aspect of the Twenty-Fourth's actions was the overtly threatening language she directed at white Americans and the nation itself. "Believe me," she wrote, "what the American white man has sown that he will reap. He has shown us just how he measures out justice and in the very near future, he will get the same returns and believe me the returns will be embarrassing." Repeating the refrain that would echo throughout both World Wars, that black men had more cause to fight and die for democracy at home than in Europe, Smith pushed this sentiment a step further.

Asserting that her race had more grievance with the "Southern Hun" than the German, she added, "and believe me the Germans know when to approach and press his arguments and I am giving you no assurance that they won't be successful." Whether genuinely announcing a willingness to conspire with the enemy or knowingly exploiting white fears about German infiltration into black communities, Smith presents an image of fighting black manhood realized in its resolute opposition to the "defiled" American nation. Both noble black manhood and the corruption of the nation were evidenced in black blood. Asking who had been punished for the "3,000 negroes lynched and burned in the south," Smith cited the deaths of the Twenty-Fourth: "No wonder our boys walked bravely to their death singing a hymn. No doubt they would rather be dead than fight for such a democracy."[77]

An editorial in the *Twin City Star*, reprinted in the *Crisis*, took a tone akin to Lillian Smith's, positioning the men's deaths as the "beginning of the end" of black oppression rather than merely a highly symbolic manifestation of it:

> [I]t is said, "They faced death bravely." The death of these men has done more to bring about a real democracy in America than the onslaughts of a thousand black heroes in Europe. The world is watching, and the Negro is awakening. These men knew the penalty and suffered the consequences. If the hell hounds of the South or anywhere choose to intimidate or in any way molest the Negro soldiers, and especially their women, then somebody must die.

"The Negro soldier can give but one life," it continued. "The question is whether it shall be in defense of his own or his country."[78]

The day after the execution, the *Brooklyn Eagle*, a white paper, printed an editorial commenting on the fate of the mutineers. It asserted that the executions were a necessary and effective deterrent and regretted that the "race problem" would now be forced into discussions of the executions by "negrophiles," malcontents, and the "negro agitators" they "misled." George Miller responded in his sermon that week that the *Eagle* was "sadly mistaken" if it imagined the execution would prevent further events like that at Houston: "Give men the same provocation, and the same thing will happen fifty times again." Asserting that there were "thousands today whose thoughts are the same as mine," Miller stated, "We should get the names of all these men. They are all heroes. They were men and only fought the wrongs of the police. We should copy their example of courage and fortitude." Miller emphasized the men's stature in death, which inspired his own stand in speaking boldly against their execution: "These men went to their death singing, that is something for us to consider, something to be prouder about. These men did not go to their deaths like dogs."[79] The men's bravery in death became just as meaningful as their violent rejection of white supremacy, a demonstration of manhood that could be celebrated even by those reluctant to wholly condone the form of resistance they undertook. The men are imagined as dying in a willed, defiant, and composed self-sacrifice, antithetical to representations of the mob victim which circulated through both the white and black press. However, Miller's assertion that his audience could be proud that the men did not die "like dogs" bears a lingering shame about those who died deaths less heroic than the men of the Twenty-Fourth.

The polysemic power of manly self-sacrifice, and how readily such symbolism was also marshaled to beckon allegiance to hegemonic nationalism is evident in an incident that took place in Richmond after the execution, recorded by an agent of military intelligence. On the evening news of the hangings becoming public, a black orator named Roscoe Conkling Simmons delivered a speech at a rally designed to bolster African American support for the war. Members of the audience, in shock and mourning, repeatedly interrupted Simmons's speech with questions about the "hanging of the Negro soldiers." From the perspective of the intelligence agent, Simmons managed to dispel the audience's initial reluctance, winning their enthusiastic applause when he declared, "The American Negro ... knows but one government, speaks but one language and claims but one flag ... [he] has but one request. He asks for the gun of war, for the uniform of his country, and for the command from the officer who fears neither life nor death."[80] Simmons's invocation of a black manhood that feared "neither life nor death" could momentarily engage the audience in a passionate patriotic display, however ambivalent many in the audience felt toward the nation that had just executed black men in its uniform.

Not all African Americans were moved by press images of the executed men's noble bearing in death. Ida B. Wells's account of the execution in her autobiography is entirely absent of any such sentimentality or related nationalist overtures. When government agents came to her office to question her over the distribution of buttons memorializing the "MARTYRED NEGRO SOLDIERS," she insisted upon her right to criticize the government. She stated that "it was a dastardly thing to hang those men as if they were criminals and put them in holes in the ground just as if they had been dead dogs." The hanging of the men and the disposal of their bodies in nameless graves was the army's placation of "Southern race hatred."[81] The symbolic union of martial manhood and death, however, was remarkably flexible and could be engaged for varied purposes.

The iron discipline of the service

A Houston journalist named C.D. Waide wrote an account of the munity in 1927 for the Houston magazine the *Gargoyle*. He titled his piece "When Psychology Failed." He offered his knowledge of both "the negro race" and life in the army as the basis of his expertise on the matter, knowledge that included such observations as, "Any Southerner, familiar with the characteristics of the negro, knows that when general shooting starts the average negro's desire is to 'get from and in a hurry.'" In the opening installment of the five-part series, Waide delineated two supposedly singular aspects of the mutiny that "psychology failed" to anticipate or explain. The first supposedly inexplicable aspect of the mutiny was the "calm manner" of "these negroes" on the morning of their execution, for which, Waide insisted, "[t]here is neither explanation in psychology nor precedent in history."

> Even the negro's well known love of pageantry and the dramatic can hardly account for the cool nerve of these men as they stood on the scaffold and practiced stepping forward to the traps through which they were in a few moments to drop to eternity. There were neither piteous wailings nor religious chantings in the air as the single pull of a lever released the thirteen traps.

The other "failure of psychology" that puzzled Waide was the behavior of white Houstonians after the Negro soldiers' march on Houston:

> It was a strange psychology that held in check the white citizens of Houston on that ghastly night when their women and children were being slain and wounded by black men gone berserk. It was one of the few times in history when such events were not followed by reprisal that equaled or exceeded the original acts in violence.[82]

Waide explains this latter mystery of white people's restraint through their spirit of wartime discipline ("a spirit the negro soldiers seemed not have embraced"); the emphasis on the strange absence of retaliatory violence and black dignity in death allows the contemplation of white victimhood while nevertheless reasserting white masculine dominance – notably the reference to "their women and children" makes clear that the "white citizens of Houston" are the white *men* of Houston. Waide furthermore counterfactually makes "women and children" the victims of the black soldiers rather than white men themselves, shifting weakness and vulnerability to violence to their natural source.

Waide does not attempt to offer an explanation for the "calm manner" and "cool nerve" of the black men at the moment of their demise. There is simply no explanation for this historically "unprecedented" moment. As a bizarre anomaly, the manly death of the soldiers does not demonstrate a truly manly nature nor disrupt their status as "berserkers" antithetical to white citizens. Waide's bewilderment at the condemned black men's bravery in death as well as his imaginative shift to slave insurrection imagery of slain white women and children highlight revealing incongruities in the discourse of the mutiny and subsequent executions.

While in August, the white press expressed indignation and disgust at "the savageness displayed by the negroes toward the white police officers ... whose bodies in nearly every instance had been hacked with bayonets," in December, many of the newspapers that reported the men's stoicism in the face of death did not mention the scale of the violence or the nature of the casualties, citing only that the men were being hung for "complicity in the riot at Houston."[83] Not all papers, of course, failed to remind their readers of the men's guilt. In its coverage of the executions, the *Washington Herald* gave no description of the actual hanging but offered a graphic description of the soldiers' hacking and mutilation of white men's bodies.[84]

Yet, even the *Houston Post*, whose readership obviously had a particular interest in the hangings, referred to the "wanton bloodshed" that the soldiers incurred, but maintained the solemn tone in its story on the men's death. Unlike the descriptions of "cowering," "terrorized," or simply inert victims of white mobs in the East St. Louis narratives, or lynching narratives more generally, the doomed men of the Twenty-Fourth are rendered "erect" and disciplined, active agents in ensuring their own dignified demise. Such imagery marks a distinct contrast from that of the rioting Negro soldier in the summer's press reports. At the August funeral of Ira D. Rainey, one of the police officers killed by the mutineers, the white Houston pastor Dr. W.S. Lockhart used his sermon to reject the "slanderous" idea that the violence had been due to "race prejudice," asserting that the mutiny was attributable to just two causes – "vice and booze": "It was simply a case of a bunch of 'bad niggers' dressed up in a uniform, given a little authority and put under very lax discipline, who, under the influence of women and booze, perpetrated this murderous crime against the army and the city of Houston."[85]

Though still continually referring to the men as "the negroes," the *Post* story emphasized their soldierly bearing in another paragraph that was commonly repeated in the national press coverage. At the moment of death, "the negroes" are portrayed as true soldiers, a striking departure from the dismissal of the mutinous soldiers as drunken brutes or the more sinister image of the black soldier as civilization destroyer in *Birth of a Nation*. "The negroes dressed in their regular uniforms as carefully as for inspection" and their singing was "that of soldiers on the march." In the final moment, "the negroes executed displayed neither bravado nor fear"; the "only expression from any of the negroes" was the "low good-bye, boys," addressed to the members of their military guard, evincing a sense of military camaraderie.[86]

A United Press story printed in another Southern paper, the Kingston, North Carolina, *Daily Free Press*, also specifically emphasizes the men's military bearing in death. The opening sentences of the article are striking: "The 13 negro non-commissioned officers and privates of the 24th Infantry hanged here yesterday for complicity in the Houston rioting, in which many persons were killed and wounded, died bravely. The iron discipline of the service that they violated at Houston counted heavily at the end."[87] The first sentence is thus structured to make the bravery of the men in death the subject, rather than their hanging for rioting. The second is even more suggestive of the possibly ameliorating aims of the story. Here the execution acts as a kind of reconciliation. Through their iron discipline "at the end," the men are symbolically reintegrated into the mantle of the authority they rebelled against. When the commander of the guard calls attention, "every man of those on the gallows unconsciously stiffened to the position of the soldier" just before the traps are released and the men are transformed into bodies "swinging in the early morning air." At the moment of death, rather than being merely "dressed up" as soldiers, their uniforms are donned "as carefully as for inspection." Their automatic response to the death call of the commander demonstrates the depth of their military training. In presenting the men as obedient soldiers, in whom the imprint of military discipline is revealed at the end, despite their terrible lapse into barbarism, the narrative works to uphold the legitimacy of the military, and its iron authority in the training, command, and obliteration of "negroes."

In reading this telling of the execution it is useful to bear in mind Alan Belkin's insightful argument that rather than a disavowal of the feminine and queer, military masculinity required a contradictory embrace of traits constructed as "unmasculine," demanding as it did obedience and subordination.[88] If black men did not embody a manly warrior ideal, the "good negro's" supposed racial gravity to subordination could be reconciled with some aspects of the "good soldier." Here the calm, soldierly disposition does not evoke the sacrifice of the black men steeled to die, and kill, for the freedom of their people but instead offers a soothing image of a well-controlled Negro soldiers ready to accept their rightful death.

In January of 1918, President Wilson was visited by a delegation from the NAACP led by James Weldon Johnson and George F. Miller. They presented Wilson with a petition signed by 12,000 people requesting that the latest round of death sentences handed out to accused mutineers be commuted.[89] Following the advice of Newton Baker, secretary of war, in August of 1918, Wilson commuted ten of the death sentences to life imprisonment. The executions of six more men who were found to have murdered, "under circumstances of shocking brutality ... peaceable disposed civilians" were confirmed. Wilson issued a statement that began by affirming the legitimacy of the first thirteen executions, claiming that "extraordinary precautions were taken to insure the fairness of the trials." He commuted the ten sentences, he explained, because the "lesson of this lawless riot" had adequately been demonstrated by the previous executions, and

> also because I desire the clemency here ordered to be a recognition of the splendid loyalty of the race to which these soldiers belong and an inspiration to the people of that race to further zeal and services to the country of which they are citizens and for the liberties of which so many of them are now bravely bearing arms at the very front of great fields of battle.[90]

Though the statement reads to confirm black citizenship, and notably does so through acknowledging black sacrifice on the battlefront, it simultaneously marks black racial abnormality. By entirely effacing the conditions against which the men rebelled, the same which made the loyalty of African Americans continually suspect, their mutiny is intelligible only as lawlessness, the forgetting of "obligations," the "break[ing] over the restraints of discipline." Though Wilson does not give racial explanation for this otherwise inexplicable rampage, it is implicit in his presentation of the commutation as fatherly benevolence. The terrible punishment is mitigated, not because it is not deserved, but as a reward and an incentive for a race still unready for the full rights and responsibilities of citizenship (as the very need for rewards, incentives, and terrible punishments demonstrates). Tellingly, in his original advice, rather than the more optimistic hope for "zeal and service," Baker suggested that Wilson express his "hope that no such incident will again disgrace the military service of the United States."[91]

As Hubert Harrison suggested, a shadow of menace could never be completely exorcised from the prospect of a Negro soldier in a state that lynched Negroes. At the same time however, the image of the rebellious soldier, whose death could be read to reaffirm the capability of black men to die and fight for freedom, could also be soft-focused to diffuse the seemingly explosive potential of black unrest and to obscure the violent apartheid the men attacked. In both configurations, as dignified resistance or obedient submission to the state, the death of the condemned is treated as the realization of manly duty rather than, primarily, the destruction of life. Even in the words of those, like Lillian Smith, who were passionately moved by the men's actions, as their brave deaths came to be treated as an achievement, a kind of victory for manhood that transcended the oppressive act of the execution itself, life and manhood are once again constructed as incompatible.

The experiences of the executed men as individuals who wanted to live, who carried out the raid on Houston with the intention of surviving it, were frequently obscured in narrative of the heroic. A short letter sent by Charles Baltimore to his brother on the eve of his execution captures something of the desolation the condemned man must have felt faced with hanging. Baltimore did not mention the righteousness of his actions. He asserted that he was innocent of bloodshed but that the execution was God's will. "Dear Brother: I write you for the last time in this world. I am to be executed tomorrow morning ... I am going to meet my father and mother and all the rest of the family gone before. Goodbye; meet me in heaven."[92] Among these filtered and fractured traces of the men's voices left to us through time, Robert Haynes identifies a particularly poignant archival fragment. After the train carrying the disarmed, heavily guarded men from Houston to Columbus, New Mexico, passed through Schulenburg, Texas, a resident there found an unused soldier's pass on the tracks. It had a message handwritten upon it, presumably by one of the men of the Twenty-Fourth who then threw it out of the window. The words he wanted to communicate to the world outside were not declarations of self-sacrifice or even assertions of manhood per se but a longing for life elsewhere. "Take Tex. and go to hell," the note read. "I don't want to go there anymore in my life. Let's go East and be treated as people."[93]

Notes

1 Haynes, *A Night of Violence*, 6. "13 Negro Soldiers Hanged for Rioting," December 12, 1917, *New York Times*, 7.
2 Haynes, "The Houston Mutiny and Riot of 1917," 430–31. Haynes, *A Night of Violence*, 169.
3 Woodrow Wilson commuted the death sentences of ten of the sixteen men to life imprisonment. Haynes, *A Night of Violence*, 438. The other six condemned men were hung at Fort Sam Houston in September 1918. "Houston Riot Case Ended," September 25, 1918, *New York Times*, 9.

 Leavenworth is the same prison to which Enrique and Ricardo Flores Magón were sentenced for sedition and where Ricardo died in 1922. For discussion of their overlapping time in the prison, see Sara M. Benson, *The Prison of Democracy: Race, Leavenworth, and the Culture of Law* (Oakland, California: University of California Press, 2019).

4 The official death count was thirty-nine African Americans and nine white people. Some observers estimated that as many as 500 black people might have been killed. Some 7,000 black people fled across the river into St. Louis, leaving behind their homes and possessions. Charles L. Lumpkins, *American Pogrom: The East St. Louis Race Riot and Black Politics* (Athens, OH: Ohio University Press, 2008), 126–27. On East St. Louis, see also McLaughlin, "Ghetto Formation and Armed Resistance in East St. Louis, Illinois." McLaughlin, *Power, Community, and Racial Killing in East St. Louis*.

5 Richard Stokes, "Massacres by Mobs in East St. Louis Riots Blamed upon Epidemic of Desperate Crimes Committed by Colored Men From the South," July 8, 1917, *Washington Post*, 3. Carlos Hurd, "Post-Dispatch Man, an Eye-Witness, Describes Massacre of Negroes," July 3, 1917, *St. Louis Post-Dispatch*, 2. "Jury Declared Negroes Guilty," October 8, 1917, *Courier Journal* (Louisville, KY), 3. Malcolm McLaughlin argues the later historiography of the violence continued to produce constructions of black helplessness. Countering such assessments, he writes that facing continual attacks from white residents and harassed rather than protected by the police, the black population had made a concerted effort to arm itself and organize for self-defense. During the riots, the white mob expressed their desire to drive out the "business negroes" but failed to penetrate the Denverside area of the city, where they were repelled by the black gunmen protecting its borders. This organized resistance also provided refuge to black people escaping the terroristic fury of the mob in the downtown area. McLaughlin, "Ghetto Formation and Armed Resistance in East St. Louis, Illinois," 438–39.

6 W.E.B. Du Bois, "Houston," *Crisis* 14, no. 6 (1917): 285–86.

7 "More Toll for Houston", undated newspaper article, Record Groups 153 and 393, Modern Military Records Branch, Textual Archives Services Division, National Archives Services Division, NARA, College Park, MD, Reel 11, image 516.

8 Du Bois, "Houston," *Crisis*: 286.

9 "The Hanging of the Negro Soldiers," *Messenger* 2, no. 1 (1918): 7.

10 Colonel G.O. Cress, "Investigation of Trouble at Houston, Texas, between Third Battalion, 24th Infantry, and Citizens of Houston, August 23, 1917," in Record Group 393, NARA, 13.

11 Ibid.

12 Hubert Harrison, "Houston vs. Waco," August 28, 1917, *Voice*, in Hubert H. Harrison and Jeffrey Babcock Perry, *A Hubert Harrison Reader* (Middletown, CT: Wesleyan University Press, 2001), 95. On the lynching of Jesse Washington, see Patricia Bernstein, *The First Waco Horror: The Lynching of Jesse Washington and the Rise of the NAACP*, 1st ed. (College Station: Texas A&M University Press, 2005).

13 Mark Ellis, *Race, War, and Surveillance: African Americans and the United States Government During World War I* (Bloomington: Indiana University Press, 2001), xvi, 18, 74–75.

14 Vincent P. Mikkelsen, "Coming from Battle to Face a War: The Lynching of Black Soldiers in the World War I Era," Ph.D. dissertation (Florida State University, 2007), 97–150.

15 Lentz-Smith, *Freedom Struggles*, 8–9.
16 Ibid.
17 Ellis, *Race, War, and Surveillance*, xvi, 18, 74–75.
18 Matthew Pratt Guterl, "The New Race Consciousness: Race, Nation, and Empire in American Culture, 1910–1925," *Journal of World History* 10, no. 2 (1999): 330. William G. Jordan, *Black Newspapers and America's War for Democracy, 1914–1920* (Chapel Hill and London: University of North Carolina Press, 2001), 94. Ellis, *Race, War, and Surveillance*, 16.
19 United States Department of Justice, "Investigation Activities of the Department of Justice: Letter from the Attorney General Transmitting in Response to a Senate Resolution of October 17, 1919, a Report on the Activities of the Bureau of Investigation of the Department of Justice against Persons Advising Anarchy, Sedition, and the Forcible Overthrow of the Government," (Washington: Government Printing Office, 1919), 165.
20 Guterl, "The New Race Consciousness," 330.
21 United States Department of Justice, "Investigation Activities of the Department of Justice," 162.
22 Ibid., 172, 184, 179.
23 Arthur I. Waskow, *From Race Riot to Sit-In: 1919 and the 1960s* (Garden City, NY: Doubleday & Company, 1967), 191.
24 Haynes, *A Night of Violence*, 61–62. "A Court Martial Tragedy," *Messenger* 2, no. 10 (1919): 24. Martha Gruening, "Houston. An NAACP Investigation," *Crisis* 15, no. 1 (1917): 14. Haynes, "The Houston Mutiny and Riot of 1917," 30–31. For a broader history of both anti-black and anti-Mexican racism in Houston, and the cultural and social relations between these groups, as well as their respective relations with white people, see Steptoe, *Houston Bound*. On black soldiers in the early twentieth century and U.S. imperialism, see Willard B. Gatewood, Jr., *Smoked Yankees and the Struggle for Empire: Letters from Negro Soldiers, 1898–1902* (Urbana: University of Illinois Press, 1971).
25 Excerpts from "Stenographer's Report of Testimony Adduced before the Board of Inquiry Appointed by the City Council of the City of Houston to Investigate and Report on Conditions Leading up to and Immediately Connected with the Mutiny or Riot of Troops of the 24th U.S. Infantry (Colored) which Occurred on the Night of Thursday, 23 August 1917, in the City of Houston, Texas," in Morris J. MacGregor and Bernard C. Nalty, eds, *Blacks in the United States Armed Forces: Basic Documents, Volume III: Freedom and Jim Crow, 1865–1917* (Wilmington, DE: Scholarly Resources, 1977), 6.
26 Haynes, "The Houston Mutiny and Riot of 1917," 424. Lentz-Smith, *Freedom Struggles*, 62.
27 Gruening, "Houston: An NAACP Investigation," *Crisis*: 14.
28 Ibid.
29 Edgar A. Schuler, "The Houston Race Riot, 1917," *Journal of Negro History* 29, no. 3 (1944): 318. Haynes, "The Houston Mutiny and Riot of 1917," 438, n.76.
30 Gruening, "Houston: An NAACP Investigation," *Crisis*, 15–16.

31 Office of the Judge Advocate General United States War Department, "United States Vs. Corporal Robert Tillman, Et Al. 24th Infantry, Volume III," in Record Groups 153 and 393, NARA, 1174.
32 Haynes, *A Night of Violence*, 122.
33 Cress, "Investigation of Trouble at Houston," 5–6. Lentz-Smith, *Freedom Struggles*, 259, n.101. United States War Department, "United States vs. Corporal Robert Tillman, et al. 24th Infantry, Volume III," 1296.
34 "Eyewitnesses Tell How Negroe [sic.] Soldiers Shot Down Whites," August 25, 1917, *Chicago Tribune*, 2.
35 Haynes, *A Night of Violence*, 175.
36 Cress, "Investigation of Trouble at Houston," 5; Haynes, *A Night of Violence*, 140–41.
37 Ibid., 165–67.
38 United States War Department, "United States vs. Corporal Robert Tillman, et al. 24th Infantry, Volume III," 1183. Haynes, *A Night of Violence*, 134–35.
39 "Martial Law Declared," August 24, 1917, *Houston Post*, 4.
40 Haynes, *A Night of Violence*, 201.
41 "Rumors of Expected Trouble with Negro Troops is Groundless," September 12, 1917, *Houston Post*, 1.
42 "Race Riot in Texas," August 24, 1917, *Los Angeles Times*, 1. "Negro Regulars Riot Near Houston, Texas; Twelve Whites Killed, a Score Wounded," August 24, 1917, *New York Times*, 1. Lumpkins notes that a black policeman told the Chicago *Defender* that the number of white people killed in East St. Louis had been considerably underreported. Rather than nine white dead, he reported having seen thirty-eight dead white people in the morgue. Lumpkins, *American Pogrom*, 127. On the other hand, in the aftermath of the 1919 riots in Chicago, the *Chicago Tribune* inversed the number of white and black casualties, inflating the number of white dead from seven to thirteen. Juan González, *News for All the People: The Epic Story of Race and the American Media* (London and New York: Verso, 2011), 225.
43 "16 Dead, 20 Injured in Race Riots: Bayonets Bring 100 Negroes to Yield," August 24, 1917, *Washington Times*, 1.
44 "Negro Rioters Given Parole," September 18, 1924, *Courier-Gazette*, 1.
45 Secretary of War Newton D. Baker to President Woodrow Wilson, August 28, 1917, in MacGregor and Nalty, *Blacks in the United States Armed Force: Basic Documents, Volume III*.
46 "Investigate Riot of Negro Troops," August 25, 1917, *Record-Argus* (Greenville, PA), 1. "Negro Troops in Riot Face Court Charge," August 26, 1917, *Commercial Dispatch* (Columbus, MS), 1.
47 Das, "Violence, Gender, and Subjectivity," 285. George L. Mosse, *The Image of Man: The Creation of Modern Masculinity* (New York and Oxford: Oxford University Press, 1996), 50–51.
48 George L. Mosse, *Nationalism and Sexuality: Middle-Class Morality and Sexual Norms in Modern Europe* (Madison: University of Wisconsin Press, 1988), 147–48, 69–70. In this regard, it is telling that, while Americans were inundated with graphic descriptions of men's bodies gassed, dismembered, and disintegrating

on the battlegrounds of World War I, once U.S. soldiers joined the conflict such reports were strictly censored. See: David W. Seitz, *World War I, Mass Death, and the Birth of the Modern US Soldier: A Rhetorical History* (New York: Lexington Books, 2018); Pearl James, *The New Death: American Modernism and World War I* (Charlottesville and London: University of Virginia Press, 2013).

49 Mosse, *Nationalism and Sexuality*, 150.
50 Margaret Humphreys, *Intensely Human: The Health of the Black Soldier in the American Civil War* (Baltimore: Johns Hopkins University Press, 2008), 13. See also: Bobby A. Wintermute, "'The Negro Should Not Be Used as a Combat Soldier': Reconfiguring Racial Identity in the United States Army, 1890–1918," *Patterns of Prejudice* 46, no. 3–4 (2012): 292–98.
51 Memorandum, Brig. Gen. Lytle Brown, Assistant to the Chief of Staff, for the Chief of Staff, "Disposal of Colored draft," June 12, 1918, in Morris J. MacGregor and Bernard C. Nalty, eds, *Blacks in the United States Armed Forces: Basic Documents, Volume IV: Segregation Entrenched 1917–1940* (Wilmington, DE: Scholarly Resources, 1977), 25–26.
52 Wintermute, "'The Negro Should Not Be Used as a Combat Soldier,'" 296–97.
53 Myrta Lockett Avary, *Dixie after the War* (New York: Doubleday, Page & Company, 1906), 377.
54 Michael Rogin, "'The Sword Became a Flashing Vision': D.W. Griffith's *The Birth of a Nation*," *Representations* 9, Winter (1985): 150. Mark E. Benbow, "Birth of a Quotation: Woodrow Wilson and 'Writing History with Lightening,'" *Journal of the Gilded Age* 9, no. 4 (2010): 512.
55 Miriam Bratu Hansen, "'Schindler's List' Is Not 'Shoah': The Second Commandment, Popular Modernism, and Public Memory," *Critical Inquiry* 22, no. 2 (1996): 293.
56 Ira Galen and Seymour Stern, eds, *D.W. Griffith's Birth of a Nation* (Victoria, BC: Friesen Press, 2014), 306. For a scene-by-scene description of the film, see the continuity script in Robert Lang, "Birth of a Nation: History, Ideology, Narrative Form," in *The Birth of a Nation: D.W. Griffith, Director*, ed. Robert Lang (New Brunswick, NJ: Rutgers University Press, 1994), 37–156.
57 Lang, "Birth of a Nation," 11.
58 In a scene later deleted by censors of the National Board of Review, a Klansman is depicted castrating Gus. In his account of the scene, for which footage is now lost, film critic Seymore Stern writes that the plunging of the Klansman's sword is synchronized to the storm music in Beethoven's *Pastoral Symphony*, the final thunder crash of the music coinciding with a view of Gus's "pain-racked face and body." See, Rogin, "'The Sword Became a Flashing Vision,'" 175.
59 Thomas Dixon, *The Clansman* (New York: Grosset & Dunlap, 1905), 323, 325, 327, 294.
60 "Paid Tribute to Officers Killed in Recent Mutiny," September 3, 1917, *Houston Post*. Lentz-Smith, *Freedom Struggles*, 69–70. Schuler, "The Houston Race Riot, 1917," 336.
61 "Not Even Washington Knew of Execution," December 12, 1917, *Houston Post*, 2. Christian, *Black Soldiers in Jim Crow Texas, 1899–1917*, 165.

62 "The Hanging of the Negro Soldiers," *Messenger* 2, no. 1 (1918): 7. For a summary of critical white editorials on the handling of the execution see the January 1918 edition of *Crisis*.
63 "Stops Army Executions," December 30, 1917, *Brooklyn Eagle*, 50.
64 Telegram from G.L. Laffer, Intelligence Officer, 34th Division, Camp Cody, Deming N.M, to Chief, Intelligence Section, War College, Washington D.C., December 3, 1917. Microfilm Publication M1440: Correspondence of the Military Intelligence Division Relating to "Negro Subversion" 1917–1941, RG 165, NARA, Roll 001. See also, Theodore Kornweibel, *Investigate Everything: Federal Efforts to Compel Black Loyalty During World War I* (Bloomington: Indiana University Press, 2002), 134–35.
65 "Soldiers Lynched to Appease South," December 17, 1917, *Brooklyn Daily Eagle*, 15.
66 Haynes, *A Night of Violence*, 4.
67 "Tillman Warns of Race Clashes," July 17, 1917, *New York Times*, 7. "New Outbreak of Race riots Brings Order for Troops to Shoot to Kill," July 3, 1917, *Washington Times*, 2.
68 "Many Arrests Made as Governor Takes Charge," July 4, 1917, *Washington Herald*, 1.
69 Walter Burns, "Work of the Mob," July 4, 1917, *Chicago Tribune*, 2. This salacious description of defiled bodies and the ubiquitous use of the term "negroes" contrasts strikingly with the survivors' testimonies recorded by Ida B. Wells, whose account includes names, ages, gender, and places of residence, their relations to the people around them – mothers, husbands, sisters. Ida Wells-Barnett, *The East St. Louis Massacre: The Greatest Outrage of the Century* (Chicago: Negro Fellowship Herald Press, 1917), 6.
70 "13 Negro Soldiers Hanged for Rioting," December 12, 1917, *New York Times*, 7. "Death Penalty Exacted of 13 Negro Soldiers," December 12, 1917, *Pittsburgh Post*, 4. "Negro Soldiers Hanged in Texas," December 12, 1917, *Eugene Morning Register*, 1. Another version suggests that a floodlight was provided for the building of the scaffold rather than bonfires. "The Negroes Pay for Texas Rioting," December 11, 1917, *Wichita Beacon*, 11.
71 "New Outbreak of Race Riots Brings Order for Troops to Shoot to Kill," July 3, 1917, *Washington Times*, 2.
72 "Court Martialed Negroes Hanged," December 12, 1917, *Great Falls Daily Tribune* (Great Falls, MT), 3. "Noose Avenges Riot Murderers," December 12, 1917, *Los Angeles Daily Times*, 5. "Singing a Hymn, 13 Negroes Soldiers Go to the Gallows," December 12, 1917, *Atlanta Constitution*, 3.
73 "Negro Rioters at San Antonio are Disposed Of," December 11, 1917, *Charlotte News*, 1. "14 Negro Rioters are Hanged at San Antonio; 41 Given Life Sentence," December 11, 1917, *El Paso Herald*, 1. "13 of Negro Soldiers in Riot Hanged," December 11, 1917, *St. Louis Post Dispatch*, 1–2.; "Noose Avenges Riot Murders," December 12, 1917, *Los Angeles Times*, 5.
74 Lucian B. Watkins, "These," *Crisis* 15, no. 4 (1918): 185.

75 Jordan, *Black Newspapers and America's War for Democracy, 1914–1920*, 95–96.
76 A.P. Sherwood, "In Re: Lillian Smith, Negress. Disloyalty Matter," January 16, 1918, Old German Files, 800–127259, Microfilm Publication M1085: Investigative Reports of the Bureau of Investigation 1908–1922, NARA, roll 515. Gruening incorrectly suggested a white girl wounded during the mutiny had been killed, "Houston: An NAACP Investigation," *Crisis*, 18. See the *Houston Post* for a list of casualties, which records "Alma Reichert, white girl" among the wounded. "Martial Law Declared," August 24, 1917, *Houston Post*, 1.
77 A.P. Sherwood, "In Re: Lillian Smith, Negress. Disloyalty Matter."
78 "The Houston Horror," *Crisis* 15, no. 4 (1918): 189.
79 "The Fate of Negro Mutineers," December 12, 1917, *Brooklyn Eagle*, 6; "Soldiers Lynched to Appease South," December 17, 1917, *Brooklyn Daily Eagle*, 15. Miller's comments are also reprinted in "The Houston Horror," *Crisis*, 189.
80 Kornweibel, *Investigate Everything*, 235.
81 Ida B. Wells and Alfreda M. Duster, *Crusade for Justice: The Autobiography of Ida B. Wells* (Chicago and London: University of Chicago Press, 2020), 316, 13.
82 C.D. Waide, "When Psychology Failed: An Unbiased Fact-Story of the Houston Race Riot of 1917," *Houston Gargoyle* 1, no. 20–24 (1928): 5.
83 "Thirteen Negroes Die on Scaffold," December 11, 1917, *Lead Daily Call* (Lead, SD), 1; "Large Number Negro Soldiers Are Executed," December 11, 1917, *Corvallis Gazette-Times*, 1. "Houston Negro Rioters Hung," December 12, 1917, *Leavenworth Post*, 1. "Noose Avenges Riot Murders," December 12, 1917, *Los Angeles Times*, 5. "Negro Troops Hanged, Buried; Remove Gibbets as Camp Sleeps," December 12, 1917, *Chicago Tribune*, 3. "13 Negro Soldiers Hanged for Rioting," December 12, 1917, *New York Times*, 7.
84 "Hang Thirteen Negro Rioters and Mutineers," December 12, 1917, *Washington Herald*, 2.
85 "Mutiny Was Caused by Vice and Booze," August 28, 1917, *Houston Post*, 5.
86 "Site of Execution Marked by Ashes of Big Bonfires," December 12, 1917, *Houston Post*, 2. The story printed in the *Post* is largely the same as the one printed in the *New York Times* and the *Chicago Tribune*. For references to "cowering" and "terrorized" victims in East St. Louis, see "Race Riot's Toll 29 Dead, 75 Hurt", July 4, 1917, *Washington Post*, 1; "Race Rioters Fire East St. Louis and Shoot or Hang Many Negroes; Dead Estimated at from 20 to 75," July 3, 1917, *New York Times*, 6.
87 "Negro Soldiers Stood at Attention as Traps Were Sprung to Hang 'Em," December 12, 1917, *Daily Free Press* (Kinston, NC), 1.
88 Aaron Belkin, *Bring Me Men: Military Masculinity and the Benign Facade of American Empire, 1898-2001* (New York: Columbia University Press, 2014), 4–5.
89 Haynes, "The Houston Mutiny and Riot of 1917," 438–39, n.79.
90 "President Saves Rioters," September 5, 1918, *New York Times*, 10.

91 Office of the Judge Advocate General United States War Department, "Secretary Newton Baker to President Woodrow Wilson, Washington, D.C, August 22," in Record Groups 153 and 393, NARA, 7.
92 "Tells Part He Played in the Houston Riot," December 29, 1917, *New York Age*, 1.
93 Haynes, *A Night of Violence*, 418.

5

War to the knife

Virgil Lott worked as a sheriff's deputy during the years of what he and other Anglo Texans referred to as the "bandit wars." In the unpublished history of the Lower Rio Grande Valley that he completed decades after the conflict was finished, he noted that it was impossible to count the number of Mexicans killed in the conflict. "[H]undreds ... were killed who had no part in the uprisings, their bodies concealed in the thick underbrush."[1] The uprisings he refers to began on July 4, 1915, with a raid in Cameron County in which several dozen Tejano and Mexican men stole supplies, killed a white teenager, burned a railway bridge, and cut telegraph lines. The two men attributed with leading the uprising, Ancieto Pizaña and Luis de la Rosa, declared that they had taken up arms to punish "with all the energy of which we are capable" the authorities and civilians who daily perpetrated outrages against Mexicans in Texas. Anglo Texans responded to the raids with a devastating wave of repression upon Mexicans in the valley.[2] *Regeneración* described the violence, citing a report of San Antonio's "bourgeois" Spanish-language newspaper, *El Presente*:

> Men have been killed hiding under their beds, and they have been killed inside their houses, in spite of having asked for a moment of peace to explain themselves. They have been taken to the jail to be hung, and even more have been shot in the back after giving up their arms and surrendering ... Nobody knows who killed the men who show up hung from the trees or riddled with shots; but the entire world points at the rangers.[3]

An Anglo lawyer named Frank Pierce wrote an account of the violence in a local history published just two years after the conflict began. He also identified the Rangers as authors of the repression, asserting that they began a "systematic manhunt" after the raids started. Pierce himself compiled a list of 102 ethnic Mexicans he knew to have been killed but noted, "it is claimed by citizens and army officers who saw many of the bodies, that at least 300 Mexicans were so killed."[4] In his full-length account of the uprising and its aftermath, the historian Benjamin Heber Johnson estimates the death toll of the repression to be in the low thousands – meaning that "a Tejano in south Texas was more likely to 'disappear' than a citizen of Argentina during that country's infamous 'Dirty War' of the 1970s."[5]

Before the raids and the retribution, a young Mexican national named Basilio Ramos was arrested carrying a document titled the Plan de San Diego. It set its sights on the "Government and country of the United States of North America," declaring two primary aims. It called for the independence of those states of which Mexico had been robbed "in a most perfidious manner by North American imperialism." It also called for the liberation of the black race from "Yankee tyranny which has held us in iniquitous slavery since the remote times."[6] To achieve these ends, it pledged to put to death "[e]very North American [man] over 16 years of age." It also promised to return to the "Apaches of Arizona as well as the Indians (redskins) of the Territory" the "lands which have been taken from them," in exchange for their assistance, and it welcomed the "Japanese race" into the rank of its liberating forces. The plan closed by reiterating the commitment to black liberty with which it began. Its final point read: "It is understood among those who may follow this movement that we shall carry in a singing voice the independence of the negroes."[7] The Congreso Revolucionario, as the signatories of the document called themselves, produced a number of other, similarly ambitious, manifestos. While the exact relationship between the authors of the Plan de San Diego and the armed raiders is unclear, at least some of the raiders acted in allegiance with its principles.[8]

The plan's aims were seemingly incomprehensible to many U.S. observers. The authorities dismissed the plan as "lunacy" when they first discovered it. When Ramos was brought to trial the judge set a bond and released him, commenting that he may be "more in need of a physician than anything else."[9] In 1919 a writer in the *New York Herald* concluded that the plan must have actually been written shortly after the Mexican–American War. Why else would the document refer to slavery and Indian uprisings? It proposed that the Mexicans who issued the plan in 1915 had somehow stumbled upon the document and were so captivated by the language that they put their own names to it.[10] The *Herald* author, clearly not a *Regeneración* subscriber, was unfamiliar with the *magonista* parlance of referring to the oppression of workers as "slavery." The misunderstanding of the document as a nineteenth-century relic reveals a deeper incommensurability, however. For the reporter in New York, U.S. domination of the land now within its borders was a concluded matter. The men on the border designating themselves the Congreso Revolucionario, for whom U.S. conquest was an ongoing experience, saw other possibilities.

This chapter will explore the multivalent discourses of civilization, savagery, and manhood that run through some of the Mexican and U.S. textual residues of the 1915 border conflict. Examining the cultural texts produced during and after the uprising and its repression offers insight into the ways in which the historical violence of U.S. expansion and its contestation were imagined by U.S. authors, law enforcement, and press, as well as ethnic Mexican radicals and militants. In the first half, I will draw on the Plan de San Diego as well as a series of other broadsides issued by the Congreso Revolucionario, apparently intended to be distributed among Tejanos, as well as one draft manifesto, handwritten in English, which is addressed to African Americans. The authors' call for an armed rebellion against U.S. brutality is framed in civilizational terms. The Congreso Revolucionario imagined new states and a different kind of American civilization, built on the ruins of a savage U.S. capitalism.

The documents' appeals to their readers are grounded in a visceral, sweeping condemnation of U.S. imperialism and capitalism, imagining a continental struggle between Anglo-Saxon barbarism and the "men of the future." Imagining an "EMANCIPATORY REVOLUTION FOR THE PEOPLES AND RACES OF AMERICA," the congress declared the abolition of race hatred as one of their primary aims, beginning with the "radical extirpation" of the oppressors who fomented this evil.[11] Their articulation of the struggle against U.S. capitalism as one of civilizational destiny sometimes relied upon problematic silences and inferences. The anti-racist pronouncements of the documents, and specifically their preoccupation with black freedom, have been frequently remarked upon. Johnson, for example, writes that the plan "focused on African Americans as much as the plight of Mexicans in the United States."[12] I will argue that the blackness the documents imagine is ambiguous, at times suggesting a more problematic reading of American history and American future than their call for common struggle might initially suggest.

In the second half of the chapter, I will examine how constructions of Mexican death and Mexican savagery in the U.S. discourse of the uprising and its repression fit into broader narratives of white Texan manhood and nation. Here I will draw on contemporary newspaper reports as well as histories written by white Texan writers later in the twentieth century. I will particularly focus on the unpublished manuscript of Virgil N. Lott, with which this chapter opened. As alluded to above, press across the nation presented Mexicans' armed resistance and the systematic killing of ethnic Mexican people during the conflict as a matter of border pacification. Many white Texans framed the border war as an episode in a long history of frontier defense against a hostile and barbaric nation at its periphery. In the graphic media accounts of anti-black violence at Slocum and other pogroms, the mass killing of African Americans was often conceptualized as a lamentable erosion of white civilization. In contrast, in the discursive framework of settlement and conquest, the killing of Mexicans is presented as the latter-day sweeping away of a decrepit Mexican sovereignty from the as yet incompletely cultivated edges of the nation. The landscape of Mexican death in such narratives signals the inexorable forward march of white U.S. nationhood.

The grounds of rebellion

While the politics of the Mexican Revolution profoundly suffused the borderlands, their propaganda suggests it was the conditions that existed in Texas that moved the s*ediciosos* to violence. The ethnic Mexican population in south Texas, who vastly outnumbered the small number of white American settlers, was somewhat insulated from the shock waves of dispossession after U.S. annexation. Until the early twentieth century, social relations and a ranching economy prevailed, marked by social and economic inequality as well as inter-ethnic accommodation. The landed elite class included ethnic Mexicans and Anglos who learned Spanish and adapted to Mexican culture, and intermarriage was common. The ranch economy was structured through labor relations emphasizing "paternalism, reciprocal obligations, and permanency" in which families of Mexican laborers were attached to the ranch of a powerful *patrón*. The introduction of the railroad to the region initiated an "acceleration of the colonization process," as Trinidad Gonzales puts it, as a surge of Anglos arrived and the economy shifted to one of industrial agriculture.

Newcomers viewed the previous order as archaic and corrupt and Mexicans as racially inferior and politically corrosive. They instilled new relations of racialized social and economic relations that subordinated both upper- and working-class Mexicans, who now found themselves subject to segregation in public spaces and pushed into separate residential districts.[13] The emergent caste-like social order would only harden further with the uprising. Mexican residents were disarmed while a registry was prepared of white men who had arms and were ready to respond to "invaders." As the Rangers, aided by local white men organized into "home guard" militias, undertook a campaign of terror to repress the threat, it opened new opportunities for some white people to acquire Tejano land and consolidate their own political and economic power. Terrorized Mexicans were forced to sell their land quickly and cheaply, often under direct threat by Rangers supporting Anglo buyers. Many Mexicans fled across the border carrying with them whatever they could, their attempt to seek safety in war-ravaged Mexico indicating the potency of the threat in Texas.[14]

The rebellion and its suppression were inevitably shaped by the wider arc of the Mexican Revolution and U.S. responses to it. Initially Venustiano Carranza, leader of the provisional revolutionary government in Mexico, offered tacit support to the raiders, allowing them to pass freely into Mexico. This support came to an abrupt end once his government was recognized by the Wilson administration.[15] Both the revolution in Mexico and the hardening of racialized caste lines in Texas intensified the radicalism and revolutionary spirit spreading among the poor ethnic Mexicans in the borderlands. Historian Dirk Raat writes that in 1906, "*Regeneración* had a circulation of between 15,000 and 20,000." Engagement with radical politics reached further than subscribers to the paper; in the first decade of the twentieth century, there were 165 *magonista* clubs in Cameron and Hidalgo counties, the two counties most affected by the border war.[16]

The lives of the men associated with the rebellion reflect these currents and counter-currents, the tightening grip of racial order in south Texas, and the electrifying philosophical and material impact of the Mexican Revolution. Agustín S. Garza was in his mid-thirties when the Plan de San Diego was issued. His revolutionary career, and that of Basilio Ramos, the young man carrying the copy of the plan that fell into the hands of the U.S. authorities, traversed the border. Both men spent time in prisons in the U.S. and Mexico. Though named the commander of the Plan de San Diego's "Liberating Army of Races and Peoples," Garza had no military experience but he was passionately opposed to U.S. imperialism. When the United States occupied the Mexican port of Veracruz in 1914, he telegraphed then President Huerta, offering to organize some men to help repel the invaders. When Garza was later incarcerated in a jail in Monterrey, the story goes, the Plan de San Diego, composed by an unnamed author, was smuggled into his cell. Garza is the only individual to have signed both the original Plan de San Diego, as well as a revised version of the plan, entitled "Manifesto to the Oppressed Peoples of America," using the alias León Caballo.[17] This second document, discussed at length below, was found at the scene of a raid. It elaborated a fervent critique of capitalism and U.S. racism against darker races and called for a social revolution.

The two Tejano men who led the raids, Luis de la Rosa and Ancieto Pizaña, were both *magonistas*. Pizaña, who worked as a stockman and owned his own ranch, was a friend of Flores Magón and contributor to *Regeneración*. A Mexican informant told an agent of the Bureau of Investigation that he had often seen Pizaña reading *Regeneración* to groups of friends at his ranch. Luis de la Rosa had met Garza in Texas, where the latter had traveled in order to foment an anti-imperialist movement. De la Rosa, who at one time in his life worked as a Cameron County deputy sheriff, was apparently already contemplating direct action and was moved by Garza's arguments. Ancieto Pizaña originally declined de la Rosa's invitation to take up arms but was pushed to action after a party of U.S. soldiers and law enforcement attacked his ranch. During the assault, they shot his twelve-year-old son, Gabriel, whose leg was later amputated as a result. While some who joined the raids envisioned a new social order, Pizaña was concerned first and foremost with ending Ranger brutalities against Tejanos. An agent of the Bureau of Investigation reported that Garza and de la Rosa worked together to distribute the Plan de San Diego in Mexico and Texas, though neither Pizaña nor de la Rosa signed the document and neither publicly affiliated themselves with it.[18]

The raiders, referred to by Mexicans as *sediciosos,* or seditionists, targeted structures of Anglo domination. In their more spectacular efforts, they attacked the large ranches of agricultural industrialists and derailed a train, the symbol of U.S. domination par excellence. As Richard Ribb points out, despite the sensationalist call for white genocide in the first Plan de San Diego document, which is not repeated in subsequent propaganda, the raiders selected their targets with rebellious or retributive aims. This sometimes included Tejanos they suspected of cooperation with authorities. In a particularly disturbing incident, raiders attacking a ranch at Las Norias shot and killed a Mexican woman because when they asked her how many Americans were in the ranch house, she told them that "they would soon find out." However, for the most part, as Gonzales writes, the raids targeted those responsible for the exploitation of or brutality against Tejanos, the owners of industrial ranches and men who had participated in the Law and Order league. The Rangers and white vigilantes who responded to the raids, on the other hand, cast a wide net.[19]

Despite suspecting the Plan de San Diego to be some kind of forgery and rejecting any connection between it and the rebellion, Ricardo Flores Magón would be identified by many Americans as the intellectual author of the uprising. This notion was actively pushed forward by the Carranza government, whose consul in Texas went so far as to offer U.S. prosecutors translated versions of supposedly incriminating articles from *Regeneración*.[20] Flores Magón denounced the idea that Mexicans had taken up arms to kill white people or restore Mexican sovereignty over the territory of the Southwest. Rather, they were defending themselves from the "attacks of which members of our race are so often victims in this country." In *Regeneración*, he stated that the "bourgeois press" insisted upon pushing the lie that the movement in Texas was a "racial clash," when in reality it was a movement for "human redemption" aimed at the creation of a "single human family composed of the working class."[21] In addition to suspecting the Plan de San Diego document to be a forgery designed to justify anti-Mexican repression, Claudio Lomnitz suggests that Flores Magón might also have worried that any "Mexican revolt in Texas was doomed to a quick and bloody end."[22] As his hesitation reflects, the documents of the Congreso Revolucionario are politically confused and pragmatically unlikely. As James Sandos notes, the materials lack a coherent focus and single philosophy. The anarchist rhetoric, he writes, was at odds with the rigid organizational hierarchy detailed in the documents and the aim to form a new republic.[23] Despite their unachievable aims and ideological vagueness, however, the documents speak to the profound discontent permeating the borderlands.

Savagery and slavery in the Plan de San Diego

The Congreso Revolucionario writers position their struggle within a New World history that envisions, if in vague terms, trajectories of violence that dispossess, denigrate, and exploit Native Americans, African Americans, Mexicans, and Asians. The Manifesto to the Oppressed Peoples of America includes provisions to outlaw racial hatred, as well as to abolish prisons, penitentiaries, and other "centers of brutalization." Describing themselves as a movement destined to recover trampled liberties and sovereignties, the proclamation urged the different peoples of the "continent of Columbus" – a revealing designation – to stand together to put an end to the abuses, infamies, and barbarism of arrogant "white skinned' savages." They insisted that the United States did not even deserve to be designated a "nation." This group of barbaric men call themselves the "'Colossus' of the United States of North America," the document reads, "just like a ton of filth randomly placed in a field of cultivation declared itself the world's granary."[24] Maintaining the binary division between the productive order of civilization and the dissolute disorder of savagery, the usual definition of savagery as the incapacity to master the land is here re-envisioned as a mode of domination whose greed, violence, and exploitation make a ruin of the land.

In their declaration of rebellion, reprinted in Monterrey's *El Democratica*, Anciento Pizaña and Luis de la Rosa also employed an idiom of civilization and barbarism, stating that just indignation at anti-Mexican abuse "impels us, orders us to punish with all the energy of which we are capable, that crowd of savages that would put to shame a hungry tiger or a loathsome hyena."[25] The imagery bears striking resemblance to that used by Mirabeau Lamar, second president of the Republic of Texas, as he addressed the Texas Congress in 1838. Mirabeau insisted that "if wild cannibals of the woods will not desist from their massacres; if they will continue to war upon us with the ferocity of Tigers and Hyenas," then an "exterminating war" would be necessary.[26] As this resonance suggests, despite making capitalism or white U.S. racism the degenerate force of "savagery," the new points of reference cannot fully expunge the terminology of the traces of its colonial origin.

The ascription of the Americas as the "continent of Columbus," seemingly designed to emphasize the pre-Anglo Hispanic presence in the region and thus delegitimize U.S. sovereignty, simultaneously reinforces the colonialist logic of European "discovery." In the Manifesto to the Oppressed Peoples of America, the authors describe the "white skinned savages" of the United States as "super-anthropophages," literally man-eaters or cannibals, who committed acts that defied the imagination. The eighteenth-century French cartographer Guillaume Delisle who produced the first map known to use the word Texas also used this striking term of otherness. Around the curve of the coastline of the Texan Gulf of Mexico, Delisle inscribed *"Indiens errans et Antropophages"* – "wandering Indians and Cannibals." However appropriate the imagery of "man-eating" may be for the voracious destruction of U.S. capitalism, the figure of the savage "cannibal" was not historically free-floating, equally fixable to any designated target. The "anthropophages" marked on Delisle's map were probably the Karankawa, a tribe whose last members were killed by a party of Tejano ranchers led by Juan Nepomuceno Cortina. Cortina, who became a Chicanx folk hero, took up arms against the dispossession of ethnic Mexicans in the nineteenth century, famously raising a Mexican flag over Brownsville in 1859 and declaring the land the Republic of the Rio Grande. Cortina's role in the genocide of the Karankawa starkly illustrates that projects of Mexican/Tejano sovereignty were not necessarily in the interests of indigenous peoples.[27]

Both the Plan de San Diego and the Manifesto to the Oppressed Peoples of America promised that the "Apaches of Arizona" and the other "Red Skins of the Territory" would have their stolen lands returned to them, in return for their assistance with the cause.[28] The simple pledge effaces the complexities of borderlands history, namely the enmity between Apaches and Mexican settlers in the region and Mexico's historical role as a colonial power in the very lands it was "robbed of in the most perfidious manner."[29] The point is not that the Congreso Revolucionario or the raiders themselves were directly implicated in this earlier violence, or that Mexico and the United States were interchangeable in their approaches to Native Americans in the borderlands. However, these violent histories linger in the idiom the documents employ. The ways in which the racially saturated framework of "savagery" inflected the authors' critique of U.S. imperialism is further evident in the documents' construction of blackness.

The invocation of black insurrection in the Plan de San Diego reflects a deep and varied discursive history in which Mexicans, African Americans, and white Americans imagined the potentialities of black and Mexican subversion and linked black freedom to Mexican territory. Before the Civil War, the very presence of Mexico undermined security for a people who deemed slavery necessary and essential to their individual and national existence. Before emancipation, Mexico's physical proximity, its ideological hostility to slavery, and its ongoing political tensions with Texas and the United States made it a landscape of promise for enslaved people in Texas. John "Rip" Ford, who served as Texas Ranger and also an officer in the Confederate Army, estimated that thousands of slaves freed themselves by making the arduous trek across the Rio Grande.[30] As the territorial presence of Mexico perpetually undermined slaveholders' physical hold on captives, Mexicans themselves were imagined as agents of discord. Texan slaveholders were perpetually worried that enslaved people would make alliances with Mexicans that would enable them to either abscond, kill their masters, or both. After the discovery of a slave conspiracy to slaughter the white population in Colorado County, the local Vigilance Committee found that "without exception every Mexican in the county was implicated" and declared that "the lower class of the Mexican population are incendiaries in any country where slaves are held."[31] Periodic fears of uprising and subversion triggered various efforts by white Texans to "[clear] our country of rascally peons," efforts which coalesced with wider streams of Anglo settlers' violence against the Mexicans in their midst.[32]

After the Civil War, Texan John H. Reagan, previously postmaster general of the Confederacy, reflected on the ominous example of Mexico for the United States.[33] As the Confederacy lay in ruins, Reagan sent a letter to the people of Texas, urging them to accept defeat and the death of slavery. He suggested that restrictions on literacy and property ownership would go a long way in preventing the political enfranchisement of the freedpeople. He asserted that Mexico and other Latin American states, where "the zeal of liberty and progress" had induced governments to give the vote to Indians, Negroes, and "mixed bloods," now provided "the saddest warning" of the policy of universal suffrage.[34] Reagan also suggested that Mexico's bizarre notions of liberty might have a silver lining for white Texans. He encouraged his despondent countrymen to look with "confidence to the future," assuring them that they would not be inundated with free black people. Instead, many of the freedpeople would probably now "go to Mexico and other countries, in search of social equality."[35] Thus Mexico's destructive racial equality would serve as a cleansing siphon for the people of the United States.

Before and after the Plan de San Diego authors called for black independence, Mexican radicals and revolutionaries on both sides of the border contemplated their relationship to, and sought solidarity with, African Americans. The possibility of such a rebellious partnership concerned the federal government. Over a third of the Bureau of Investigation's surveillance of alleged black subversion during the World War I era focused on alleged German and Mexican conspiracies to manipulate the black population, with a large proportion of these cases coming from Texas. Years after the border conflict had been quelled, agents reported concerns about "secret meetings" in Houston in which black and Mexican speakers "are disseminating anti-American and anti-white propaganda," and in which African Americans were encouraged to "join forces" with Mexico in any conflict between that country and the United States.[36] As Mexicans in the United States were "exposed to being killed from one moment to another," in 1913 a *Regeneración* writer named José Garcia urged, "we must not waste time but declare the revolution in the border states: the black race must support this emancipatory movement." He suggested that a "box of matches will make very good luminaries in the Louisiana plantations," just as a "a good bloodletting" could destroy the cattle of those "savage cowboys" in Texas." The revolutionary movement begun in Mexico, he asserted, should "extend from Greenland to the Panama Canal."[37]

Within these examples, the Plan de San Diego is unique in the centrality it gives black liberation, which, as described at the outset of this chapter, is delineated as an aim in itself rather than a means to an end. The Manifesto to the Oppressed Peoples of America likewise envisions a multi-racial workers' movement against capitalism. Unlike the Mexican editorials discussed in Chapter 3 that angrily rejected the supposedly degrading association made between the Mexican and the Negro who "has no country," the Revolutionary Congress passionately asserted common cause with all "proletarians ... who also have the misfortune of being a different race" from the Yankee oppressors. Toward this aim, they frequently used the imagery of slavery. The U.S. capitalists designated "anthropophages" and "'white skinned' savages" are also described in the manifesto as *negreros* (slave drivers, literally, "drivers of blacks") who commit "unprecedented robberies" against the workers and exclude the "Mexican, black [and] yellow," from schools, theaters, and public establishments.[38] In another broadside, the authors accuse thieving *negreros* of holding "Mexican, black and Latino origin workers" in debt slavery. The Plan de San Diego's first provision, as noted in the introduction to this chapter, proclaims the independence of "the black race [from] the Yankee tyranny which has held us in iniquitous slavery since the remote times."[39] While "slavery" to Yankee tyranny is seemingly imagined as a common condition of all oppressed peoples of color and the grounds for common action, as we will begin to see, the civilizational destinies of black and Latin race in the documents are far from interchangeable. While the particular history of black captivity in the Americas is occluded in the documents' universalist framing of slavery, its traces nevertheless become apparent.

In another broadside, entitled "LEVANTEMONOS!!" (Let Us Rise Up), the Congreso Revolucionario describe the "Revolutionary Movement" developing along the border using a broad-based language of class: "It is the war of the hungry against the potentates and authorities ... It is the SOCIAL WAR that stirs in these moments ... spreading throughout all the peoples of the globe, bearing by motto: Redemption for all the disinherited!" On the rubble of the "expired regime of the bourgeoise" the disinherited would build a society of peace and freedom. Toward this end, the broadside calls on "virile Mexicans and races of color" to push forward in revolutionary effort, "beheading [parasites] and everything that stands in the way of the incontrovertible march of progress!" The broadside also denounces the violence of the United States ruling class against those who had previously rebelled against its injustices. As a particularly important example, it invokes the eight Chicago anarchists imprisoned and executed by the U.S. government in 1886, after a dynamite bomb was thrown at police during a labor demonstration in Haymarket Square.

The authors might have read about the Haymarket martyrs in *Regeneración*, in which the Flores Magón brothers and English-language contributors memorialized the men as spiritual precursors to the revolutionary Mexican proletariat.[40] The broadside recounts the tragedy of these men, who "suffered ... relentless lashes on their backs" to redeem their class but fell victim to the "wild beasts of this Country." In order to further emphasize the depraved nature of American capitalism, the authors then use colonial constructions of African savagery as they urge readers to remember all attacks against liberty "in this country of hyenas and hottentots."[41] Thus, the authors use the imagery of slavery to imagine oppression and righteous resistance – the Haymarket martyrs suffer "relentless lashes" – but retain the racial idiom of blackness as anti-civilization in this invocation of the hyena and the "hottentot," two figures of African wilderness. Steeped in the racisms of both transatlantic slavery and imperialism in Africa, the "hottentot," as Jimmy Casas Klausen has written, has long featured in the Western philosophical imagination as the "conventional, ultimate limit case of humanity," the "rightless [bearer] of naked human life."[42]

In describing the savage United States as "this land of hyenas and hottentots," the Congreso Revolucionario paint U.S. capitalism as an anticivilization and moral wilderness. This likening of American capitalists to black "hottentots" does not sit in opposition to their description of the same American capitalists as "the *negreros* of the land," a phrase which invokes the "driving of blacks" as the quintessential form of oppression.

Each figure, the black African savage and the cruel "driver of blacks," is meant to illustrate the backward, brutal nature of the white U.S. civilization. The ascription of capitalist exploitation and racism to "savagery" here uses the familiar teleologic understanding of civilization as the progressive achievement of the virile, just, and capable, casting those outside civilization as "primitive." If shared oppression makes African Americans caught in the grinding U.S. tyranny recognizable as potential fellow revolutionaries and a "virile race of color," the primitive "hottentot" in the unhistory of the jungle remains the emblematic figure of bare humanity, an evocative point of reference for barbaric capitalists. This reference to "hottentots" reflects how deeply the construction of racialized blackness was imbricated with discourses of civilization and progress, even in their radical deployments.

The equation of the capitalist enemy to "the hottentot" draws our attention back to the political alliances offered to African Americans. The positioning of black race outside of the currents of history is latent in the documents in more subtle ways. In another broadside, entitled "To our Brothers of America," which does not mention African Americans or black liberation, the authors of the Congreso Revolucionario urge their comrades, in well-established tradition, to break their chains: "The time has come to shake the iron yoke, the object of our slavery." Here the brotherhood called upon to combat the "Saxon race" was envisioned specifically as Latin: "We are the budding of a civilization; We embody the heroic spirit of the Latin race." As in some nationalist discourses of mestizaje, the Latin race imagined as bearing regenerative possibilities for the continent:

> We are the advanced of America; We are the men of the future. We are going to a holy fight, to a noble war ... of that country founded with the detritus of civilizations, we will found a new country, a heroic country, a Latin country. We are first that we wield the flag of rebellion in this soil where we have been pariahs, poor helots, miserable wretches.
>
> No more oppressions, no more tyrannies, no more preponderance of the Saxon race. ... Help us conquer a freedom that will be continental freedom. The colossus falters and trembles and we fight to destroy it.[43]

Ties of personal and racial history, the broadside asserts, bound these men to the land where they grew up and which "once belonged to a Latin country."[44] Rather than a reconstitution of a lost past, then, as characterized in some of the U.S. interpretations of the Plan de San Diego, the author or authors here imagine the birth of something new. How does this vision of a "a new country ... a Latin country" fit with the movement's proclaimed aim of African American independence?

"The Negro Free"

While the movement may have failed to recruit large numbers of black supporters for very practical reasons, the construction of black insurrectionary agency in its extant manifestos is ambiguous.[45] Among the broadsides in the archive is a handwritten draft manifesto addressed to potential "Negro recruits." There is a marked and revealing difference in the pleas made to potential black revolutionaries and those made to "Latin brothers." The author of the draft apparently intended to give the impression that it had been written by an African American supporter of the Plan de San Diego. As Charles Harris and Louis Sadler point out, this seems unlikely given the syntax and spelling of the English used, which strongly suggest the author's primary language was Spanish.[46] The author begins by calling for his "Negro Brothers to come to Life and Liberty," rejecting the "false civilization" and the "social cancer that is slavery." In an energetic rush of words, the author reminds the imagined black reader of the abuse experienced in service to "the infernal white man as a master." Written after the Battle of Carrizal, in which black soldiers of the U.S. Tenth Cavalry fought Carranza's troops in Chihuahua, the draft manifesto urges its black readers to refuse to fight for the white man:

> [Never] think of taking up arms againts [sic.] Mexico the only country in the world that offers you the ... shadow of a chance, and give you social rights is the country he is telling you to fight [...] don't fight Mexico but turn your gun the other way and march through Texas, demonstrating you [sic.] rights as a citizen and defending the Plan of San Diego, which means the Negro Free.[47]

The author declares the commitment of the Latin race to racial equality and black freedom. In contrast, though the heroes Washington and Lincoln "fought for your Liberty ... and [won victories] for you," their ideals were betrayed by white men who could not fathom an America built upon the principle of "equal rights for all man."[48]

Being subject to the generalized "slavery" of the proletariat and despised races makes the figure of the oppressed Negro intelligible as a potential historical actor – in stark distinction to the bestial figure of the "hottentot." However, though Yankee tyranny is frequently positioned as a seamless condition holding all subject races in thrall, in the written materials of the movement, Negro and Latin agency are far from interchangeable. In contrast to the appeal addressed to the Latin race in "Brothers of America," which invites men to participate in the building of a new world, the appeal to "the black race" frames a choice of allegiance between two national frameworks not of their own making. The would-be Latin revolutionaries are "men of the future" who will found a new and heroic nation; black men should remember that Mexico is the "only country in the world" that would accept them on terms of equality. While it is hoped that black men will rise up, "march in groups and columns" to defend the Plan de San Diego and thus their own freedom, "the Negro" is again constructed as having heretofore not acted for his own liberation. Washington and Lincoln had fought "for" him.

The draft manifesto author urged his purported "black brothers" to rise from their slumber and demonstrate their worth by fighting for their liberty: "Human natur[e] is equal in the black as well as the white, therefore the Negro must be free and to be Free you must fight for your Freedom."[49] This language of struggle and manhood, typical to revolutionary discourses of all stripes, unintentionally recalls the assertions and admonishments of white Americans that black men had not fought for their freedom and thus had not earned citizenship. The author's projected black speaker does not just urge black men to realize manhood through resistance but emphasizes their shameful lack thereof: "We this poor suppressed Race we poor foot stools of the [white] man the most degraded people of the world we are a disgrace to mankines [sic.]." The author implores his audience to free themselves by casting their "lot with a nation that will give you rights and justice. Free yourself from the grip of the hated gringos and be a man and not food for his cañon [sic.]."[50] Black agency is seemingly a latent force, waiting to be activated.

In his manuscript, Virgil Lott wrote that the Plan de San Diego promised "a land of milk and honey" to "every poor Mexican and to every poor negro and to every man of off-color."[51] It is noteworthy, however, that the documents of the Congreso Revolucionario do not promise a multi-racial utopia. After declaring the intention to liberate "the black race" from "Yankee tyranny," the Plan de San Diego declares:

> When we shall have obtained independence for the Negroes, we shall grant them a banner, which they themselves shall be permitted to select, and we shall aid them in obtaining six States of the American Union … and they may form from these six States a republic, and they may be independent.[52]

Apart from the patronizing language (the Congreso Revolucionario will "grant them a banner"), it is striking that the authors' vision for liberating black people is completed through the creation of a separate territorial homeland. In the Manifesto to the Oppressed Peoples of America, after describing the provisions for a new society free of prisons, racial hatred and grounded in love and education, the authors reiterate their aim to obtain independence for black people and to secure a new state for them from the territory of the Southern U.S. The Negroes would be free to organize their new state however they deemed appropriate, "provided it was communal."[53]

Thus, whereas the Latin race is imagined as the vanguard of a new continental freedom, and the "redskins of the territory" are promised the return of their land from that wrested from the "white skinned savages," the final vision of the congress's struggle against the U.S. colossus culminates in the departure of African Americans from the new "Latin country." Alongside the professions of radical solidarity with those who had felt the sting of the "Yankee whip," and the calls to workers and pariahs to join the social revolution and "bring war to capital," a conventional nationalist logic lingers.[54] In the movement's discourse, if both African Americans and Mexicans had been "wretches and outcasts," Mexicans' previous sovereignty and settlement in the region imbued their relationship with the land with a different order of historical meaning. If slavery is metaphorized as a general condition of oppression, Mexicans' claim to the land, of which they were "robbed in a most perfidious manner by North American imperialism," is implicitly treated as particular. Though the promise of a sovereign territory confirms a sense of black peoplehood, the future of the "Negro Free" is projected elsewhere, away from the land in which they and generations of their ancestors had lived, worked, bled, and died. That they are envisioned as outside of the Congreso Revolucionario's new republic implicitly reconstructs blackness as, once again, present in the imagined America but not of it.

Landscapes of death and the Texan nation

For the remainder of this chapter, I will turn to examine the discourses of death and violence produced by white Americans during the uprising and the repression, which also drew heavily on the imageries of savagery and civilization emergent from the violence of New World settlement. Roland G. Usher, the professor of history at Washington University discussed in Chapter 3 who asserted that Mexico was "a collection of, loosely organized ... sundered Indian tribes" rather than a nation, offered quite a different view of the emergence of U.S. nationhood. In his 1914 *The Rise of the American People*, he wrote:

> There is something of an epic splendor about this growth to rugged physical manhood of a great people. Like Antaeus, we drew our strength from the ground. We built our house with our bare hands and fashioned our national physical body in an incredibly short time out in a cleansing wilderness.[55]

This mythical image of the white Americans carving their national manhood out of the wilderness, of course, offers the racial foil to the chaotic tribal stagnation of Mexican half-civilization. In the U.S. press coverage of the Texas rebellion and repression, the physical landscape of the border was tied to the construction of both Mexican otherness and white Texan manhood.

In a syndicated series that appeared in several newspapers on the East Coast, a journalist named Frederick J. Haskin regaled his readers with the details of the Texas "bandit wars." As with other accounts of the violence, Haskin's narrative oscillates between diminishing the prowess of the so-called bandits, for example scoffing that the "little Spanish [language] newspapers" trumpeted the raiders' successes as if they were "serious warfare," and presenting them as an insidious threat to life and social order – 5,000 U.S. troops guarded "American lives and homes along the Mexican border." In Haskin's account, the bandits are inferior to American fighting men, but are able to attack and retreat through the desolate wilderness at the border. "'The Mexicans disappeared in the brush,'" he writes, is a sentence repeated "again and again in the annals of the bandit war."

> To a great extent the brush, the tangled thickets of mesquite and chaparral is the crux, the heart to the whole situation. Without the brush the war would have been over long ago. The brush is the bandits' strongest ally. The iron tough mesquite flourishes in the rich soil all the way from a little brush to a tree two feet in diameter. It is dense and impenetrable from the ground to a height of thirty feet. Scattered through it are great piles of broad-leaved cactus and hundreds of sword like yuccas perched on their prickly pedestals like little palms. Where the ground is moist this confusion is worse confounded by a luxuriant growth of cane and willow. The whole is worse than an African jungle.[56]

Further emphasizing the symbiotic relationship between Mexican lawlessness and the confounding tangles of impenetrable growth, Haskin writes that for the "Mexican native" the brush is both a refuge and, if necessary, a home. Like the Congreso Revolucionario's reference to "hyenas and hottentots," his assertion that the brush is "worse than an African jungle" momentarily invokes the imperialist imaginary of the so-called Dark Continent. Adjoining the border landscape to Africa, commonly treated in early twentieth-century U.S. and European discourse as nature not merely untamed but hostile, dangerous and disease-ridden (the "White Man's Grave"), accentuates the alien racial otherness of the "Mexican native" who seamlessly disappears into its darkness.[57]

The *St. Louis Post Dispatch* reporter Clair Kenamore approvingly relayed one Texas ranchman's proposal to end the "lawlessness" that made the eradication of the brush central to both the restoration of social order as well as the control of the potentially dangerous Mexican population. The solution would be to establish martial law and then "round up all Mexicans living north of the line," placing them in "concentration camps along the river from Rio Grande City to the Gulf." The inmates of the camp would be compelled to clear the northern bank of the river of the "semitropical" vegetation that was almost impenetrable for American soldiers," but which the bandits "seem to go through at will."[58] Unlike the "cleansing wilderness" in which Usher envisioned that Americans forged their nation, the Mexican brush is at once over-ripe and fruitless, producing only a dark "confusion" of hard, virtually weaponized vegetation. Haskin's reference to the territory's "rich soil" hints at the productive capacities of the land, were it to be properly managed, further insinuating the Mexicans' native backwardness. The worse-than-jungle Mexican brush maps the sterile and decrepit nature of Mexican sovereignty.

While Mexicans are linked to the primitive landscape of the brush, white Texans, as rugged men of the frontier, are repeatedly figured as having a masterful, disciplinary relationship to the territory. The *Houston Post* asserted that the "Rangers know the brush as well as the Mexicans," noting in October, 1915, that 200 "marauding Mexicans" had paid the penalty for twenty-one Americans killed.[59] The Rangers' knowledge of the brush is evidenced in their violent subjection of Mexicans, who in turn are likened to fauna. The Lynford *Courant*, for example, reported that "[h]unting bandits is more like hunting coyotes than organized warfare."[60] In his piece, Haskin wrote that "[t]he Texas Rangers, a band of picked fighting men, are beating the brush for Mexicans as hunters beat thickets for deer." While a dozen ranchmen and some forty soldiers had been killed in the fighting, the Plan de San Diego dreamers had paid in blood. "The number of Mexicans that lie unburied in the brush about Brownsville is variously estimated at 300 to 500."[61] As well as a site from which Mexican lawlessness leaks, the brush thus also becomes site of Mexican death, decay, and containment by the policing agents of white civilization, signifying both the threat of barbarous Mexican masculinity and its ultimate doom.

Applauding their efforts to rid the country of "bandits," the *Courier-Gazette* in McKinney, Texas, noted appreciatively how the Rangers refrained from "boasting" about their deeds: "The way they speak of their heroic acts when a dead Mexican is found among the cactus bushes, is a jocular statement that said 'greaser' must have suffered an attack of 'sunstroke' or some other term equally as witty." The author claimed to "deplore death in any manner" but opined that the "marauding bands which have infested the lower Rio Grande Country for the past fortnight are getting what is coming to them."[62] Even some more circumspect about the Rangers' tactics found them to be ultimately justifiable if not essential. Clair Kenamore allowed that the de-facto policy of mass punishment could have unfortunate consequences. "When a certain man is discovered to have taken part in a bandits' raid, is captured or killed in such a raid, his brothers, half-brothers and brothers-in-law are assumed to be guilty and are immediately arrested or killed." However, if such methods seemed "archaic" to the outsider in the present day and age, Kenamore reminds the reader that they were rooted in the Rangers' historical duty to "uphold and emphasize the fact that [Texas] is and will remain a white man's country."[63]

In a series of investigative hearings convened in 1919 by the Tejano legislator J.T. Canales into the conduct of the Rangers, a number of witnesses referred euphemistically to the frequent "evaporations" of Mexicans during the trouble. Robert E. Lee Knight, the attorney acting on behalf of the Adjutant General's Department to defend the Rangers, sought to evade the more ominous readings of the term, suggesting that there were different forms of "evaporations." He prompted R.B. Creager, an Anglo resident of Brownsville who sharply criticized the Rangers, to agree that "evaporations" might refer to Mexicans that merely "disappeared back into Mexico" rather than executions. Creager responded, "You know there were large numbers of bodies found in the brush."[64] The landscape of death was marked both by disappearance as well as exposure. The bodies of many murdered men were left unburied to decompose, their relatives unable to claim them for fear of reprisal by the Rangers. J.T. Canales testified that this "condition existed until it was nauseating, nauseating, it was terrible."[65] In other instances, Rangers made a greater spectacle of their killings. Memoirs of both white and Mexican residents from the region recall Rangers burning the bodies of Mexicans in piles. A photograph of three white men, two of whom were Rangers, posing with the bodies of two dead Mexican men was sold as a postcard in Brownsville and appeared in newspapers.[66] In the contemporary national press, the killing was presented as the byproduct of the endemic violence of Mexico's chaos and accepted as a function of national self-defense: "The daily discovery of dead Mexicans along the border," the *Los Angeles Tribune* noted, "is presumptive evidence that the pacification of our sister republic goes on apace."[67]

The Unburied at San Jacinto

Contemporary and later historical accounts of the killing in 1915 drew meaning from and reinforced settler mythology of the founding of the Texan nation, in which mass Mexican death was a recurring trope. D.P. Gay, an immigration inspector who took part in a gun battle with *sediciosos* at Norias ranch, later wrote that during the battle he could not help but remember the "immortal" heroism of the Alamo, when "a hundred and eighty red-blooded Americans fought about five thousand greasers."[68]

The memorialization of the defeat of the Mexican Army at the Battle of San Jacinto, the decisive battle of the Texas Revolution, in both granite and text, illustrates how nationalist narratives used portrayals of mass Mexican death to emphasize white Texan manhood and sovereignty. A brief reflection on the imagery of San Jacinto gives illuminating context to narratives of the mass killing of Mexicans in the 1910s. William S. Taylor, who participated in the 1836 battle, later wrote for the annals of Texas history: "as we overtook them, we felt compelled to kill them, and did so, though on their knees crying for quarter, and saying, 'Me no Alamo.'" Despite the attempts of their officers to moderate the killing, the Texan forces killed defeated Mexican soldiers as they attempted to surrender. Taylor and his comrades were disinclined to show mercy to the Mexicans, knowing that despite "solemn treaty stipulations," the Mexican General Santa Anna had killed Texian prisoners "in cold blood."[69] Thus the Texans' primal brutality is called forth from the Mexicans' barbarism and disregard for the laws of nations. Their massacre of men attempting to surrender is presented as the ruthless punishment of a treacherous enemy, demonstrating the unbridgeable distance between Texan and Mexican manhood. As historian John E. Dean notes, in the U.S. cultural memory of the battle, the furious manly cry of "Remember the Alamo" is met by the cringing, inarticulate plea of "Me no Alamo," signifying the difference between the unflinching fortitude of Anglo Texans and the decadence of Mexican sovereignty.[70]

In the 1930s, Texans erected a nearly 570-foot monument at the site of the battle. As part of the monument, the eight Texans who died in the battle were honored with a grave marker whose inscription notes that nothing in the annals of war or the natural world itself, not "the loud roaring thunder, the desolating tornado, and the withering simoom of the desert," inspired emotion like that evoked by the soldiers' sacrifice.[71] No marker was erected for the 630 dead Mexicans. Some indication of the gruesome nature of the battle is recorded in the solemn inscription on the monument. After setting out the conditions of Mexican tyranny against which the Texan colonists struggled, the inscription describes the battle itself: "The Texans asked no quarter and gave none. The slaughter was appalling, victory complete, and Texas free!" (It is striking that Walter Webb, author of a romanticized history of the Rangers, used precisely this language to morally qualify what he referred to as the "orgy of bloodshed" white Americans unleashed in 1915: "Of bandits they asked no quarter and gave none."[72]) Unlike the struggles against "Negro domination" during Reconstruction in Pauline Buck Hohes's history of Anderson County, memorialized as the fatherly punishment of impudent racial children, the crushing of the Mexican enemy at San Jacinto is given grave historical and military import. Santa Anna is described as "the Napoleon of the West." "Measured by its results," the inscription concludes, "San Jacinto was one of the decisive battles of the world ... Almost one-third of the present area of the American Nation, nearly a million square miles of territory, changed sovereignty."[73]

The victorious Texan army refused to bury the hundreds of Mexican dead after the battle, leaving them to decompose where they lay. A Mexican survivor of the battle wrote despondently, "they had not the generosity to burn or bury after the time-honored custom, regardless of their own comfort and health and those of the surrounding settlements." A correspondent from the *New Orleans Bulletin* at Galveston visited the site of the battle three days after it had finished and produced a more visceral and degrading imagery for his readers. "The ground was strewn with dead men" and debris, he wrote. The unburied Mexican corpses had become "disgusting masses of corruption." Illustrating the symbolic potency of blackness in the U.S. racist imagination to signify corrosion, the unnamed correspondent observed that "[t]he faces of most of the dead were as black as negroes."[74]

Capturing the shifting tones of lofty glorification and profane humor that frequently mark cultural narratives of violence, the exposure of the Mexican casualties at San Jacinto is recorded in the subsequent historiography with a tone of derision that reverberates in U.S. accounts of the border wars in the twentieth century. The field of mass decay is rendered to illustrate Mexican ineptitude and the grim and unrelenting will of Texan frontiersmen. In 1935, James T. Shields published an account of the Texas Revolution, *Tall Men with Long Rifles*, purportedly drawn from the memories of a participant in the event, Creed Taylor. Recounting the Battle of San Jacinto, Taylor describes the jovial conversations of the white soldiers as the field of dead, exposed to sun and drenching rain, became a "fearful, most ghastly sight" of forms that had lost human proportions. Here again the effeminate nature of the Mexican enemy is emphasized: "it was jocosely suggested that a dead 'greaser' would turn to a mummy … that there was not vitality enough about them to cause decomposition."[75] In contrast to the towering solemn monument describing the "Napoleon of the West," Walter Webb offers a passing vision of the field of San Jacinto dead, writing that carrion animals ate the horses but "refused to eat the Mexicans because of their peppery skins." Relating an anecdote reproduced in numerous accounts, he notes that the local people finally relented and "buried the Mexican remains in self-defence" because their cows were chewing the bones of the dead, which spoiled the milk.[76] The utter eradication of sovereign Mexican power from the land is signified in the grotesque, as the Mexican Army is reduced to bone and a lingering taste of defilement on the palates of Anglo settlers.

At the 1919 hearings investigating Rangers' misconduct, H.J. Kirk, a Chicago native who was a justice of the peace in Cameron County, testified about his experiences during the border violence four years previously. A local Mexican man, he told the committee, came to see him during the troubles, to ask him to accompany some families to bury the decomposing bodies of four men. Kirk asked why the man did not bury the bodies himself, and the man replied that the people were afraid the Rangers would shoot them should they attempt it. When Kirk attended the site where the bodies lay, there were "five or six hacks [trucks] filled up with men and women who finally went out to this place of burial."[77] Observing that there can be no obituary for the casualties produced by the United States' War on Terror, Judith Butler has written that the obituary, a public text of mourning, works as an act of nation-building, mapping out the boundaries at which life is recognizable as life, and death is intelligible as loss. "[I]f a life is not grievable, it is not quite a life ... It is already the unburied, if not the unburiable."[78] During the border violence, as after the Battle of San Jacinto, Mexicans were literally made unburiable, a tactic of terror heavy with symbolic ramifications. In 1915, the exposure of Mexican bodies was clearly intended to intimidate local Mexican people, while it also worked to strip the bodies themselves of intimate social and human meaning. A paper in San Antonio observed that "the finding of dead bodies of Mexicans suspected for various reasons of being connected with the troubles, has reached a point where it creates little or no interest. It is only when a raid is reported or an American is killed that the ire of the people is aroused."[79] Rather than the deprivation of life, the Mexican unburiable offer evidence of the processes in place to protect life (that is, "grievable" life) and order. As in the fields of San Jacinto, Mexican death is construed as a precondition for the perpetuity of American destiny.

Emerging from the brush unscathed: savagery and manhood

Before pursuing his aspirations as a writer of history in his later life, Virgil Lott worked as a reporter and an immigration inspector. As noted in the introduction to this chapter, he also participated in the border conflict as a deputy sheriff. His manuscript, "A History of the Lower Rio Grande Valley," completed shortly before his death, given to flourishing, if repetitive, turns of phrase, portrays the border conflict as part of Texans' longer struggles of settlement and sovereignty. Like other U.S. authors, Lott uses Indianness to reveal the nature and historical meaning of Mexicans' and white Texans' violence. In his assessment of the troublesome Mexicans, Lott sketches the standard U.S. vision of "duped and deluded peons" in thrall to treacherous and corrupt rulers. Lott portrays Venustiano Carranza as the mastermind of the raids, obsessed with fanatical dreams of reconquering "a land richer than far Cathay, a land of green fields and happy homes," whose fruitfulness had been developed by the "indomitable will and efforts" of the very American race that Carranza despised. Lott's Carranza, "the chauvinistic dreamer," is emblematic of the failed mestizo settler, incapable of productively dominating the land he had once occupied and now filled with treacherous jealousy. As well as "peons" duped by the false promises of a life of "ease and indolence," Lott also characterizes the Plan de San Diego raiders as driven by an insensate brutality, each tendency – that of indolence and meaningless violence – indicative of the savage's essential historical inertia. He recounts an incident in which a group of raiders mounted the head of a young U.S. private they had captured and killed on a lance on the Mexican side of the border, in view of the man's comrades on the American side of the river. "The actions of the bandits in this horrible drama proves them to be the same today, yesterday and tomorrow – the Indian in them will drive them to brutality in spite of their vaunted civilization."[80] Like many U.S. accounts of the Mexican Revolution, the violence of the bandits is a maelstrom, perpetuating chaos; unlike the progress-making violence of the "frontiersmen," as Lott revealingly refers to white Texans, it is unproductive and unchanging. While the Mexicans' desecration of the soldier's body is an act of telltale savagery, the expression of a barbarism that is the same today, yesterday and forever, the Mexican bodies left by Rangers in the brush are the unfortunate remains of the often-savage march of civilization.

In his concluding passage on the Plan de San Diego, Lott uses the archetypal figure of the Indian to situate the historical significance of the conflict.

> There were bloody "battles" along the entire river front in which both Mexicans and Americans fought desperately. Death and fear and terror reigned throughout this inchoate land of ours. Homes were barricaded and guarded like frontier forts of old. Mothers trembled for their own and their children's lives while their menfolk were riding the chaparral with rifle and pistol in hand blazing the way to peace and security for the generation that followed. It was war to the knife and no quarter, and the youth of today who walks the streets of our Valley cities should be made to realize that he owes more than he can ever repay to those valiant pioneers who grimly went about the business of exterminating a horde more savage than any red man that ever lifted a scalp.[81]

Lott invokes the act of scalping as the "red man's" distinctive mode of savage violence, that which supposedly distinguishes him from civilized peoples. In fact, scalping was an activity through which Mexicans and white Texans expressed their national sovereignty. After slaughtering the retreating Mexican soldiers at San Jacinto, Texan soldiers removed the scalps of some of the dead on the battlefield.[82] In the mid-nineteenth century four northern states in Mexico passed legislation that offered rewards for the scalps or heads of Apache, Comanche, Kiowa, and Seri Indians, an offer eagerly taken up by white American bounty hunters, as well as some Mexican Indians, Native Americans, and African Americans, with individuals of the latter groups using this "service" to the state as a means of securing Mexican citizenship.[83] As María Josefina Saldaña-Portillo argues, the Mexican bounty laws worked to place the "savage tribe" outside the realm of citizenship, as well as to establish a racial parity between Mexican and U.S. nationals, positioned against a mutual, alien enemy.[84] Lott's designation of Mexican raiders as "more savage" than the scalping "red man" places the Mexican enemy beyond the limits of civilized humanity. It also works to endow the Rangers' and white vigilantes' repression against ethnic Mexicans with a nineteenth-century frontier piety. Lott critiques the "school-master" Woodrow Wilson, whose over-concern for diplomatic formalities led to his disastrous lack of vigorous action. Lott mocks the "ridiculous" restrictions placed on federal soldiers and gives thanks that no such rules bound the Rangers. "They have been the saviors of the settlers on the Texas frontier from the founding of this republic."[85]

In paring the true conflict down to a struggle between pioneers and savages, white men's "business of exterminating" the horde is given a cleansing historical logic. The potentially troubling persecution of Mexicans and Mexican Americans, persons holding the formal rights of national citizenship, however inferior, is obscured. In this regard, it is also significant that in his envisioned march of white civilization, Lott notes that "to their everlasting credit, men of the Latin race" were among the Rangers who faced the "bandit hordes"; their "courage and devotion to their state and nation were never doubted." Like their forefathers who fought for Texas against the Mexican Army at San Jacinto, these men "were never found wanting when there was grim business to attend to."[86] Thus these Rangers of the "Latin race" are set apart from the Indian-like Mexicans of the "savage horde" by their Texan patriotism as well as their willingness to undertake the "grim business" of killing those (bad) Mexicans tainted with the lawlessness of Mexico and the savagery of the "horde."

Lott's narrative of anti-Mexican violence makes it foundational to but temporally outside of Texan modernity. As cited in the passage above, he reminds the contemporary young man of the valley's modern cities that he owes "more than he can ever repay to those valiant pioneers" who waged this bloody war against dangerous savages. This instructive moral lesson echoes the fervent assertions of nineteenth-century cataloger of "Indian depredations" John Wesley Wilbarger, who wrote in 1890 that the "present generation can at best have but a faint idea" of the sacrifices of the pioneers who founded a civilization under threat of "the tomahawk and scalping knife."[87] Rather than the violent expression of new social relations established through the twentieth-century surge of white American immigration into south Texas, the landscape of Mexican death, with its still-present skeletons, is the distant work of grim pioneers forging civilization in a rugged land. In fighting "a war to the knife and no quarter" against a primitive and formidable enemy, white Texans are the manly bringers of civilization fumigating an "inchoate land" for the entrenchment of modernity. It is not a dirty war targeting fellow citizens merely a few decades before, but the final cycle in the pioneers' epic victorious struggle through the wilderness.

Like the white man as lyncher in U.S. discourses of anti-black violence, the construction of the Texas Ranger as defender of white life and civilization along the border depended upon his ambivalent relationship to savagery. Both the Ranger and the lyncher are cast as men who engage with a primitive masculine violence to discipline and dominate subracial enemies. However there are revealing differences in the emotive tone these narratives, reflecting the distinctive histories from which they emerge. Whereas the stern-faced white men of the lynch mob temporarily revert to primitivity in order to repress the black barbarism that threatens white civilization from within, the Ranger patrols the borders of civilization, unbound by its confines, to punish and expel the barbaric transgressors from without. It is in the very different ways in which their respective forms of white savagery are imagined and given meaning in relation to racial others that their different historical positioning becomes clear.

Designed to morally justify the terrorization of a socially and economically subordinated black population as well as to circumscribe the freedom of white women, supposedly under continual threat from the brute in their midst, the lynching narrative evokes a tone of dread and sorrow.[88] Felipe Smith writes that in the discourse of lynching apologia, any imagined expression of Negro wrongdoing, "from theft to economic ascendancy, constituted an attempt to restage Reconstruction's 'rape' of the 'prostrate South.'" Thus the continually conjured image of the brutalized defenseless woman 'ruined' by bestial black sexual violence doubled as the image of the white race laid defenseless – for a time – before the barbarism of their own former slaves.[89] In the lynching encounter, white sovereignty is demonstrated and confirmed through the violation and dismemberment of the bodies of the white woman and the "negro." Throughout the lynching narrative the white man remains powerful, intact, impenetrable, yet the moral of the narrative is the need for constant vigilance, the unceasing threat of undoing and corruption. In his now-infamous defense of lynching from the Senate floor, Tillman insisted that there was nothing carnivalesque about the practice, rather the lyncher experienced "the feeling of participating as mourner at a funeral" – not because of the impending death of the "creature in human form" but because of the horror of the crime being punished. Once provoked by the rape of a woman, a "deadly and cruel" blow against civilization and a "death in life" for the ravaged woman herself, the white man is transformed beyond the restrictions of rationality:

> It is idle to reason about it; it is idle to preach about it. Our brains reel under the staggering blow and hot blood surges to the heart. Civilization peels off us, any and all of us who are men, and we revert to the original savage type whose impulses under any and all such circumstances has [sic.] always been to "kill! kill! kill!"[90]

Even as he proclaimed the necessity of lynching in the South, and indeed cast the lynching impulse as essential to white manhood, this instinctual fury is righteous but melancholy.

As we have already seen in Chapter 2, Northern critiques of anti-black mob violence also imagined it as white men's reversion to savagery. After the killing at Slocum, an editorial printed in the *Literary Digest* condemned the massacre as "damnable a crime as if it had been committed by ... red Sioux warriors on white men."[91] In such discourse, by indulging in such excesses and flouting the rule of law, the white man became as base as the "red Sioux warrior" or as the black man he sought to purge and punish. In contrast to the fantasy of frontier violence as a process by which white American manhood was honed and hardened through its encounter with savagery, here savagery ate away at the white man's own ability to maintain civility. James E. Cutler, the sociologist and military intelligence consultant discussed in Chapter 2, hypothesized that it was the utterly incomprehensible nature of black crime that called forth heinous methods of white punishment that threatened the order of national civilization.[92]

U.S. cultural narratives of border violence and imagined Mexican lawlessness differ starkly from those of anti-black lynching and imagined black criminality. In contrast to the lynch mob as an erosion of white civilization from within, the Rangers emerged from the forward thrust of the white race. After his investigation of the border violence, Clair Kenamore contrasted the hardened Rangers, men of thirty to forty years, who were lean and serious, with the U.S. soldiers sent to the region, "many of whom are pasty-faced youths."[93] The Rangers, as Lott put it, were "in the vanguard of every new colonization project." Unlike the lyncher who reverts to savage type in the face of a cancerous racial depravity, in Walter Webb's portrait of idealized twentieth-century Ranger Frank Hamer, Hamer works to develop Indian-like abilities through his intimate relationship with the land. Webb's choice of Hamer as an embodiment of the modern virtues of the Ranger is interesting considering that J.T. Canales, the Tejano legislator who led the 1919 investigation into the Rangers' misconduct, testified that Hamer stalked and threatened him for pursuing the investigation. Webb begins Hamer's biography with his avid childhood consumption of tales of

"Indian depredations, massacres, and thefts" and battles between Rangers and Indian warriors. This early education leads Hamer to make up his mind "to be as much like an Indian as I could," an ambition he cultivates in the "unspoiled forests and streams" of the rugged Texas landscape now devoid of actual indigenous people. Hamer develops uncanny "Indian" tracking and sensory powers, perhaps not as "acute as those of the Indian, but ... certainly far sharper than those of the average man."[94] Thus in contrast to the incomprehensible black inhumanity that drives white men to primitive brutality, the absent Indian spiritually enhances white manhood.

As agent of civilizational advance but not himself bound within its constraints, the Ranger's learned savagery – his ability to "track like an Indian" and "to know the brush as well as a Mexican" – facilitates his unique capacity and prowess as a defender of the American "colonization project." Capturing the dynamic in his reflections on the period, Lott would later write, "The wilderness of chaparral and mesquite blazed with gunfire as the grim Texas Rangers went about their business ... The chaparral was putrid with the dead of the 'Army of Independence.' The Rangers, strangely enough, always emerged unscathed."[95] Texans, whose manhood is produced and expressed through their relationship to the land, "know the brush as well as Mexicans," but also know how to call forth its bounty and to discipline its dangers. The Mexican enemy's "disappearance" – often permanent – "into the brush" is emblematic of his racial indolence and his unfitness for sovereignty. The Ranger's ability to enter and know the brush demonstrates the streak of virile masculine savagery necessary for frontier defense. His unscathed emergence from the wilderness demonstrates his manly mastery of savage land and savage people.

In contrast to the image of the lyncher constantly surveilling the black threat lodged within civilization, the Ranger, according to Lott, gazes outward: "Ever restless and always longing for new fields to conquer, with their faces always towards the sun, few of the Rangers ever settle down to domestic life ... and when they do settle, it is always as far removed from the commerce of the world as possible."[96] Lott accordingly imagined the Rangers' ruthless eradication of the bandits who terrorized the frontier as a concluding episode in the global journey of the white race from the Old World to outward edge of the New:

> [This race] had fought for all it had ever gained, and it had gained much since its trek from the shores of Albion to the chaparral fringes of the Rio Grande, therefore fighting was not new to it as attested by the gruesome skeletons found even at this late day, twenty years after, in the wilderness, lying in neatly arranged rows, side by side, each with a trim, round hole in the forehead squarely between the empty eye-sockets – "Brands" of the Texas Rangers' "irons," the never failing 45-colts.[97]

Again, the landscape of Mexican death becomes the grounds upon which U.S. civilization will flourish. Unlike the savagery of the white lyncher which many observers judged to degrade the white race, the violence of the white men on the border, in the narratives cited here, is accepted as the necessary force for the realization of national destiny.

The men of the Congreso Revolucionario who called for the overthrow of U.S. sovereignty envisioned their people's destiny to culminate in a new society forged across the American continent through an effort of manly determination undertaken together with "all oppressed peoples [and] all maltreated races."[98] Each vision of destiny bears its own inscriptions of global tides of conquest and enslavement. In imagining the possibility of a new world, the Congreso Revolucionario repurposed – however incompletely – the colonial idiom of "savagery" and progress to denounce the racism and misery of U.S. capitalism. Using the metaphorical language of slavery, the elemental oppression, to frame a common struggle for the disinherited, they subtly rearticulated constructions of black race as historically inert. In contrast to the Congreso Revolucionario's dream of an unrealized future, Virgil Lott's narrative offered a consecrating saga of the Texan present. His histrionic depiction of the remains of executed Mexicans as testament to the white race's transcontinental sojourn illustrates the very different nature of their projects as well the precarity of the *sediciosos*' utopian aspirations for the Americas' disinherited.

Notes

1 Virgil N. Lott, "The Rio Grande Valley, Part II," part of the unpublished manuscript, Virgil N. Lott Narrative, 1953, in the Dolph Briscoe Center for American History, University of Texas at Austin, 1953, 120.
2 Ribb, "*La Rinchada*," 66. Consul Garrett to Secretary of State Lansing, August 26, 1915, NARA 812.00/15929, pp. 1–2.
3 "The Uprising in Texas," 2 October, 1915, *Regeneración*, in Flores Magón, Cowen Verter, and Bufe, *Dreams of Freedom*, 202–5.
4 Frank C. Pierce, *A Brief History of the Lower Rio Grande Valley* (Menasha, WI: George Banta Publishing Co., 1917), 114.
5 Johnson, *Revolution in Texas*, 120. Sandos found that the raiders killed thirty-three Americans and wounded twenty-four. He does not indicate the ethnicity of these casualties. James Sandos, "The Plan of San Diego: War and Diplomacy on the Texas Border 1915–1916," *Arizona and the West* 14, no. 1 (1972): 23.
6 Committee on Foreign Relations, "Investigation of Mexican Affairs," 1205.
7 Ibid., 1206.

8 For a discussion of the distinct Tejano social and political formations operating in South Texas at the time and their relationship to the armed rebellion, see Gonzales, "The Mexican Revolution, *Revolución de Texas*, and *Matanza de 1915*."
9 Sandos, *Rebellion in the Borderlands*, 85. "Reduced Bond of Ramos", May 14, 1915, *Houston Post*, 2.
10 Webb, *The Texas Rangers*, 483–84. "A Cruel Hoax," December 2, 1919, *St. Louis Post-Dispatch*, 26.
11 El Congreso Revolucionario, "¡¡A los Pueblos Oprimidos de América!!" Agustín S. Garza Collection (ASGC), Margaret H. McAllen Memorial Archives, Museum of South Texas, Edinburg, Texas, p. 2.
12 Johnson, *Revolution in Texas*, 80.
13 Sandos, *Rebellion in the Borderlands*, 64. Johnson, *Revolution in Texas*, 189, 77–78, 21, 81, 97. Montejano, *Anglos and Mexicans in the Making of Texas, 1836–1986*, 81–82, 113–125. Gonzales, "The Mexican Revolution, *Revolución de Texas*, and *Matanza de 1915*," 110.
14 Johnson, *Revolution in Texas*, 121, 81, 97. Pierce, *A Brief History of the Lower Rio Grande Valley*, 115.
15 Gonzales, "The Mexican Revolution, *Revolución de Texas*, and *Matanza de 1915*."
16 Raat, *Revoltosos: Mexico's Rebels in the United States*, 27. Sandos, *Rebellion in the Borderlands*, 77–78.
17 Harris and Sadler, *The Plan de San Diego: Tejano Rebellion, Mexican Intrigue*, 18. René A. Ballesteros, "Agustín S. de la Garza Collection Finding Aid," in *Agustín S. de la Garza Collection, 1906–1952* (Edinburg, Texas: Margaret H. McAllen Memorial Archives, Museum of South Texas, 2013), 4–5.
18 Sandos, *Rebellion in the Borderlands*, 72–74, 81–82. Ballesteros, "Agustín S. de la Garza Collection Finding Aid," 5. Johnson, *Revolution in Texas*, 93.
19 Gonzales, "The Mexican Revolution, *Revolución de Texas*, and *Matanza de 1915*," 71–72. Frederic Haskin, "The Mexican Muddle III. The Bandit War," November 21, 1915, *Evening Star* (Washington, D.C.), 12.
20 Lomnitz Adler, "The Return of Comrade Ricardo Flores Magón," 452.
21 "The Uprisings in Texas," October 2, 1915, *Regeneración*, in Flores Magón, Cowen Verter, and Bufe, *Dreams of Freedom: A Ricardo Flores Magón Reader*, 202, 207, 210.
22 Flores Magón was not alone in his suspicion of the plan. Some American radicals thought that border raids were plotted by American conspirators to create an excuse for invasion of Mexico. As Heber Johnson notes, the call for a black insurrection and the killing of all the white people seem "particularly well suited to create mass hysteria." After the discovery of the Zimmerman telegram, some Americans, such as Walter Webb, recast the rebellion as a nefarious German ploy, taking advantage of an erstwhile "ignorant but simple-hearted and kindly people." The historians Sadler and Harris have argued that the movement was essentially masterminded, in terms of both manpower and propaganda, by agents of Mexican President Venustiano Carranza, who used Tejanos as a fifth column, "skillfully playing on their hopes and fears as a means of exerting pressure on

the United States." Lomnitz similarly notes that Carranza's officers aided in printing the plan but that once Carranza received recognition from the U.S., "he came down hard on the Texas rebels," extraditing Pizaña from Mexico to the U.S. Sandos, *Rebellion in the Borderlands*, 158–59. Harris and Sadler, *The Plan de San Diego*, 281–82. Johnson, *Revolution in Texas*, 81–82. Webb, *The Texas Rangers*, 483–84.

23 Sandos, *Rebellion in the Borderlands*, 84.
24 El Congreso Revolucionario, "¡¡A los Pueblos Oprimidos de América!!," ASGC, 1.
25 Garrett to Lansing, August 26, 1915, NARA 812.00/15929, pp. 1–2, forwarded to the State Department by the U.S. Consul in Nuevo Laredo, Alonzo Garrett.
26 Ben Kiernan, *Blood and Soil: A World History of Genocide and Extermination from Sparta to Darfur* (New Haven, CT, and London: Yale University Press, 2007), 342–43.
27 Thomas Wolff, "The Karankawa Indians: Their Conflict with the White Man in Texas," *Ethnohistory* 16, no. 1 (1969). Jerry D. Thompson, *Cortina: Defending the Mexican Name in Texas* (College Station: Texas A&M University Press, 2007), 11. See Guidotti Hernández for an analysis of how Texan-Mexican anti-Indian violence has been effaced from Tejano and Chicano narratives of history. Guidotti-Hernández, *Unspeakable Violence*, 143–47. Delisle's map can be seen at www.thehistorycenteronline.com/exhibits/grid/imagining-texas-an-historical-journey-with-maps/674 (accessed February 1, 2021).
28 Committee on Foreign Relations, "Investigation of Mexican Affairs," 1226. El Congreso Revolucionario, "¡¡A los Pueblos Oprimidos de América!!" ASGC, 4.
29 Brian DeLay, *War of a Thousand Deserts: Indian Raids and the U.S.–Mexican War* (New Haven, CT: Yale University Press, 2008), 60–61.
30 Ronnie C. Tyler, "Fugitive Slaves in Mexico," *Journal of Negro History* 57, no. 1 (1972): 6. Aptheker, "American Negro Slave Revolts," 343–47.
31 Francis White Johnson and Ernest William Winkler, *A History of Texas and Texans* (Chicago and New York: American Historical Society, 1914), 515. Carrigan, "Slavery on the Frontier," 82. James David Nichols, "The Line of Liberty: Runaway Slaves and Fugitive Peons in the Texas–Mexico Borderlands," *Western Historical Quarterly* 44, no. 4 (2013): 425–26. Aptheker, "American Negro Slave Revolts," 346–47. Jerry D. Thompson, *Cortina,* 61–62.
32 Lack, "Slavery and Vigilantism in Austin, Texas, 1840–1860," 5. Carrigan, "Slavery on the Frontier."
33 In 1910 Reagan's grandson, Captain Rees Fowler, an officer in the National Guard and native of Palestine, Texas, worked with sheriff's deputies to restore order after white men there staged an anti-black pogrom, the subject of Chapter 3. Bills, *The 1910 Slocum Massacre*, 16, 41.
34 John H. Reagan and Walter Flavius McCaleb, *Memoirs, with Special Reference to Secession and the Civil War* (New York and Washington, D.C.: Neale Publishing Company, 1906), 309.
35 Ibid., 295. For antebellum iterations of the argument that Mexico would act as a "safety valve" for unwanted African Americans, see Stephen Hartnett,

"Senator Robert Walker's 1844 *Letter on Texas Annexation*: The Rhetorical 'Logic' of Imperialism," *American Studies* 38, no. 1 (1997): 43.
36 Kornweibel, *Investigate Everything*, 53. Alfredo Aguilar, "Uprooted: African Americans in Mexico; International Propaganda, Migration, and the Resistance against US Racial Hegemony," in *Human Rights, Race, and Resistance in Africa and the African Diaspora*, ed. Toyin Falola and Cacee Hoyer (New York: Routledge, 2017), 201–2.
37 Katz, *The Life and Times of Pancho Villa*, 527. Sandos, *Rebellion in the Borderlands*, 79. Jose Garcia, "Dos Notas," December 13, 1913, *Regeneración*, 1.
38 El Congreso Revolucionario, "¡¡A los Pueblos Oprimidos de América!!" ASGC, 2.
39 Committee on Foreign Relations, "Investigation of Mexican Affairs," 1205.
40 See Shelley Streeby, *Radical Sensations: World Movements, Violence, and Visual Culture* (Durham, NC: Duke University Press, 2013), chs 1 and 2.
41 El Congreso Revolucionario, "LEVANTEMONOS!!" ASGC.
42 Jimmy Casas Klausen, "Hannah Arendt's Antiprimitivism," *Political Theory* 38, no. 3 (2010): 395.
43 El Congreso Revolucionario, "¡¡A nuestros Hermanos de América!!" AGSC.
44 Ibid.
45 In July of 1916, the body of a black doctor named Jesse Mosely was found in an arroyo outside of Laredo. Mosely had lived in Mexico, reportedly serving as the personal physician of the governor of the Mexican state of Tamaulipas. He made statements printed in the black press that in Mexico "a man could be a man," pointing to his own advancement there as evidence. Later working as a surgeon in Carranza's army, Mosely apparently sympathized with the San Diego movement and traveled through Texas and Oklahoma trying to enlist black people to join the cause. According to the reports of agents of the Bureau of Investigation, Tom Ross, a Texas Ranger and Bureau agent, was charged with Mosely's murder but was not convicted. Harris and Sadler, *The Plan de San Diego*, 125–26. Horne, *Black and Brown*, 163–64.
46 Harris and Sadler, *The Plan de San Diego*, 202.
47 Ibid.; Revolutionary Congress of San Diego, "Draft Manifesto to Negro Recruits," ASGC, 1–2.
48 Ibid., 5–6. The authors' grasp on the details of U.S. history were tenuous. They suggest that Lincoln was assassinated by "C Guiteau" rather than John Wilkes Booth. Charles Guiteau assassinated President Garfield in 1881.
49 Ibid., 2–3.
50 Ibid., 4.
51 Lott, "The Rio Grande Valley," 90.
52 Committee on Foreign Relations, "Investigation of Mexican Affairs," 1206.
53 El Congreso Revolucionario, "Manifesto ¡¡A los Pueblos Oprimidos de América!!" ASGC, 2.
54 El Congreso Revolucionario, "A Nuestros Hermanos de América!!" and "Basta ...!!!", ASGC.
55 Usher, "The Real Mexican Problem," 45. Roland G. Usher, *The Rise of the American People: A Philosophical Interpretation of American History* (New York: Century Co., 1914), 7.

56 Frederick Haskin, "Mexican Muddle. III. The Bandit War," November 21, 1915, *Sunday Star* (Washington, D.C.), 34.
57 Lucy Jarosz, "Constructing the Dark Continent: Metaphor as Geographic Representation of Africa," *Geografiska Annaler. Series B, Human Geography* 74, no. 2 (1992): 106–7.
58 Clair Kenamore, "What Texans on Mexican Border Would Do to End Rio Grande Lawlessness," November 14, 1915, *St. Louis Post-Dispatch*, 1 and 8.
59 "21 Americans Have Been Killed Along the Rio Grande Border", October 29, 1915, *Houston Post*, 1.
60 Cited in Ribb, "*La Rinchada*," 75.
61 Frederick Haskin, "The Mexican Muddle II. The Plan of San Diego," November 27, 1915, *Pittsburg Telegraph*, 10.
62 "Kickback," August 23, 1915, *Courier-Gazette* (McKinney, TX), 2.
63 Kenamore, "What Texans on Mexican Border Would Do to End Rio Grande Lawlessness," *St. Louis Post-Dispatch*, 8.
64 Texas Legislature, "Proceedings of the Joint Committee," vol. 1, 303.
65 Ibid., vol. 2, 868. Johnson, *Revolution in Texas*, 119. Johnson writes that one witness to such a burning, Francisco Sandoval, said that some of the people burned by the Rangers were still alive when the fire started.
66 Texas Legislature, "Proceedings of the Joint Committee," vol. 1, 365.
67 Johnson, *Revolution in Texas*, 119. "Short Snatches from Elsewhere," October 5, 1915, *El Paso Herald*, 12.
68 Johnson, *Revolution in Texas*, 200.
69 William S. Taylor, "Pursuit of Santa Anna and His Cavalry after They Had Commenced Their Flight from the Battlefield of San Jacinto," in *The Texas Almanac for 1868* (Galveston, TX: W. Richardson & Co., 1868), 44.
70 John Emory Dean, *How Myth Became History: Texas Exceptionalism in the Borderlands* (Tuscon: University of Arizona Press, 2016), 38.
71 Stephen Harrigan, "Eighteen Minutes," *Texas Monthly* 14, no. 4 (1986): 144–45 and 187.
72 Webb, *The Texas Rangers*, 478.
73 "San Jacinto Monument, San Jacinto Battlefield," Historical Marker Database, www.hmdb.org/marker.asp?marker=6702 (accessed February 1, 2021).
74 Untitled, June 20, 1836, *Adams Sentinel* (Gettysburg, PA), 1.
75 Creed Taylor and James T. DeShields, *Tall Men with Long Rifles: The Glamorous Story of the Texas Revolution, as Told by Captain Creed Taylor who Fought in that Heroic Struggle from Gonzales to San Jacinto* (Washington, D.C.: Library of Congress Photoduplication Service, 1935), 233. A 2010 paper by Jeff Dunn, "The Mexican Soldier Skulls of San Jacinto Battleground," published on the Friends of San Jacinto website, www.friendsofsanjacinto.com/sites/default/files/uploads/MexicanSkulls4-1-10.pdf (accessed February 20, 2020), provides a very useful overview of historical sources on the subject. Dunn also writes that some of the skulls of Mexican soldiers were given to race scientist Samuel Morton.
76 Webb, *The Texas Rangers*, 41.
77 Texas Legislature, "Proceedings of the Joint Committee," vol. 1, 602.

78 Judith Butler, *Precarious Life: The Powers of Mourning and Violence* (London: Verso, 2006), 34.
79 Johnson, *Revolution in Texas*, 3.
80 Lott, "The Rio Grande Valley," 65. For more on the killing of Private Johnson, see Johnson, *Revolution in Texas*, 84.
81 Lott, "The Rio Grande Valley," 90.
82 Stephen Hardin, *Texian Iliad: A Military History of the Texas Revolution, 1835–1836* (Austin: University of Texas Press, 1994), ch. 10. Harrigan, "Eighteen Minutes," 187.
83 Saldaña-Portillo, *Indian Given*, 113–14.
84 Ibid., 129, 137. In this sense the bounty laws operated a racial logic similar to that in the Treaty of Guadalupe Hidalgo, in which the United States, after having devoured half of Mexico's territory, pledged to protect its citizens from the "incursions" of "savage tribes."
85 Lott, "The Rio Grande Valley," 70.
86 Ibid., 24.
87 Wilbarger, *Indian Depredations in Texas*, 14. Lott, "The Rio Grande Valley," 90.
88 Jacqueline Dowd Hall has observed narratives of lynching became an acceptable form of "folk pornography." She argues that the construction of the black rapist also emerged just at the time when the Southern women's rights movement emerged and thus offered a "fantasy of aggression against boundary-transgressing women as well as a weapon of terror against blacks." Hall, *Revolt against Chivalry*, 150–51. In the Senate speech referred to in this chapter, Ben Tillman led his fellow senators in imagining the hypothetical rape of the daughter of their colleague who denounced lynching, in lingering and brutal detail, as "her body [is] prostituted and her purity destroyed." "Congressional Record, January 21," 1441.
89 Smith, *American Body Politics*, 139–40.
90 "Congressional Record, January 21," 1441.
91 "The Texas Race Riot," August 13, 1910, *Literary Digest*, 226.
92 Cutler, "Capital Punishment and Lynching," 183.
93 Kenamore, "What Texans on Mexican Border Would Do to End Rio Grande Lawlessness," *St. Louis Post-Dispatch*, 8.
94 Webb, *The Texas Rangers*, 521–23. On Hamer's threats to Canales, see: "Proceedings of the Joint Committee of the Senate and the House in the Investigation of the Texas State Ranger Force," vol. 1, 884–87. Johnson, *Revolution in Texas*, 174–75.
95 Lott, "The Rio Grande Valley," 22.
96 Ibid., 71–72.
97 Ibid., 24.
98 El Congreso Revolucionario, "¡¡A los Pueblos Oprimidos de América!!", ASGC, 2.

Epilogue

Across the previous chapters, I have traced cultural, nationalist, scientific, and political narratives of death and killing, examining their iterations across the late nineteenth and early twentieth centuries. By examining how these particular violent encounters were understood within broader historical struggles for sovereignty and freedom in the Americas, I have suggested that they offer insight beyond the finite moments in which they occurred, into the sprawling histories of domination in which we still live. The stark language of evolutionary racism and manhood, the "savage song" of racial conquest that Jack London exalted in 1903 had limited longevity. Overt declarations of white racial superiority and the doom of enfeebled racial others lost considerable public traction with the waning of scientific racism and the political need to repudiate the unsettling links between U.S. racism and Nazi genocide.[1] Rather than a complete rupture in racial imagery, as the twentieth century progressed there was a reconfiguration of threat and punishment, savagery and civilization, vulnerability and aggression in U.S. racial imaginaries.

These changes also reflect the evolving relationship between legal and extra-legal violence. Over the passage of the twentieth century, historians argue, the power of the lynch mob was subsumed within expanding powers of the state to execute, punish, contain, deport, and expel.[2] This is not to suggest that state violence replaced extra-legal violence, as the two had always coexisted. In south Texas, Rangers worked with white citizen groups. Police and white citizens in Houston engaged in the violence that the soldiers of the Twenty-Fourth retaliated against, and police and national guardsmen facilitated and participated in the mass killing of African Americans in East St. Louis in 1917.[3] However, over the course of the twentieth century, the public legitimacy of extra-legal killing and mob violence eroded, in large part due to the various forms of resistance taken up by African American and ethnic Mexican actors.[4] At the same time, as the border and the carceral walls of the ghetto hardened, distinct discourses of the nation's racial struggles emerged to describe these new circumstances. As a final reflection, I will examine two key conjunctures to draw links between the early twentieth century and its future: the emergence of the "illegal alien" and the suppression of rebellion in Watts, each of which produced their own ideological landscapes of race and death.

Prevention and deterrence

During the final years of the 1920s, Congressional hearings were held to debate legislation proposed to restrict Mexican immigration.[5] Despite the very recent history of bloodshed and so-called banditry along the border, restrictionists warned that the exploitability of the imagined deluge of Mexicans would erode American democracy and the standing of American working men. A historical parallel was continually drawn between Mexicans and enslaved African Americans in order to establish the former as a naturally subservient, and therefore corrosive, racial population. While the problem of Mexicans as bandits, criminals, and potential "revolutionists" was also occasionally given voice during these hearings, those demanding the restriction of Mexican immigration, as well as those championing it, highlighted the supposed racial submissiveness of "the peon."[6]

Capturing some of the key themes of the racist philosophy that saturated the debates, in his testimony, Henry Ward, of the Boston Immigration Restriction League, admitted there was "no doubt that most Mexican peons are good 'raw' laborers"; they were willing to carry out all sorts of work, from farm-work to building railroads and they were "as a rule, peace-loving, docile, and obedient." In Ward's view, it was precisely this docility that was toxic to American manhood, as the Mexicans' abasement ruined working conditions for the "self-respecting white laborer," who could not accept the same degrading living conditions or wages. The letter of one Texas citizen neatly sums up the usual complaints: "Landlords … prefer them, for they can be driven almost like slaves [and] will live in barns, sheds, or tents."[7]

Those defending the use of Mexican labor emphasized Mexicans' agreeable temperament as well as their transience in the national body, which made their presence benign. This healthful quality was often accentuated through comparisons to the irreparably permanent black population. In a report submitted to the Committee on Immigration and Naturalization during the hearings on Mexican immigration, the California Agricultural Legislative Committee argued that Mexicans presented Californians' safest source of labor. In a section titled "Shall the Negro Problem be Spread More Widely," the report read: "The Mexican is closer to home and can, and does, return there sooner or later in large numbers ... The American negro, the Porto Rican negro, and the Filipinos can not be deported if they prove later to be a crime menace. The Mexican can be."[8] The sanguine assertion that "the Mexican" returns in large numbers is underscored by the more violent attribution of deportability.

In her history of the Border Patrol, Kelly Lytle Hernández argues that in its mid-century iterations the Border Patrol had painted the Mexican as pathetic and slave-like, subject to exploitation by farmers and thus in need of return, an effort supported by Mexican Americans. After the Bracero Program began to regulate contract labor between Mexican migrants and U.S. farmers, however, the Border Patrol's mission shifted to a frame of policing and punishment, resonant with broader discourses of social order and control in the late twentieth century. This drew new racial lines around the category of "illegality."[9] Rather than the "poor, emaciated, Mexican worker" seeking to feed his starving family, as one official of the Border Patrol put it, "today's apprehensions consist in the main part of criminals, often vicious in type, and of hardened and defiant repeaters."[10] While Mexicans had long been subject to violence by white citizens and law enforcement as dangerous unwanted invaders, the construction of racialized illegality envisioned a new relationship between "the Mexican" and the nation. In the "inchoate" frontier, Mexican raiders and bandits, figures who could be used to attack any Mexican, were driven back. In the iteration of the Mexican as a "fraudulent citizen" or illegal alien, the crime is in the attempt to insert himself permanently in the national body, to be pursued not just along the border but deep into the nation's cities. This was made clear after the 1992 Los Angeles uprising when Border Patrol agents rode around the city with police apprehending Mexican and Central American migrants.[11]

Militias and vigilante groups, whose membership and affinities had long been entangled with Rangers and Border Patrol, also participated in policing the imagined criminals violating the nation's borders.[12] In reference to the violent campaigns of Arizona vigilantes targeting Mexican immigrants in the first decade of this century, William Carrigan and Clive Webb note that mainstream discussions of "border killings have rarely placed them in the long history of conflict and violence between Anglos and Mexicans in the United States." However, as they argue, Mexican and Chicanx people retained a cultural memory, in folklore, song, and oral history of Ranger violence and lynching.[13] The rupture in the mainstream U.S. imagination between the violence of the 1910s and that of the late twentieth century reflects an underlying discourse of Mexican foreignness that denies and distorts the ongoing Mexican presence in the borderlands. In 1942, the *Brownsville*

Herald Sunday edition reflected on the city's "birthpains" and ultimate triumph from "raw frontier country" to a developed modern city. Like other Anglo accounts, the paper rooted the "terrible 'Bandit Days'" in the "breakdown of law and order on the Mexican side of the Rio Grande," rather than the consolidation of a new racial order in Texas. The article concludes with a faint allusion to the repression: "It was one of the most bloody and trying periods in the history of the Valley – particularly since in the drastic steps taken to stamp out the bandit raids some innocent persons suffered."[14] The killings are thus resolutely lodged in a distant, formative but pre-national past. As removable and unlawful aliens, Mexicans are perpetually new invaders who have never been part of the fabric of the nation.

In the racialized imagery of the border landscape in 1915, the figure of the Mexican bandit was depicted as disappearing into the brush at will, his racial savagery symbiotic with that of the savage, raw landscape of the not fully settled frontier. After the border was constructed as sacred and inviolable, the movement of the "illegal alien" through the landscape produced quite a different imagery at the end of the century. Through a strategy of "Prevention through Deterrence," the Border Patrol sought to weaponize the terrain against migrants, making it more difficult to cross except through the most deadly routes of travel. Juanita Sundberg and Bonnie Kaserman have examined how government agencies and media in this period began to construct "illegals" as an insidious ecological threat to the integrity and beauty of "America's most beautiful desert treasures." The website of a group called "Desert Invasion" described the threat:

> Our fragile National Monuments, National Wildlife Refuges, National Parks, and National Forests along the U.S. southern border are being annihilated, not by natural forces or by unwitting tourists, but instead by an overwhelming number of illegal aliens ... who rampage through and destroy these supposedly protected areas.

In such narratives, the migrants' movement through these sites of national beauty scarred the land with garbage, graffiti, and bodily substances, endangering the legacy for "future generations."[15] Like the repression unleashed by Rangers and white citizen militia, "Prevention by Deterrence" has also created a landscape of death that renders Mexicans and other Latinx migrants "unburiable." In contrast to the bullet hole in the skull, in the context of "Prevention by Deterrence," Jason de León argues, nature is conscripted as enforcer, the desert is personified "as a perpetrator of violence." The lives and deaths of migrants, as well as the violence of the enforcing state, are always out of public view.[16] Like the families of the Rangers' victims in 1915 and 1916, unable to claim their loved ones in the brush for fear of retaliation, the families of missing migrants are unable to call authorities. A century after the Rangers' victims lay in the brush, volunteers, many of them migrants themselves, would wake up at dawn once a month to spend the day searching the desert for remains, to be marked, buried, prayed for, and named.[17]

A captive nation within a nation[18]

In 1965 Watts became the epicenter of a rebellion in south Los Angeles, catalyzed by the police assault of a black woman and her grown sons at a traffic stop. Once a multi-ethnic neighborhood of Mexican, African American, and white families, by 1965 an NAACP investigator likened it to a concentration camp. It was virtually all black and home to the poorest 80,000 people in Los Angeles, a shift that reflects the singularly ruthless residential apartheid applied to African Americans.[19] The uprising, as Mike Davis and Jon Wiener write, did not have central leadership or a platform of specific aims, but it did have "explicit grievances (police abuse, mercantile exploitation, unemployment and so on) ... and an emotionally infused but *rational* strategy (the destruction of white-owned property as a means to force reforms and create a sense of urgency that nonviolent protest had been unable to achieve)."[20]

The suppression of rebellion in Watts was created into a national spectacle that offers insight into the reconfiguration of racialized masculinities, savagery, civilization, and death in the late twentieth century. Like previous epochs of black people's protest against structural violence, the rebellion in south Los Angeles was, as Trouillot observes of slave resistance, "drained of its political content" by many white observers and framed as an explosion of Negro "maladjustment." The official investigation into the "riots" suggested that the "dismal spiral of failure" in the ghetto could be traced to the "unpreparedness" of migrants from the South, drawn to California by the state's generous welfare system.[21] While the racialized effluent of Watts regurgitated the same discourse of corrosive black freedom and failure that had circulated since the end of Reconstruction, it reordered other features of earlier anti-black discourses of violence. In its presentation of the threat of insurrection, Watts differed markedly from Slocum, where the continual refrain of press coverage had been, "not one white man was hurt." When the anxieties that black men would rise up were in some fashion realized in Houston, many white media at first seemed to have difficulty accepting dead white men, "more or less mutilated by bayonets." In Los Angeles, however, the press indulged in a heavy imagery of endangered white people.

Whites were not savage enforcers of brutal justice, or bloodthirsty men looking to exercise their racial instincts as in some early twentieth-century narratives. Rather they were law-abiding citizens or agents of law enforcement under constant threat. Reporters flocked to Watts and offered lurid accounts of insensate attacks on hapless white people by crowds of black people chanting, "Kill, Kill, Kill!" The *Los Angeles Times* printed the story of an observer ("A Negro," the editor noted) who asserted: "It's a wonder anyone with white skin got out of there alive."[22] As the historian Gerald Horne notes, despite white Angelenos' horror of armed black men coming for retribution, the police suppressed the uprising with a "monster-like ferocity." After five days, thirty-four people were dead, most of them killed by the police or National Guard and all but nine of them were black.[23]

The stories of East St. Louis and Slocum featured detailed and spectacular accounts of black people being killed and hunted by white aggressors. Black death was presented as an unquantifiable mass, narrated with lurid and graphic detail of black people's terror and suffering. The accounts from Slocum reported that they were "hunted like sheep," and that they prayed that their "lives may be spared" but the mob's "lust ... for blood" only increased.[24] In stark contrast, in Watts – though constant reference was made to the fact that more than thirty people had died – the death and injury of black people was effaced, as was the fact that it was white police and National Guard who were killing. Bayard Rustin noted that the McCone Report specified that of the deaths, "'one was a fireman, one was a deputy sheriff, and one was a Long Beach policeman,' but it does not tell us how many Negroes were killed or injured by police or National Guardsmen."[25] While the deaths of black people were erased, black people were imagined as bringers of death and decay. An article in a Texas paper reported, for example, that "[t]he looters fattened off what was left of the corpse of Watts. They set fire to business places and the flames leaped upward to the sky for a hundred or more feet." Later it suggested that the violence spread out of Watts because "[i]ts skeleton offered no enticement."[26]

In East St. Louis narratives of black migrants' "intolerable" insolence and "desperate crimes" were saturated with the graphic description of their horrifying vulnerability to violence as the white mob killed them "without distinction for age or sex, innocence or guilt."[27] Black vulnerability to white violence was a central feature of constructions of racial abnormality, and was firmly linked to discourses of black crime. In 1965, this link had been undone. There were no narratives of black men's abject subjection to mastery, violence, and punishment. The press coverage of Slocum and East St. Louis described an ungendered mass of lifeless black bodies. The print media coverage of Watts emphasized the corrosive activity of its denizens, whose amorality continues to be illustrated in the absence of normative boundaries of gender and generation. "Men, women and children, some no older than

3, climbed through the store windows to reach merchandise ... Parents led their youngsters on raids, squeezing them through broken glass store fronts. When the looting was all over, the place looked like a ghost town."[28] In their wake, then, the "looters" leave urban space deathlike and eviscerated, a skeleton and a ghost town. As I will reflect below, the construction of the ghetto as a space of death and anti-civilization would become a potent landscape for imagining heroic white masculinity.

A 1968 *Esquire Magazine* interview with James Baldwin captured how the "looting" of carceral urban space was interpreted as threatening by white Americans. After commenting that he objected to the term "looter," the white interviewer asked Baldwin how he would define "someone who smashes in the window of a television store and takes what he wants."

> JB: On television you always see black hands reaching in, you know. And so the American public concludes that these savages are trying to steal everything from us. And no one has seriously tried to get where the trouble is. After all, you're accusing a captive population who has been robbed of everything of looting. I think it's obscene.
> Esquire: Would you make a distinction between snipers, fire bombers, and looters?
> JB: I've heard a lot [about] snipers, baby, and then you look at the death toll.
> Esquire: Very few white men, granted. But there have been a few.
> JB: I know who dies in the riots.
> Esquire: Well, several white people have died.
> JB: Several, yeah, baby, but do you know many Negroes have died?[29]

Baldwin's response highlights the deep aggression in white Americans' fear of dispossessed captive blacks "taking everything," which is unintentionally underscored by the interviewer's shift to "snipers." The "snipers" he referred to were rumored black assassins taking shots at white police and National Guard from housing projects during ghetto unrest. In grouping together "looters," "someone who takes what he wants," and "snipers and fire bombers," the latter two seemingly agents of the white deaths he imagined, the interviewer draws a continuum of threat between black "taking" and black killing. It is the "several" white deaths that need to be accounted for, whose meaning needs to be determined in order to understand the nature of the unrest; black death is an expected and unmeasurable backdrop to the conflict. Black politics are again framed as transgression and abrogation. Baldwin, like Frederick Douglass and others before him, warned that it was their own violence that endangered white people's future and the future of the nation: "you may think that my death or diminution, or my disappearance will save you, but it won't ... All that can save you now is your confrontation with your own history ... which is not your past, but your present."[30]

White men as agents of repression

The hangings at Houston were presented in media and state discourse as reconciling the rebellious black soldiers to military discipline and thus the disaffected black population to the nation. In contrast, the more common representations of state violence at the end of the century were deeply pessimistic. As we have seen, the lynch mob's passion and the disciplined, uniformed violence of the state were not completely distinct. W. Fitzhugh Brundage notes that from the early 1950s, "At the moment when the actual practice of lynching virtually ceased, the trivialization of lynching gathered momentum." Westerns and later films about urban crime glorified vigilante violence, continuing to infuse protective white masculinity with the wielding of unregulated violence.[31] In the twentieth century the figure of the Ranger was revered as an exemplar of untamed masculinity, whose exercise of excessive violence signifies his resilience against both racial savagery and the emasculating erosion of civilization. Early twentieth-century historian Walter Webb's reverent history of the Rangers opens with a celebratory description of the force originally penned during the Mexican American War: "He is ununiformed, and undrilled, and performs his active duties thoroughly, but with little regard to order or system." This portrait of the chivalrous but anti-authoritarian and unwavering apostle of necessary violence reflected a virulent settler masculinity reproduced in twentieth-century narratives of the Rangers' anti-Mexican violence, casting a nostalgic innocence around the repression. Indeed, admiration for state agents disregarding "order and system" in their handling of "savages" and "enemies" reverberates more widely through narratives of police violence in the United States. Sparks, the policeman who beat the two black soldiers and catalyzed the Houston Mutiny, testified that a white police officer on patrol in a black neighborhood could find himself quickly inundated by several hundred black people, and therefore had to "do things that you know aren't absolutely legal in order to keep the vicious negro from running over you."[32]

In contrast to early twentieth-century assertions of white wrath and genocidal urges, in later twentieth-century discourses of police struggles with racial others, the police are continually positioned as vulnerable, as indicated in the coverage of Watts, with its continual calculation of police injury and death. In 1992, the police officers who brutally assaulted Rodney King were acquitted by a white jury who judged that King was "in control" the entire time. Rather than the graphic narratives of black terror and submission of the early twentieth-century folk pornography of lynching, the officers claimed that King "had superhuman strength." "I was completely in fear for my life, scared to death that if the guy got up again he was going to take my gun and there would be a shooting," Officer Laurence

Powell testified.[33] The transmutation of brutalization into manipulation and vulnerability into aggression illustrates the "fiction of legitimate violence" that, as criminologist Tyler Wall has argued, renders state violence always defensive.[34]

The Los Angeles Police Chief William Parker, in office during the Watts uprising, famously asserted that the police formed "a thin blue line of defense ... upon which we must depend to defend the invasion from within."[35] While his identification of society's enemies included communists and unionists, Parker was predictably racist. He referred to black people in Watts as "monkeys in a zoo" and claimed that "[t]he Negro committed eleven times as many crimes as other races." Many Mexicans in Los Angeles, he suggested, were "not too far removed from the wild tribes of the district of the inner mountains of Mexico." It is perhaps telling that, when drunk, Parker was wont to clumsily perform a "Sioux Indian dance" he had learned in his youth in South Dakota, the display of mimetic Indianness in keeping with the white guardian of civilization's frontier.[36] When asked about the rush of white people to buy guns after Watts, a deluge that saw sales increase by 500 percent, Parker declined to discourage citizens from exercising their "their legal right" to arm themselves, commenting, "I think there are a lot of terrified citizens in this community."[37] Despite championing the professionalization of the police and their singular social role as agents of state violence, Parker's dark law-and-order vision of a society at war could accommodate the white civilian's enrolment into the war on crime.

Like the colonial mythology that positions the settler as constantly endangered by the "savage hordes at our border," the thin-blue-line mythology imagines a frontier between savagery and civilization. However, the wilderness on the wrong side of the line is not the cleansing wilderness of the frontier or the land to be "reclaimed for civilization," as William Randolph Hearst described Mexico in his imperialist fantasy. In 1908 sociologist Alfred A. Stone described the Southern white man's victory in the perverse racial siege of Reconstruction:

> In the face of handicaps and obstacles which might well have palsied a less determined people, [he] has demonstrated his ability to control his domestic affairs, regardless of the Negro within or the white man without. It cannot be questioned that he will do so in the future as he has in the past. Whatever share in that control the Negro masses may be permitted to have, can come only as a grant from those who hold it within the hollow of an iron hand.[38]

In contrast to Stone's confident assertion of dominance, or Thomas Dixon's and Benjamin Tillman's intimations at the expulsion or extermination of the black population, the threat imagined in thin-blue-line rhetoric is insurmountable, threatening to overwhelm from all sides. In 1981, Ronald Reagan opined to the International Association of Chiefs of Police that "the thin blue line … holds back a jungle which threatens to reclaim this clearing we call civilization." The imagery evokes a sense of being submerged, even as the apartheid walls of the ghetto and the border were well-fortified. As Wall notes, the very thinness of the blue line, "perpetually on the brink of being broken or obliterated by bestial hordes," signifies both the constant insecurity of society and the heroism and endangerment of the police. It is a war without victory and thus without end.[39]

In 1915, the *St. Louis Post Dispatch* reporter Clair Kenamore observed that it was the "Rangers' duty to uphold and emphasize the fact that this is and will remain a white man's country."[40] The waning legitimacy of private collective violence in the mid- and late twentieth century did not cleave ties of affinity between law enforcement and militia and far-right groups but made such ties more covert and, as such, enhanced their paranoid sensibility. The discourse of such groups and activists in the contemporary period often emphasize a particular defensive nationalist masculinity: only the few truly understand the nature of the war; only the few are willing to die to defend the nation against it. The critiques of police violence and even questions about the nature of police itself that are entering mainstream public and political forums have intensified the sense of a war of decay being waged against the vulnerable white nation.[41]

In the wake of four years in which the nation's president publicly expressed approval and encouragement for the far right, the nebulous relationship between state and private violence is again being recalibrated. The armed mob that ransacked the Capitol building in January, 2021, to defend "their country", as some security and law enforcement stood by or even posed for selfies with the rioters, demonstrated the corrosive combination of politically sanctioned belligerence and a fervid sense of endangerment.[42] If these latest articulations of violent white manhood emphasize the grim continuity of terror in the United States and the enduring flexibility of racism, this very flexibility betrays how the boundaries and claims that terror seeks to enforce have always been and continue to be refused by those they constrain.

Notes

1 Elazar Barkan, *The Retreat of Scientific Racism: Changing Concepts of Race in Britain and the United States between the World Wars* (Cambridge: Cambridge University Press, 1992).
2 Ethan Blue, "From Lynch Mobs to the Deportation State," *Law, Culture and the Humanities,* October (2017). Brundage points out that state violence did not

replace lynching as the two coexisted and furthermore their impact and function were distinct. The brutality of police or prison officers was "an instrument of terror, not a violent ritual that could give expression to or harness the deepest fears and convictions of the white community." Brundage, *Lynching in the New South*, 256.

3 On police and national guardsmen participating in the mob in East St. Louis, see Lumpkins, *American Pogrom*, 1.
4 On the fight against lynching, see Brundage, *Lynching in the New South*; Carrigan and Webb, *Forgotten Dead*; Dray, *At the Hands of Persons Unknown*; Smith, *An Old Creed for the New South*; Hall, *Revolt against Chivalry*.
5 Mark Reisler, *By the Sweat of Their Brow: Mexican Immigrant Labor in the United States, 1900–1940* (Westport, CT: Greenwood Press, 1976), 56. Reisler gives a detailed account of the various bills introduced in these years to restrict "Western Hemisphere" immigration, all of which were ultimately unsuccessful, not because the measures lacked support but because the State Department intervened through diplomatic fears over the impact of such legislation in Mexico and Latin American.
6 Margarita Aragon, "'The Mexican' and 'the Cancer in the South': Discourses of Race, Nation and Anti-Blackness in Early Twentieth-Century Debates on Mexican Immigration," *Immigrants and Minorities* 31, no. 1 (2017).
7 Committee on Immigration and Naturalization, "Hearings: Immigration from Countries of the Western Hemisphere," ed. House of Representatives (Washington, D.C.: United States Government Printing Office, 1928), 16, 48.
8 U.S. Congress, "Hearings before the Committee on Immigration and Naturalization: Immigration from the Western Hemisphere" (Washington, D.C.: United States Government Printing Office, 1930), 238.
9 Kelly Lytle Hernández, *Migra!: A History of the U.S. Border Patrol* (Berkeley: University of California Press, 2010), 222, 634–35.
10 Ibid., 205.
11 Mike Davis, "An Interview with Mike Davis by the *Covertaction Information Bulletin*," in *Reading Rodney King/Reading Urban Uprising*, ed. Robert Gooding-Williams (New York and London: Routledge, 1993), 145.
12 Greg Grandin, *The End of the Myth: From the Frontier to the Border Wall in the Mind of America* (New York: Metropolitan Books, 2019), 164, 223–24.
13 Carrigan and Webb, *Forgotten Dead*, 16. See also Muñoz Martinez, *The Injustice Never Leaves You* for a discussion of the enduring cultural memory around the lynching of Antonio Rodriguez.
14 "Bandit Era Was Trying One for Youthful Valley," December 6, 1942, *Brownsville Herald*, 1, 6. "Birth Pains Experienced in 1912–22 Era for the Valley," December 6, 1942, *Brownsville Herald*, 1.
15 Jason de León, *The Land of Open Graves: Living and Dying on the Migrant Trail* (Oakland: University of California Press, 2015). Juanita Sundberg and Bonnie Kaserman, "Cactus Carvings and Desert Defecations: Embodying Representations of Border Crossings in Protected Areas on the Mexico–US Border," *Environment and Planning D: Society and Space* 25 (2007): 732.
16 De León, *The Land of Open Graves*, 28–29.

17 See the website for Águilas del Desierto, www.aguilasdeldesierto.org (accessed February 1, 2021). Simon Romero, "They Have a Mission: Finding the Bodies of Border Crossers," July 13, 2018, *New York Times*, www.nytimes.com/interactive/2018/07/13/us/california-border-deaths.html (accessed February 1, 2021).
18 James Baldwin, "How Can We Get the Black People to Cool It?" (Interview), July 1, 1968, *Esquire*, 52.
19 Mike Davis and Jon Wiener, *Set the Night on Fire: L.A. In the Sixties* (London: Verso, 2020), 208. Gerald Horne, *Fire This Time: The Watts Uprising and the 1960s* (Charlottesville: University Press of Virginia, 1995), 51, 54–55. On the changing demographics of Watts and Mexican and African Americans' different experiences of residential segregation, see Josh Sides, *L.A. City Limits: African American Los Angeles from the Great Depression to the Present* (Berkeley and London: University of California Press, 2003), 109–11. "Summer Task Force – Watts, a Confidential Report Submitted to the NAACP, 1966," National Association for the Advancement of Colored People, Region I, Records, 1942–1986 (Bancroft Library, University of California, Berkeley), 1.
20 Davis and Wiener, *Set the Night on Fire*, 210.
21 Trouillot, *Silencing the Past*, 83. John A. McCone, *Violence in the City: An End or a Beginning? A Report by the Governor's Commission on the Los Angeles Riots* (Los Angeles: State of California, 1965), 4. Bayard Rustin, "The Watts Manifesto and the McCone Report," March, 1966, *Commentary*, 29–35.
22 Robert Richardson, "'Get Whitey,' Screams Blood-Hungry Mob," August 14, 1965, *Los Angeles Times*, 1.
23 Horne, *Fire This Time*, 75.
24 "Not Race War: Just Murder," August 1, 1910, *New York Sun*, 1.
25 Rustin, "The Watts Manifesto and the McCone Report."
26 "Negro Rioters Swarm into LA Streets Again," August 15, 1965, *Fort Worth Star-Telegram*, 16.
27 Richard Stokes, "Massacres by Mobs in East St. Louis Riots Blamed upon Epidemic of Desperate Crimes Committed by Colored Men from the South," July 8, 1917, *Washington Post*, 3.
28 "Terror of Los Angeles – Looting, Violence, Fires," August 16, 1965, *St. Albans Daily Messenger* (St. Albans, VT), 2.
29 James Baldwin, "How Can We Get the Black People to Cool It?" 51.
30 Ibid., 116.
31 Brundage, *Lynching in the New South*, 259.
32 Webb, *The Texas Rangers*, 1. Lentz-Smith, *Freedom Struggles*, 55.
33 Associated Press, "'Thin Blue Line' Argument Heeded," *Spokane Chronicle*, A10."
34 Tyler Wall, "The Police Invention of Humanity: Notes on the 'Thin Blue Line'", *Crime, Media, Culture* 16, no. 3 (2020): 321.
35 Ibid., 323.
36 Davis and Wiener, *Set the Night on Fire*, 39, 41. 323.
37 "Whites Buying Guns," August 16, 1965, *York Dispatch* (York, PA), 1. Horne, *Fire This Time*, 80.

38 Alfred H. Stone, *Studies in the American Race Problem* (New York: Doubleday, Page & Company, 1908), 402.
39 Wall, "The Police Invention of Humanity", 321.
40 Clair Kenamore, "What Texans on Mexican Border Would Do to End Rio Grande Lawlessness," *St. Louis Post-Dispatch*, 8.
41 This is attested to by the armed citizen and militia groups patrolling Black Lives Matter demonstrations across the country in the Spring and Summer of 2020. Thanks to Aaron Winter for his insights on this point. Mike Giglio, "A Pro-Trump Militant Group Has Recruited Thousands of Police, Soldiers and Veterans," November, 2020, *Atlantic*. Michael German, "Hidden in Plain Sight: Racism, White Supremacy, and Far-Right Militancy in Law Enforcement," policy report (New York: Brennan Centre for Justice, 2020). Nicolle Okoren, "The Birth of a Militia: How an Armed Group Polices Black Lives Matter Protests," July 27, 2020, *Guardian*. Mara Hvistendahl and Alleen Brown, "Armed Vigilantes Antagonizing Protestors Have Received a Warm Reception from Police," June 19, 2020, *Intercept*.
42 Aaron Winter, "Charlottesville, Far-Right Rallies, Racism and Relating to Power," August 17, 2017, *Open Democracy*, www.opendemocracy.net/en/charlottesville-far-right-rallies-racism-and-relating-to-power (accessed March 3, 2021). Lois Beckett, "From Charlottesville to the Capital: how rightwing impunity fueled the pro-Trump mob," January 8, 2021, *Guardian*, www.theguardian.com/us-news/2021/jan/07/capitol-mob-attack-rightwing-rallies-trump (accessed March 3, 2021). Bernard E. Harcourt, "The Fight Ahead," January 7, 2021, *Boston Review*, https://bostonreview.net/race-politics/bernard-e-harcourt-fight-ahead (accessed March 3, 2021).

Bibliography

Archival sources

Agustín S. Garza Collection (ASGC), Margaret H. McAllen Memorial Archives, Museum of South Texas, Edinburg, Texas.

Correspondence of the Military Intelligence Division Relating to "Negro Subversion" 1917–1941, Microfilm Publication M1440, RG 165, National Archives and Records Administration (NARA), Goldsmiths Library, University of London.

National Association for the Advancement of Colored People, Region I, Records, 1942–1986, Bancroft Library, University of California at Berkeley.

Old German Files, Microfilm Publication M1085: Investigative Reports of the Bureau of Investigation 1908–1922, National Archives and Records Administration (NARA), Fold 3.

Records of the Department of State Relating to Internal Affairs of Mexico 1910–1929, National Archives and Records Administration (NARA), Cambridge University Library, Cambridge.

Record Groups 153 and 393, Modern Military Records Branch, National Archives and Records Administration (NARA), South Texas College of Law Digital Collection, Houston.

Virgil N. Lott Narrative, 1953, Dolph Briscoe Center for American History, University of Texas at Austin.

Periodicals

Colliers
Crisis
Literary Digest
Messenger
Mother Jones
National Geographic
Regeneración

Works cited

Abbot, Benjamin H. "'That Monster Cannot Be a Woman': Queerness and Treason in the Partido Liberal Mexicano." *Anarchist Developments in Cultural Studies* 1 (2018): 9–28.

Aguilar, Alfredo. "Uprooted: African Americans in Mexico; International Propaganda, Migration, and the Resistance against US Racial Hegemony." In *Human Rights, Race, and Resistance in Africa and the African Diaspora*, edited by Toyin Falola and Cacee Hoyer, 188–209. New York: Routledge, 2017.

Allen, James S. "The Struggle for Land During the Reconstruction Period." *Science & Society* 1, no. 3 (1937): 378–401.

Anderson, Mark C. "'What's to Be Done with 'Em?' Images of Mexican Cultural Backwardness, Racial Limitations, and Moral Decrepitude in the United States Press, 1913–1915." *Mexican Studies/Estudios Mexicanos* 14, no. 1 (1997): 23–70.

Anderson, Mark Cronlund. *Pancho Villa's Revolution by Headlines*. Norman: University of Oklahoma Press, 2000.

Aptheker, Herbert. *American Negro Slave Revolts*. New York: International Publishers, 1993.

Aragon, Margarita. "'The Mexican' and 'the Cancer in the South': Discourses of Race, Nation and Anti-Blackness in Early Twentieth-Century Debates on Mexican Immigration." *Immigrants and Minorities* 31, no. 1 (2017): 59–77.

Avary, Myrta Lockett. *Dixie after the War*. New York: Doubleday, Page & Company, 1906.

Baker, Ray Stannard. *Following the Color Line: An Account of Negro Citizenship in the American Democracy*. New York: Doubleday, 1908.

Ballesteros, René A. "Agustín S. de la Garza Collection Finding Aid." In *Agustín S. de la Garza Collection, 1906–1952*. Edinburg, TX: Margaret H. McAllen Memorial Archives, Museum of South Texas, 2013.

Banner, Stuart. *The Death Penalty: An American History*. Cambridge, MA, and London: Harvard University Press, 2002.

Barkan, Elazar. *The Retreat of Scientific Racism: Changing Concepts of Race in Britain and the United States between the World Wars*. Cambridge: Cambridge University Press, 1992.

Bederman, Gail. *Manliness and Civilization: A Cultural History of Gender and Race in the United States, 1880–1917*. Chicago: University of Chicago Press, 1995.

Belkin, Aaron. *Bring Me Men: Military Masculinity and the Benign Facade of American Empire, 1898–2001*. New York: Columbia University Press, 2014.

Benbow, Mark E. "Birth of a Quotation: Woodrow Wilson and 'Writing History with Lightening'". *Journal of the Gilded Age* 9, no. 4 (2010): 509–33.

Benson, Sara M. *The Prison of Democracy: Race, Leavenworth, and the Culture of Law*. Oakland: University of California Press, 2019.

Bernstein, Patricia. "An 'Exciting Occurrence': The Lynching." In *Anti-Black Violence in Twentieth-Century Texas*, edited by Bruce A. Glasrud, 38–66. College Station: Texas A&M University Press, 2015.

Bernstein, Patricia. *The First Waco Horror: The Lynching of Jesse Washington and the Rise of the NAACP*. 1st ed. College Station: Texas A&M University Press, 2005.

Bills, E.R. *The 1910 Slocum Massacre: An Act of Genocide in East Texas*. Charleston: The History Press, 2014.

Blackhawk, Ned. *Violence over the Land: Indians and Empires in the Early American West*. Cambridge, MA, and London: Harvard University Press, 2006.

Blight, David W. *Race and Reunion: The Civil War in American Memory*. Cambridge, MA, and London: Belknap Press, 2001.

Blue, Ethan. "From Lynch Mobs to the Deportation State." *Law, Culture and the Humanities* October (2017): 1–24.

Brading, D.A. "Social Darwinism and Nationalism in Mexico." In *Nations and Their Histories: Constructions and Representations*, edited by Susana Carvalho and Francois Gemenne, 111–35. Basingstoke: Palgrave Macmillan, 2009.

Bratu Hansen, Miriam. "'Schindler's List' Is Not 'Shoah': The Second Commandment, Popular Modernism, and Public Memory." *Critical Inquiry* 22, no. 2 (1996): 292–312.

Britton, John A. *Revolution and Ideology: Images of the Mexican Revolution in the United States*. Lexington: University Press of Kentucky, 1995.

Brown, Vincent. "Social Death and Political Life in the Study of Slavery." *American Historical Review* 114, no. 5 (2009): 1231–49.

Brundage, W. Fitzhugh. *Lynching in the New South: Georgia and Virginia, 1880–1930*. Urbana: University of Illinois Press, 1993.

Buck Hohes, Pauline. *A Centennial History of Anderson County Texas*. San Antonio, TX: Naylor Company, 1936.

Butler, Judith. *Precarious Life: The Powers of Mourning and Violence*. London: Verso, 2006.

Carby, Hazel V. *Race Men*. Cambridge, MA: Harvard University Press, 1998.

Carby, Hazel V. *Reconstructing Womanhood: The Emergence of the Afro-American Woman Novelist*. New York and Oxford: Oxford University Press, 1987.

Carrigan, William. "Slavery on the Frontier: The Peculiar Institution in Texas." *Slavery and Abolition* 20, no. 2 (1999): 63–86.

Carrigan, William D. *The Making of a Lynching Culture: Violence and Vigilantism in Central Texas, 1836–1916*. Urbana: University of Illinois Press, 2004.

Carrigan, William D., and Clive Webb. *Forgotten Dead: Mob Violence against Mexicans in the United States, 1848–1928*. New York: Oxford University Press, 2013.

Carrigan, William D., and Clive Webb. "*Muerto por Unos Desconocidos* (Killed by Persons Unknown): Mob Violence against Blacks and Mexicans." In *Beyond Black and White: Race, Ethnicity, and Gender in the U.S. South and Southwest*, edited by Stephanie Cole and Alison M. Parker, 35–60. College Station: Texas A&M University Press, 2004.

Casas Klausen, Jimmy. "Hannah Arendt's Antiprimitivism." *Political Theory* 38, no. 3 (2010): 394–423.

Christian, Garna L. *Black Soldiers in Jim Crow Texas, 1899–1917*. College Station: Texas A&M University Press, 1995.

Clark, David Anthony Tyeeme, and Joane Nagel. "White Men, Red Masks: Appropriation of 'Indian' Manhood in Imagined Wests." In *Across the Great Divide: Cultures of Manhood in the American West*, edited by Matthew Basso, Laura McCall, and Dee Garceau, 109–30. New York: Routledge, 2001.

Clavin, Matthew J. *Toussaint Louverture and the American Civil War: The Promise and Peril of a Second Haitian Revolution*. Philadelphia: University of Pennsylvania Press, 2010.

Committee on Foreign Relations. "Investigation of Mexican Affairs." Edited by Sixty-Sixth Congress Second Session. Washington, D.C.: Government Printing Office, 1920.

Committee on Immigration and Naturalization. "Hearings: Immigration from Countries of the Western Hemisphere." Edited by House of Representatives, 1–805. Washington, D.C.: United States Government Printing Office, 1928.

Commons, John R. *Races and Immigrants in America*. New York: Macmillan Company, 1907.

"Congressional Record, January 21." Edited by Second Session, Fifty-Ninth Congress. Washington D.C.: Government Printing Office, 1907.

Coronil, Fernando, and Julie Skurski. "Dismembering and Remembering the Nation: The Semantics of Political Violence in Venezuela." *Comparative Studies in Society and History* 33, no. 2 (1991): 288–337.

Cox, Mike. *The Texas Rangers: Wearing the Cinco Peso, 1821–1900*. New York: Tom Doherty Associates, 2008.

Craven, David. "Lineages of the Mexican Revolution (1910–1940)." *Third Text* 28, no. 3 (2014): 223–34.

Crouch, Barry A. "A Spirit of Lawlessness: White Violence; Texas Blacks, 1865–1868." *Journal of Social History* 18, no. 2 (1984): 217–32.

Curry, Tommy J. "The Fortune of Wells: Ida B. Wells-Barnett's Use of T. Thomas Fortune's Philosophy of Social Agitation as a Prolegomenon to Militant Civil Rights Activism." *Transactions of the Charles S. Peirce Society: A Quarterly Journal in American Philosophy* 48, no. 4 (2012): 456–82.

Cutler, J.E. "Capital Punishment and Lynching." *Annals of the American Academy of Political and Social Science* 29 (1907): 182–85.

Cutler, James Elbert. *Lynch-Law: An Investigation into the History of Lynching in the United States*. New York: Longmans, Green, and Co., 1905.

Darder, Antonia, and Rodolfo D. Torres. *After Race: Racism after Multiculturalism*. New York: New York University Press, 2004.

Das, Veena. "Violence, Gender, and Subjectivity." *Annual Review of Anthropology* 38 (2008): 283–99.

Davis, Angela Y. *Women, Race and Class*. London: Penguin Books, 1981.

Davis, David Brion. *The Problem of Slavery in the Age of Revolution, 1770–1823*. New York: Oxford University Press, 1999.

Davis, Mike. "An Interview with Mike Davis by the *Covertaction Information Bulletin*." In *Reading Rodney King/Reading Urban Uprising*, edited by Robert Gooding-Williams, 142–56. New York and London: Routledge, 1993.

Davis, Mike, and Jon Wiener. *Set the Night on Fire: L.A. in the Sixties*. London: Verso, 2020.

Day, Ikyo. "Being or Nothingness: Indigeneity, Antiblackness, and Settler Colonial Critique." *Critical Ethnic Studies* 1, no. 2 (2015): 102–21.

De León, Jason. *The Land of Open Graves: Living and Dying on the Migrant Trail*. Oakland: University of California Press, 2015.

Dean, John Emory. *How Myth Became History: Texas Exceptionalism in the Borderlands*. Tuscon: University of Arizona Press, 2016.

DeLay, Brian. "Independent Indians and the U.S.–Mexican War." *American Historical Review* 112, no. 1 (2007): 35–68.

DeLay, Brian. *War of a Thousand Deserts: Indian Raids and the U.S.–Mexican War*. New Haven, CT: Yale University Press, 2008.

Dixon, Thomas. *The Clansman*. New York: Grosset & Dunlap, 1905.

Dobie, James F. *A Vaquero of the Brush Country*. New York: Pennant Books, 1954.

Domínguez-Ruvalcaba, Héctor. *Modernity and the Nation in Mexican Representations of Masculinity: From Sensuality to Bloodshed*. 1st ed. New York: Palgrave Macmillan, 2007.

Douglass, Frederick. "Lecture on Haiti: The Haitian Pavilion Dedication Ceremonies Delivered at the World's Fair, in Jackson Park, Chicago, Jan 2d, 1893." In *African Americans and the Haitian Revolution: Selected Essays and Historical Documents*, edited by Maurice Jackson and Jacqueline Bacon, 202–12. New York: Routledge, 2010.

Douglass, Frederick. "Lynch Law in the South." *North American Review* 155 (1892): 17–24.

Douglass, Frederick. *Why Is the Negro Lynched? Reprinted with Permission from the Ame Church Review for Memorial Distribution, by a Few of His English Friends*. Bridgewater: John Whitby and Sons, 1895.

Dray, Philip. *At the Hands of Persons Unknown: The Lynching of Black America*. New York: Modern Library, 2002.

Drewry, William Sidney. *Slave Insurrections in Virginia, 1830–1865. A Dissertation, Etc.* Washington, D.C.: Neal Company, 1900.

Du Bois, W.E.B. *Black Reconstruction in America 1860–1880*. New York: Free Press, 1992.

Du Bois, W.E.B. *The World and Africa: An Inquiry into the Part which African Has Played in World History*. New York: International Publishers, 1992.

Dubois, Laurent. *Haiti: The Aftershocks of History*. New York: Metropolitan Books, 2012.

Dunn, Jeff. "The Mexican Soldier Skulls of San Jacinto Battleground." www.friendsofsanjacinto.com/sites/default/files/uploads/MexicanSkulls4-1-10.pdf (accessed February 20, 2020).

Ellis, Mark. "'Closing Ranks' and 'Seeking Honors': W.E.B. Du Bois in World War I." *Journal of American History* 79, no. 1 (1992): 96–124.

Ellis, Mark. *Race, War, and Surveillance: African Americans and the United States Government During World War I*. Bloomington: Indiana University Press, 2001.

Emberton, Caroline. *Beyond Redemption: Race, Violence and the American South*. Chicago: University of Chicago Press, 2013.

Equal Justice Initiative. "Lynching in America: Confronting the Legacy of Racial Terror." Report. Montgomery, AL: Equal Justice Intiative, 2017.

Fick, Carolyn E. *The Making of Haiti: The Saint Domingue Revolution from Below*. Knoxville: University of Tennessee Press, 1990.

Flores, Richard R. *Remembering the Alamo: Memory, Modernity, and the Master Symbol*. 1st ed. Austin: University of Texas Press, 2002.

Flores Magón, Ricardo. "An Appeal of Mexico to American Labor, March 11, 1911." *Mother Earth* 6, no. 2 (1911): 46.

Flores Magón, Ricardo, Mitchell Cowen Verter, and Chaz Bufe. *Dreams of Freedom: A Ricardo Flores Magón Reader*. Oakland: AK Press, 2006.

Foley, Neil. "Partly Colored or Other White: Mexican Americans and Their Problem with the Color Line." In *Beyond Black and White: Race, Ethnicity, and Gender in the U.S. South and Southwest*, edited by Stephanie Cole, Alison M. Parker, and Laura F. Edwards, 123–44. College Station: Texas A&M University Press, 2004.

Foley, Neil. *The White Scourge: Mexicans, Blacks, and Poor Whites in Texas Cotton Culture*. Berkeley: University of California Press, 1997.

Foner, Eric. *Reconstruction: America's Unfinished Revolution, 1863–1877*. New York: Perennial, 2002.

Foner, Eric. "The Meaning of Freedom in the Age of Emancipation." *Journal of American History* 81, no. 2 (1994): 435–60.
Foner, Phillip, and Yuval Taylor, eds. *Frederick Douglass: Selected Speeches and Writings*. Chicago: Lawrence Hill Books, 1999.
Fortune, Timothy Thomas. *Black and White: Land, Labor and Politics in the South*. Good Press, 2019.
Foucault, Michel. *Society Must Be Defended: Lectures at the College de France, 1975–76*. Edited by Mauro Bertani, Alessandro Fontana, Francois Ewald, and David Macey. 1st ed. New York: Picador, 2003.
Friend, Craig Thompson. "'The Crushing of Southern Manhood': War, Masculinity, and the Confederate Nation State, 1861–1865." In *Masculinities and the Nation in the Modern World: Between Hegemony and Marginalization*, edited by Pablo Dominguez Andersen and Simon Wendt, 19–38. New York: Palgrave Macmillan, 2015.
Fulop, Timothy E. "'The Future Golden Day of the Race': Millennialism and Black Americans in the Nadir, 1877–1901." *Harvard Theological Review* 84, no. 1 (1991): 75–99.
Furstenberg, François. "Beyond Freedom and Slavery: Autonomy, Virtue, and Resistance in Early American Political Discourse." *Journal of American History* 89, no. 4 (2003): 1295–330.
Galen, Ira, and Seymour Stern, eds. *D.W. Griffith's Birth of a Nation*. Victoria, BC: Friesen Press, 2014.
Garland, David. "Penal Excess and Surplus Meaning: Public Torture Lynchings in Twentieth-Century America." *Law & Society Review* 39, no. 4 (2005): 793–833.
Gatewood, Willard B., Jr. *Smoked Yankees and the Struggle for Empire: Letters from Negro Soldiers, 1898–1902*. Urbana: University of Illinois Press, 1971.
German, Michael. "Hidden in Plain Sight: Racism, White Supremacy, and Far-Right Militancy in Law Enforcement." New York: Brennan Centre for Justice, 2020.
Glenn, Evelyn Nakano. *Unequal Freedom: How Race and Gender Shaped American Citizenship and Labor*. Cambridge, MA: Harvard University Press, 2002.
Goldberg, David Theo. "Racial Comparisons, Relational Racisms: Some Thoughts on Method." *Ethnic and Racial Studies* 32, no. 7 (2009): 1271–82.
Gompers, Samuel. "The Negro in the A.F. of L." *American Federationist* 18 (1911): 34–37.
Gonzales, Trinidad. "The Mexican Revolution, *Revolución de Texas*, and *Matanza de 1915*." In *War Along the Border: The Mexican Revolution and Tejano Communities*, edited by Arnoldo de León, 107–33. College Station: Texas A&M University Press, 2012.
Gonzales-Day, Ken. *Lynching in the West, 1850–1935*. Durham, NC and London: Duke University Press, 2006.
Gonzalez, Jovita. "America Invades the Border Towns." *Southwest Review* 15, no. 4 (1930): 469–77.
González, Juan. *News for All the People: The Epic Story of Race and the American Media*. London and New York: Verso, 2011.
Grandin, Greg. *The End of the Myth: From the Frontier to the Border Wall in the Mind of America*. New York: Metropolitan Books, 2019.
Guidotti-Hernández, Nicole Marie. *Unspeakable Violence: Remapping U.S. and Mexican National Imaginaries*. Durham, NC: Duke University Press, 2011.

Guterl, Matthew Pratt. "The New Race Consciousness: Race, Nation, and Empire in American Culture, 1910–1925." *Journal of World History* 10, no. 2 (1999): 302–52.

Gutiérrez, Natividad. *Nationalist Myths and Ethnic Identities: Indigenous Intellectuals and the Mexican State*. Lincoln: University of Nebraska Press, 1999.

Hahn, Steven. *A Nation under Our Feet: Black Political Struggles in the Rural South, from Slavery to the Great Migration*. Cambridge, MA, and London: Belknap Press, 2003.

Hall, Jacquelyn Dowd. *Revolt against Chivalry: Jessie Daniel Ames and the Women's Campaign against Lynching*. Rev ed. New York: Columbia University Press, 1993.

Hall, Linda B. *Oil, Banks and Politics: The United States and Postrevolutionary Mexico, 1917–1924*. Austin: University of Texas Press, 1995.

Hall, Stuart. "Race, Articulation, and Societies Structured in Dominance." In *Black British Cultural Studies: A Reader*, ed. Houston A. Baker Jr., Manthia Diawara, and Ruth H. Lindeborg (Chicago: University of Chicago Press, 1996).

Haller, John S., Jr. *Outcasts from Evolution: Scientific Attitudes of Racial Inferiority, 1859–1900*. Carbondale: Southern Illinois University Press, 1995.

Hardin, Stephen. *Texian Iliad: A Military History of the Texas Revolution, 1835–1836*. Austin: University of Texas Press, 1994.

Harrigan, Stephen. "Eighteen Minutes." *Texas Monthly* 14, no. 4 (1986): 136–44 and 187.

Harris, Charles H., and Louis R. Sadler. *The Plan de San Diego: Tejano Rebellion, Mexican Intrigue*. Lincoln: University of Nebraska Press, 2013.

Harrison, Benjamin T. "Wilson and Mexico." In *A Companion to Woodrow Wilson*, edited by Ross A. Kennedy, 193–205. Oxford: Wiley-Blackwell, 2013.

Harrison, Hubert H., and Jeffrey Babcock Perry. *A Hubert Harrison Reader*. Middletown, CT: Wesleyan University Press, 2001.

Hart, John M. *Empire and Revolution: The Americans in Mexico since the Civil War*. Berkeley: University of California Press, 2002.

Hart, Paul M. "Beyond Borders: Causes and Consequences of the Mexican Revolution." In *War Along the Border: The Mexican Revolution and Tejano Communities*, edited by Arnoldo de León, 8–30. College Station: Texas A&M University Press, 2012.

Hartman, Saidiya. "The Belly of the World: A Note on Black Women's Labor." *Souls* 18, no. 1 (2016): 166–73.

Hartman, Saidiya. *Lose Your Mother: A Journey Along the Atlantic Slave Route*. New York: Farrar, Straus and Giroux, 2007.

Hartman, Saidiya. *Scenes of Subjection: Terror, Slavery, and Self-Making in Nineteenth-Century America*. New York and Oxford: Oxford University Press, 1997.

Hartnett, Stephen. "Senator Robert Walker's 1844 *Letter on Texas Annexation*: The Rhetorical 'Logic' of Imperialism." *American Studies* 38, no. 1 (1997): 27–54.

Haynes, Robert V. *A Night of Violence: The Houston Riot of 1917*. Baton Rouge: Louisiana State University Press, 1976.

Haynes, Robert V. "The Houston Mutiny and Riot of 1917." *Southwestern Historical Quarterly* 76, no. 4 (1973): 418–39.

Hegel, Georg W.F., and J. Sibree (translator). *The Philosophy of History*. New York: Cosimo Classics, 2007.

Hernández, Kelly Lytle. *Migra!: A History of the U.S. Border Patrol*. Berkeley: University of California Press, 2010.

Hine, Darlene Clark. "Rape and the Inner Lives of Black Women in the Middle West: Preliminary Thoughts on the Culture of Dissemblance." *Signs* 14, no. 4 (1989): 912–20.

Hine, Darlene Clark, and Earnestine Jenkins. *A Question of Manhood: A Reader in U.S. Black Men's History and Masculinity*. Bloomington: Indiana University Press, 1999.

Hoffman, Frederick L. "The Race Traits and Tendencies of the American Negro." *Publications of the American Economic Association* 11, no. 1, 2 and 3 (1896): 1–329.

Hooker, Juliet. *Theorizing Race in the Americas: Douglass, Sarmiento, Du Bois, and Vasconcelos*. New York: Oxford University Press, 2017.

Horne, Gerald. *Black and Brown: African Americans and the Mexican Revolution, 1910–1920*. New York: New York University Press, 2005.

Horne, Gerald. *Fire This Time: The Watts Uprising and the 1960s*. Charlottesville: University Press of Virginia, 1995.

HoSang Martinez, Daniel, and Natalia Molina. "Introduction: Toward a Relational Consciousness of Race." In *Relational Formations of Race: Theory, Method, Practice*, edited by Daniel HoSang Martinez, Natalia Molina, and Ramón Gutiérrez, 1–18. Oakland: University of California Press, 2019.

Humphreys, Margaret. *Intensely Human: The Health of the Black Soldier in the American Civil War*. Baltimore: Johns Hopkins University Press, 2008.

James, Joy. "Profeminism and Gender Elites: W.E.B. Du Bois, Anna Julia Cooper, and Ida B. Wells-Barnett." In *Next to the Color Line: Gender, Sexuality and W.E.B. Du Bois*, edited by Susan Gillman and Als Eve Weinbaum, 69–95. Minneapolis and London: University of Minnesota Press, 2007.

James, Pearl. *The New Death: American Modernism and World War I*. Charlottesville and London: University of Virginia Press, 2013.

Jarosz, Lucy. "Constructing the Dark Continent: Metaphor as Geographic Representation of Africa." *Geografiska Annaler Series B, Human Geography* 74, no. 2 (1992): 105–15.

Jaspin, Elliot. *Buried in the Bitter Waters: The Hidden History of Racial Cleansing in America*. New York: Basic Books, 2007.

Jefferson, Thomas. *Notes on the State of Virginia*. Richmond, VA: J.W. Randolph, 1853.

Jiménez Ramos, Maricela. "Black Mexico: Nineteenth Century of Race and Nation." Ph.D. dissertation. Providence, RI: Brown University, 2009.

Johnson, Benjamin Heber. *Revolution in Texas: How a Forgotten Rebellion and Its Bloody Suppression Turned Mexicans into Americans*. New Haven, CT: Yale University Press, 2003.

Johnson, Benjamin Heber, and Andrew R. Graybill. "Borders and Their Historians in North America." In *Bridging National Borders in North America: Transnational and Comparative Histories*, edited by Benjamin Heber Johnson and Andrew R. Graybill, 1–29. Durham, NC: Duke University Press, 2010.

Johnson, Francis White, and Ernest William Winkler. *A History of Texas and Texans*. Chicago and New York: American Historical Society, 1914.

Johnson, Lyman L. *Death, Dismemberment, and Memory: Body Politics in Latin America*. Albuquerque: University of New Mexico Press, 2004.

Jones, Gareth Stedman. "The Specificity of US Imperialism." *New Left Review*, no. 60 (1970): 59–86.

Jordan, William G. *Black Newspapers and America's War for Democracy, 1914–1920.* Chapel Hill and London: University of North Carolina Press, 2001.
Kaplan, Amy. *The Anarchy of Empire in the Making of U.S. Culture.* Cambridge, MA, and London: Harvard University Press, 2002.
Katz, Friedrich. *The Life and Times of Pancho Villa.* Stanford: Stanford University Press, 1998.
Keene, Jennifer. "Wilson and Race Relations." In *A Companion to Woodrow Wilson,* edited by Ross A. Kennedy, 133–51. Oxford: Wiley-Blackwell, 2013.
Kelley, Robin D.G. "The Rest of Us: Rethinking Settler and Native." *American Quarterly* 69, no. 2 (2017): 267–76.
Kelley, Robin D.G. "'We Are Not What We Seem': Rethinking Black Working-Class Opposition in the Jim Crow South." *Journal of American History* 80, no. 1 (1993): 75–112.
Kiernan, Ben. *Blood and Soil: A World History of Genocide and Extermination from Sparta to Darfur.* New Haven, CT, and London: Yale University Press, 2007.
Kim, Claire Jean. "The Racial Triangulation of Asian Americans." *Politics & Society* 27, no. 1 (1999): 105–38.
Knight, Alan. "Racism, Revolution and *Indigenismo*: Mexico, 1910–1940." In *The Idea of Race in Latin America, 1870–1940,* edited by Richard Graham. Austin: University of Texas Press, 1990.
Knight, Alan. "U.S. Anti-Imperialism and the Mexican Revolution." In *Empire's Twin: U.S. Anti-Imperialism from the Founding Era to the Age of Terrorism,* edited by Ian R. Tyrrell and Jay Sexton, 97–117. Ithaca, NY, and London: Cornell University Press, 2015.
Knudson, Jerry W. "The *Mexican Herald*: Outpost of Empire, 1895–1915." *Gazette* 63, no. 5 (2001): 387–98.
Kornweibel, Theodore. *Investigate Everything: Federal Efforts to Compel Black Loyalty During World War I.* Bloomington: Indiana University Press, 2002.
Lack, Paul D. "Slavery and the Texas Revolution." *Southwestern Historical Quarterly* 89, no. 2 (1985): 181–202.
Lack, Paul D. "Slavery and Vigilantism in Austin, Texas, 1840–1860." *Southwestern Historical Quarterly* 85, no. 1 (1981): 1–20.
Lang, Robert. "Birth of a Nation: History, Ideology, Narrative Form." In the *Birth of a Nation: D.W. Griffith, Director,* edited by Robert Lang, 3–24. New Brunswick, NJ: Rutgers University Press, 1994.
Lentz-Smith, Adriane. *Freedom Struggles: African Americans and World War I.* Cambridge, MA: Harvard University Press, 2009.
Leroy, Justin. "Black History in Occupied Territory: On the Entanglements of Slavery and Settler Colonialism." *Theory and Event* 19, no. 4 (2016).
Levario, Miguel Antonio. *Militarizing the Border: When Mexicans Became the Enemy.* 1st ed. College Station: Texas A&M University Press, 2012.
Litwack, Leon F. *Been in the Storm so Long: The Aftermath of Slavery.* London: Athlone Press, 1980.
Livermore, Abiel Abbot, *The War with Mexico Reviewed.* Boston, MA: American Peace Society, 1850.
Loewen, James W. *Sundown Towns: A Hidden Dimension of American Racism.* New York: New Press, 2005.
Logan, Rayford W. *The Negro in American Life and Thought: The Nadir 1877–1901.* New York: Dial Press, 1954.

Lomnitz, Claudio. "Los Orígenes de Nuestra Supuesta Homogeneidad. Breve Arqueología de la Unidad Nacional en México." *Prismas* 14 (2010): 17–36.
Lomnitz Adler, Claudio. *The Return of Comrade Ricardo Flores Magón*. New York: Zone Books, 2014.
London, Jack. *The Radical Jack London: Writings on War and Revolution*, edited by Jonah Raskin. Berkeley and Los Angeles: University of California Press, 2008.
London, Jack. "Troublemakers of Mexico, June 13." *Colliers*, 1914, 13–14.
Lumpkins, Charles L. *American Pogrom: The East St. Louis Race Riot and Black Politics*. Athens, OH: Ohio University Press, 2008.
MacGregor, Morris J., and Bernard C. Nalty. *Blacks in the United States Armed Forces: Basic Documents, Volume III: Freedom and Jim Crow, 1865–1917*. Wilmington, DE: Scholarly Resources, 1977.
MacGregor, Morris J., and Bernard C. Nalty, eds. *Blacks in the United States Armed Forces: Basic Documents, Volume IV: Segregation Entrenched, 1917–1940*. Wilmington, DE: Scholarly Resources, Inc., 1977.
Manrique, Linnete. "Dreaming of a Cosmic Race: José Vasconcelos and the Politics of Race in Mexico, 1920s–1930s." *Cogent Arts & Humanities* 3, no. 1 (2016): 1–13.
Manrique, Linnete. "Making the Nation: The Myth of *Mestizajes*." *Anthropol 5*, no. 3 (2017): 1–7.
Marentes, Luis A. *José Vasconcelos and the Writing of the Mexican Revolution*. New York: Twayne Publishers, 2000.
Mbembe, Achille. "Necropolitics." *Public Culture* 15, no. 1 (2003): 11–40.
McCone, John A. *Violence in the City: An End or a Beginning? A Report by the Governor's Commission on the Los Angeles Riots*. Los Angeles: State of California, 1965.
McKillen, Elizabeth. *Making the World Safe for Workers: Labor, the Left, and Wilsonian Internationalism*. Urbana: University of Illinois Press, 2013.
McLaughlin, Malcolm. "Ghetto Formation and Armed Resistance in East St. Louis, Illinois." *Journal of American Studies* 41, no. 2 (2007): 435–67.
McLaughlin, Malcolm. *Power, Community, and Racial Killing in East St. Louis*. Basingstoke: Palgrave Macmillan, 2005.
Mikkelsen, Vincent P. "Coming from Battle to Face a War: The Lynching of Black Soldiers in the World War I Era." Ph.D. dissertation. Florida State University, 2007.
Milford, Mike. "The Rhetorical Evolution of the Alamo." *Communication Quarterly* 6, no. 1 (2013): 113–30.
Miller, Albert George. *Elevating the Race: Theophilus G. Steward, Black Theology, and the Making of an African American Civil Society, 1865–1924*. Knoxville: University of Tennessee Press, 2003.
Montejano, David. *Anglos and Mexicans in the Making of Texas, 1836–1986*. Austin: University of Texas Press, 1987.
Morena Figueroa, Mónica G., and Emiko Tanaka Saldívar. "'We Are Not Racists, We Are Mexicans': Privilege, Nationalism and Post-Race Ideology in Mexico." *Critical Sociology* 42, no. 4–5 (2016): 515–33.
Mosse, George L. *Nationalism and Sexuality: Middle-Class Morality and Sexual Norms in Modern Europe*. Madison: University of Wisconsin Press, 1988.
Mosse, George L. *The Image of Man: The Creation of Modern Masculinity*. New York and Oxford: Oxford University Press, 1996.
Muhammad, Khalil Gibran. *The Condemnation of Blackness: Race, Crime, and the Making of Modern Urban America*. Cambridge, MA, and London: Harvard University Press, 2010.

Muñoz Martinez, Monica. *The Injustice Never Leaves You: Anti-Mexican Violence in Texas*. Cambridge, MA: Harvard University Press, 2018.

Ngai, Mae M. *Impossible Subjects: Illegal Aliens and the Making of Modern America*. Princeton: Princeton University Press, 2004.

Nichols, James David. "The Line of Liberty: Runaway Slaves and Fugitive Peons in the Texas–Mexico Borderlands." *Western Historical Quarterly* 44, no. 4 (2013): 413–33.

Paredes, Américo. *With His Pistol in His Hand: A Border Ballad and Its Hero*. Austin: University of Texas Press, 1958.

Parsons, Elaine Frantz. "Klan Skepticism and Denial in Reconstruction-Era Public Discourse." *Journal of Southern History* 77, no. 1 (2011): 53–90.

Patterson, Orlando. *Rituals of Blood: Consequences of Slavery in Two American Centuries*. Washington, D.C.: Civitas/CounterPoint, 1999.

Patterson, Orlando. *Slavery and Social Death*. Cambridge, MA: Harvard University Press, 1982.

Pérez, Emma. *The Decolonial Imaginary: Writing Chicanas into History*. Bloomington: Indiana University Press, 1999.

Pierce, Frank C. *A Brief History of the Lower Rio Grande Valley*. Menasha, WI: George Banta Publishing Co., 1917.

Prince, K. Stephen. *Stories of the South: Race and the Reconstruction of Southern Identity, 1865–1915*. Chapel Hill: University of North Carolina Press, 2014.

Raat, W. Dirk. *Revoltosos: Mexico's Rebels in the United States, 1903–1923*. 1st ed. College Station: Texas A&M University Press, 1981.

Rable, George C. *But There Was No Peace: The Role of Violence in the Politics of Reconstruction*. Athens, GA: University of Georgia Press, 1984.

Reagan, John H., and Walter Flavius McCaleb. *Memoirs, with Special Reference to Secession and the Civil War*. New York and Washington, D.C.: Neale Publishing Company, 1906.

Reisler, Mark. *By the Sweat of Their Brow: Mexican Immigrant Labor in the United States, 1900–1940*. Westport, CT: Greenwood Press, 1976.

Ribb, Richard. "*La Rinchada*: Revolution, Revenge, and the Rangers, 1910–1920." In *War Along the Border: The Mexican Revolution and Tejano Communities*, edited by Arnoldo de León, 56–106. College Station: Texas A&M University Press, 2012.

Rice, Harvey F. "The Lynching of Antonio Rodriguez." M.A. thesis. University of Texas at Austin, 1990.

Richardson, Heather Cox. *The Death of Reconstruction: Race, Labor and Politics in the Post-Civil War North, 1865–1901*. Cambridge, MA, and London: Harvard University Press, 2001.

Richter, William L. *Historical Dictionary of the Civil War and Reconstruction*. 2nd ed. Lanham, MD: Scarecrow Press, 2012.

Riggs, Arthur Stanley. "A Tonic for Mexico: A Plea for Peaceful Armed Occupation." *Forum* 62 (1919): 428–37.

Rogin, Michael. "'The Sword Became a Flashing Vision': D.W. Griffith's *The Birth of a Nation*." *Representations* 9, Winter (1985): 150–95.

Roosevelt, Theodore. *The Winning of the West*. New York: G.P. Putnam's Sons, 1889.

Rosales, Francisco A. "*Pobre Raza!*": *Violence, Justice, and Mobilization among Mexico Lindo Immigrants, 1900–1936*. 1st ed. Austin: University of Texas Press, 1999.

Runstedtler, Theresa. *Jack Johnson, Rebel Sojourner: Boxing in the Shadow of the Global Color Line*. Berkeley: University of California Press, 2012.

Sadler, Jerry, and James Neyland. *Politics, Fat-Cats and Honey-Money Boys: The Mem-Wars of Jerry Sadler*. Santa Monica, CA: Roundtable Publishing, 1984.

Saldaña-Portillo, María Josefina. *Indian Given: Racial Geographies across Mexico and the United States*. Durham, NC, and London: Duke University Press, 2016.

Sanchez, Rosaura, and Beatrice Pita. "Rethinking Settler Colonialism." *American Quarterly* 66, no. 4 (2014): 1039–55.

Sanders, James E. "Race and Nation in the Age of Emancipations." In *"All the Inhabitants of this America Are Citizens": Imagining Equality, Nation, and Citizenship in an Atlantic Frame*, edited by Whitney Nell Stewart and John Garrison Marks, 164–83. Athens, GA: University of Georgia Press.

Sandos, James. "The Plan of San Diego: War and Diplomacy on the Texas Border 1915–1916." *Arizona and the West* 14, no. 1 (1972): 5–24.

Sandos, James A. *Rebellion in the Borderlands: Anarchism and the Plan of San Diego, 1904–1923*. Norman: University of Oklahoma Press, 1992.

Schechter, Patricia A. *Ida B. Wells Barnett and American Reform, 1880–1930*. Chapel Hill and London: University of North Carolina Press, 2001.

Schuler, Edgar A. "The Houston Race Riot, 1917." *Journal of Negro History* 29, no. 3 (1944): 300–38.

Scott, Daryl Michael. *Contempt and Pity: Social Policy and the Image of the Damaged Black Psyche, 1880–1996*. Chapel Hill: University of North Carolina Press, 1997.

Scott, James C. *Domination and the Arts of Resistance: Hidden Transcripts*. New Haven, CT, and London: Yale University Press, 1990.

Seitz, David W. *World War I, Mass Death, and the Birth of the Modern US Soldier: A Rhetorical History*. New York: Lexington Books, 2018.

Sexton, Jared. "People-of-Color-Blindness: Notes on the Afterlife of Slavery." *Social Text* 28, no. 2 (2010): 31–56.

Shapiro, Herbert. *White Violence and Black Response: From Reconstruction to Montgomery*. Amherst: University of Massachusetts Press, 1988.

Sides, Josh. *L.A. City Limits: African American Los Angeles from the Great Depression to the Present*. Berkeley and London: University of California Press, 2003.

Silver, Andrew. *Minstrelsy and Murder: The Crisis of Southern Humor, 1835–1925*. Baton Rouge: Louisiana State University Press, 2006.

Slayden, James L. "Some Observations on Mexican Immigration." *Annals of the American Academy of Political and Social Science* 93, no. 1 (1921): 121–26.

Smallwood, James, Barry A. Crouch, and Larry Peacock. *Murder and Mayhem: The War of Reconstruction in Texas*. 1st ed. College Station: Texas A&M University Press, 2003.

Smith, Felipe. *American Body Politics: Race, Gender, and Black Literary Renaissance*. Athens, GA: University of Georgia Press, 1998.

Smith, John David. *An Old Creed for the New South: Proslavery Ideology and Historiography, 1865–1918*. Carbondale: Southern Illinois University Press, 2008.

Speed, Sharon. "Structures of Settler Capitalism in Abya Yala." *American Quarterly* 69, no. 4 (2017): 783–90.

Steptoe, Tyina L. *Houston Bound: Culture and Color in a Jim Crow City*. Oakland: University of California Press, 2015.

Steward, Theophilus G. *The Haitian Revolution, 1791 to 1804; or, Side Lights on the French Revolution*. New York: Thomas Y. Crowell Company, 1914.

Stoddard, Lothrop. *Re-Forging America: The Story of Our Nationhood*. New York: Charles Scribner's Sons, 1927.

Stoddard, T. Lothrop. *The French Revolution in San Domingo*. Boston, MA, and New York: Houghton Mifflin Company, 1914.

Stoddard, Theodore Lothrop. *The Rising Tide of Color against White World-Supremacy*. London: Chapman and Hall, 1920.

Stone, Alfred A. "Is Race Friction Growing and Inevitable." *American Journal of Sociology* 13, no. 5 (1908): 676–97.

Stone, Alfred A. *Studies in the American Race Problem*. New York: Doubleday, Page & Company, 1908.

Streeby, Shelley. *Radical Sensations: World Movements, Violence, and Visual Culture*. Durham, NC: Duke University Press, 2013.

Sue, Christina A. *Land of the Cosmic Race: Race Mixture, Racism, and Blackness in Mexico*. New York: Oxford University Press, 2013.

Summers, Martin. "Manhood Rights in the Age of Jim Crow: Evaluating 'End-of-Men' Claims in the Context of African American History." *Boston Law Review* 93, no. 3 (2013): 749–65.

Summers, Martin. "'Suitable Care of the African When Afflicted with Insanity': Race, Madness, and Social Order in Comparative Perspective." *Bulletin of the History of Medicine* 84 (2010): 58–91.

Sundberg, Juanita, and Bonnie Kaserman. "Cactus Carvings and Desert Defecations: Embodying Representations of Border Crossings in Protected Areas on the Mexico–US Border." *Environment and Planning D: Society and Space* 25 (2007): 727–44.

Taylor, Alan. *The Internal Enemy: Slavery and War in Virginia, 1772–1832*. New York: W.W. Norton & Company, 2013.

Taylor, Creed, and James T. DeShields. *Tall Men with Long Rifles: The Glamorous Story of the Texas Revolution, as Told by Captain Creed Taylor who Fought in that Heroic Struggle from Gonzales to San Jacinto*. Washington, D.C.: Library of Congress Photoduplication Service, 1935.

Taylor, William S. "Pursuit of Santa Anna and His Cavalry after They Had Commenced Their Flight from the Battlefield of San Jacinto." In *The Texas Almanac for 1868*, 43–45. Galveston, TX: W. Richardson & Co., 1868.

Texas State Legislature. *Proceedings of the Joint Committee of the Senate and the House in the Investigation of the Texas State Ranger Force*, 36th Legislature, Regular Session, vol. 1–3, Austin, 1919.

Thompson, Jerry D. *Cortina: Defending the Mexican Name in Texas*. College Station: Texas A&M University Press, 2007.

Thompson, Jerry D., and Juan N. Cortina. *Juan Cortina and the Texas–Mexico Frontier, 1859–1877*. El Paso: Texas Western Press, University of Texas at El Paso, 1994.

Torget, Andrew J. *Seeds of Empire: Cotton, Slavery, and the Transformation of the Texas Borderlands, 1800–1850*. Chapel Hill: University of North Carolina Press, 2015.

Toro, Alfonso. "Influencia de la Raza Negra en ka Formación del Pueblo Mexicano." *Ethnos* 8–12 (1920–1921): 215–19.

Tourgee, Albion. *A Fool's Errand, by One of the Fools*. New York: Fords, Howard, & Hulbert, 1880.

Trouillot, Michel-Rolph. *Silencing the Past: Power and the Production of History*. Boston, MA: Beacon Press, 1995.

Turner, Frederick C. "Anti-Americanism in Mexico, 1910–1913." *Hispanic American Historical Review* 47, no. 4 (1967): 502–18.
Tyler, Ronnie C. "Fugitive Slaves in Mexico." *Journal of Negro History* 57, no. 1 (1972): 1–12.
United States Department of Justice. "Investigation Activities of the Department of Justice: Letter from the Attorney General Transmitting in Response to a Senate Resolution of October 17, 1919, a Report on the Activities of the Bureau of Investigation of the Department of Justice against Persons Advising Anarchy, Sedition, and the Forcible Overthrow of the Government." Washington, D.C.: Government Printing Office, 1919.
U.S. Congress. "Hearings before the Committee on Immigration and Naturalization: Immigration from the Western Hemipshere." Washington, D.C.: United States Government Printing Office, 1930.
Usher, Roland G. "The Real Mexican Problem." *North American Review* 200, no. 704 (1914): 45–52.
Usher, Roland G. *The Rise of the American People: A Philosophical Interpretation of American History*. New York: Century Co., 1914.
Vasconcelos, José. *The Cosmic Race: A Bilingual Edition*. Baltimore, MD: Johns Hopkins University Press, 1997.
Vaughn, Bobby. "México Negro: From the Shadows of Nationalist Mestizaje to New Possibilities in Afro-Mexican Identity." *Journal of Pan African Studies* 16, no. 1 (2013): 227–40.
Velázquez, María Elisa. "Africanos y Afrodescendientes en México: Premisas Que Obstaculizan Entender su Pasado y Presente." *Cuicuilco* 18 (2011): 11–22.
Villanueva, Nicholas, Jr. *Lynching of Mexicans in the Texas Borderlands*. Albuquerque: University of New Mexico Press, 2017.
Vincent, Ted. "The Blacks who Freed Mexico." *Journal of Negro History* 79, no. 3 (1994): 257–76.
Vincent, Theodore G. "The Contributions of Mexico's First Black President, Vicente Guerrero." *Journal of Negro History* 86, no. 2 (2001): 148–59.
Vinson III, Ben. "Afro-Mexican History: Trends and Directions in Scholarship." *History Compass* 3, no. LA 156 (2005): 1–14.
Vinson III, Ben. "Fading from Memory: Historiographical Reflections on the Afro-Mexican Presence." *Review of Black Political Economy* 33, no. 1 (2005): 59–72.
Vinson III, Ben. *Flight: The Story of Virgil Richardson, a Tuskegee Airman in Mexico*. New York: Palgrave Macmillan, 2004.
Virdee, Satnam. "Racialized Capitalism: An Account of Its Contested Origins and Consolidation." *Sociological Review* 67, no. 1 (2019): 3–27.
Waide, C.D. "When Psychology Failed: An Unbiased Fact-Story of the Houston Race Riot of 1917." *Houston Gargoyle* 1, no. 20–24 (1928): 5–6; 10–11; 11–12; 10–11.
Wall, Tyler. "The Police Invention of Humanity: Notes on the 'Thin Blue Line'". *Crime, Media, Culture* 16, no. 3 (2020): 319–36.
Waskow, Arthur I. *From Race Riot to Sit-In: 1919 and the 1960s*. Garden City, NY: Doubleday & Company, 1967.
Webb, Walter Prescott. *The Story of the Texas Rangers*. New York: Grosset & Dunlap, 1957.
Webb, Walter Prescott. *The Texas Rangers: A Century of Frontier Defense*. Austin: University of Texas Press, 1991.
Wells, Ida B. *The Red Record*. Cirencester: Echo Library, 2005.

Wells, Ida B., and Alfreda M. Duster. *Crusade for Justice: The Autobiography of Ida B. Wells*. Chicago and London: University of Chicago Press, 2020.

Wells-Barnett, Ida B. *Southern Horrors: Lynch Law in All Its Phases*. Frankfurt: Outlook Verlag, 2018.

Wells-Barnett, Ida B. *The East St. Louis Massacre: The Greatest Outrage of the Century*. Chicago: Negro Fellowship Herald Press, 1917.

West, Michael O., and William G. Martin. "Haiti, I'm Sorry: The Haitian Revolution and the Forging of the Black International." In *From Toussaint to Tupac: The Black International since the Age of Revolution*, edited by Michael O. West, William G. Martin, and Fanon Che Wilkins, 72–106, Chapel Hill: University of North Carolina Press, 2009.

White, Walter. *Rope and Faggot: A Biography of Judge Lynch*. n.p.: Knopf, 1929.

White, William W. "The Texas Slave Insurrection of 1860." *Southwestern Historical Quarterly* 52, no. 3 (1949): 259–85.

Wiegman, Robyn. "The Anatomy of Lynching." *Journal of the History of Sexuality* 3, no. 3 (1993): 445–67.

Wilbarger, J.W. *Indian Depredations in Texas*. Austin, TX: Hutchings Printing House, 1890.

Williams, Kidada E. *They Left Great Marks on Me: African American Testimonies of Racial Violence from Emancipation to World War I*. New York: New York University Press, 2012.

Willoughby-Herard, Tiffany. "More Expendable than Slaves? Racial Justice and the After-Life of Slavery." *Politics, Groups, and Identities* 2, no. 3 (2014): 506–21.

Wilson, Woodrow. *A History of the American People, Volume V: Reunion and Nationalization*. New York and London: Harper & Brothers Publishers, 1902.

Winter, Aaron. "Charlottesville, Far-Right Rallies, Racism and Relating to Power." *Open Democracy*, August 17, 2017. www.opendemocracy.net/en/charlottesville-far-right-rallies-racism-and-relating-to-power (accessed February 1, 2021).

Wintermute, Bobby A. "'The Negro Should Not Be Used as a Combat Soldier': Reconfiguring Racial Identity in the United States Army, 1890–1918." *Patterns of Prejudice* 46, nos 3–4 (2012): 277–98.

Wolfe, Patrick. "Race and the Trace of History: For Henry Reynolds." In *Studies in Settler Colonialism*, edited by F. Bateman and L. Pilkington, 272–96. London: Palgrave Macmillan, 2011.

Wolff, Thomas. "The Karankawa Indians: Their Conflict with the White Man in Texas." *Ethnohistory* 16, no. 1 (1969): 1–32.

Wood, Amy Louise. *Lynching and Spectacle: Witnessing Racial Violence in America, 1890–1940*. Chapel Hill: University of North Carolina Press, 2009.

Woodward, C. Vann. *Reunion and Reaction: The Compromise of 1877 and the End of Reconstruction*. New York and Oxford: Oxford University Press, 1991.

Woodward, C. Vann. *The Strange Career of Jim Crow. Third Revised Edition*. New York: Oxford University Press, 1974.

Index

African American and ethnic Mexican
    solidarity 101–2, 159–60
anarchism
    Congreso Revolucionario 157
    Haymarket Square 161
    PLM 45
anti-black mob violence
    black uprising fears 17, 56–7, 77,
        79, 60–4, 65–6, 127, 159,
        190–1
    calls for armed resistance 35–6,
        121–2
    constructions of internal enemy,
        domestic enemy 65, 91, 121
    depictions of black suffering in U.S.
        press 75, 132–4
    expulsion/racial cleansing 64, 86
        n.63
    "Negro Domination" 56, 70–1, 169
    "Santo Domingo" 29–30
    see also lynching
anti-Mexican mob violence
    calls for armed resistance 16
    early twentieth century 12
    fears of slave revolt 159
    history 90–1, 112 n.11, 185–6
    see also lynching; Texas Rangers
Austin, Stephen 65

Baldwin, James 189
bandits
    "Army of Independence" 176
    in the brush 166–7
    as fauna 167, 169
    Indians 172
    law and order in Mexico 186
Battle of San Jacinto 168–70
Birth of a Nation 130–1, 141, 147
    n.58
Buck Hohes, Pauline 58–9, 65, 70–1
Bureau of Investigation 121, 122–3,
    136, 155, 156, 160, 180 n.45

Canales, J.T. 168, 175
Congreso Revolucionario 152–3,
    157–8, 160–5, 177
criminality
    construction of "illegal alien"
        184–5
    media images of "black crime" and
        punishment 74–5
    East St. Louis 119
    in Mexico 105–5
    post-emancipation discourses 11,
        28, 57, 73–4, 83 n.11
    rape 35, 56–7, 75, 130–1, 174, 182
        n.88
    see also bandits
Cuautémoc 105–7, 109–10

death
    anti-black narratives of extinction
        10–11, 71–4
    burial 168, 170, 171, 176, 186
    construction of racial others 3, 9,
        129–30

death of white people 119, 133, 152, 146–7 n.8
East St. Louis 132–3
execution of Twenty-Fourth Infantry
  military discipline 139–41
  resistance 135–8
manhood 3, 11, 108–11, 36–7, 40, 46, 122–3, 128–9, 134–9, 140–1
Mexican death during San Diego uprising in U.S. press 165–8
Mexican death in Texas Revolution 13, 170–1
Watts 188–9
de la Rosa, Luis 16–17, 151, 155–6, 157
Dixon, Thomas 27, 57, 72, 131, 191
Du Bois, W.E.B. 10, 15, 23, 35, 92, 119–20, 122, 136

East St. Louis Massacre 2, 75, 119, 121, 125, 126, 128, 140, 144 n.4
  Ida B. Wells 148 n.69
  self-defense 144 n.5, 183, 188
  white press 132–4

Flores Magón, Ricardo 10–11, 30, 57, 62, 66, 67–71, 130–1, 169, 174, 187, 191
Fortune, T. Thomas 34–5, 36, 68–9

Gamio, Manuel 41
Garza, Agustín S. 155–6

Haiti 29–34, 36, 44
Harrison, Hubert 121, 142
Hearst, William Randolph 93, 191
Houston Mutiny *see* Twenty-Fourth Infantry
humor
  violence 69–70, 85 n.47, 167, 170

indigenous Mexicans
  Mexican discourses of mestizaje 42, 99, 101
  U.S. discourses of Mexican Indianness 96, 97, 171–2, 173

Johnson, Jack 101–2, 104

Ku Klux Klan 62, 68–9, 70, 130

London, Jack 9, 25, 26, 43, 50 n.1, 183
Lott, Virgil 151, 164, 171–3, 175–7
lynching
  African American response 33–7, 60–1, 62, 63, 69, 78–80, 121, 136–8
  black soldiers in World War I 121
  Birth of a Nation 130, 147 n.54
  Bureau of Investigation 123
  ethnic Mexican response 16, 87–90, 103–8, 109–11, 151
  execution of Twenty-Fourth Infantry as military lynching 132
  "folk pornography" 109, 182 n.88
  London, Jack 9
  lynching culture 5–6
  lynching as national humiliation for Mexicans 89
  narratives of black criminality 11, 73–4
  narratives of frontier justice 14
  narratives white manhood 171–7

manhood
  African American discourses 15, 33–7, 68–9, 78–9, 121–3, 136–8
  civilization 8–9
  constructions of submission 3, 15, 17, 25, 26–8, 37, 39–40, 41, 43–9, 69, 109–10, 190
  death 3, 110, 120, 128–9, 136–8
  imperialism 9, 25–6
  Mexican discourses 16–17, 45–6
  resistance to oppression 33–7, 45–6, 68, 121–3, 164
  white manhood and violence 5, 9, 37–9, 72–4, 165–9, 173–7, 190–2
Messenger 101, 120, 123, 131
mestizaje 41–2, 99, 100–1
Mexico
  African Americans 101–2, 159
  discourses of blackness 98–100, 105–8
  discourses of Mexican race 100–1, 95–6, 99

Mexican Revolution 4, 12, 25, 41, 43–4, 45, 58, 101, 154, 155
   national identity and U.S. racism 92–3, 104–8
   U.S imperialism 4, 12, 42, 92–4, 98, 152–3, 191
   white American colonists 105–6
Miller, George 132, 137, 138, 142

National Association for the Advancement of Colored People (NAACP) 11, 35, 88, 124, 125, 132, 141, 187
nationhood
   blackness 89–90, 99–101
   constructions of black nationlessness 28–9, 44, 89, 92, 96, 106–8, 165
   death and gendered belonging 3, 129
   exclusion of African Americans from U.S. narratives of nation 14, 27–30, 44, 81, 130
   Haiti and black nationhood 29, 31–2, 34
   Mexican discourses of nationhood 40–2, 92–3, 106
   Texas 58, 168–70
   U.S. settler colonial narratives 37–40, 165
Native Americans
   "Indian fighters" 5, 12
   narratives of U.S. history 7, 13–14, 38–40, 58, 67, 81
   violence of settlement and lynching culture 5
   white masculinity 7, 38–40, 175–6, 191
   see also indigenous Mexicans

Parker, William 191
Partido Liberal Mexicano (PLM) 17, 44–5, 48–9
Pizaña, Ancieto 16–17, 151, 155–6, 157, 179 n.22
Plan de San Diego 152, 157–8
   Mexican state violence 172–3
   "outside enemies" 13
   Texas Rangers 175–6

Plan de San Diego uprising 2, 17, 151–4
   conditions in south Texas 154–7
   documents 152, 155–7, 164–5
   narratives of white civilization 171–7
   repression 12, 168, 171
   response in U.S. press 166–7
police violence
   after Jack Johnson fight 105
   East St. Louis 144 n.5
   Houston 118, 119, 124–5, 136–7
   King, Rodney 190–1
   narratives of savagery 190–2
   "thin blue line" 191–2
   see also Texas Rangers

Reagan, John H. 159, 179 n.33
Reconstruction 10–11, 30, 57, 66, 67–71, 130–1, 169, 174, 187, 191
relational analysis of racism 6–8
Regeneración 16, 17, 45, 46, 47, 48, 49, 94, 103, 151, 152, 155, 156, 160, 161
retribution for U.S. racist violence 33, 77–9, 137
Riva Palacio, Vicente 41, 100, 107
Rodriguez, Antonio
   citizenship 94–5
   lynching 87
   reports of bearing in death 108–9
Roosevelt, Theodore 38–9

segregation 14, 21 n.27, 22–3 n.41, 44, 103, 124–35, 154
scientific racism 10–11
   African American soldiers 129
   construction of black criminality 57, 71–2
   Mexican soldiers 181 n.75
   in Mexico 40–1, 42, 45, 99
settler colonialism 5, 7, 21 n.24
   constructions of frontier warfare 14, 40, 76, 154, 172–3, 175–6
   narratives of U.S. nationhood 14, 37–40, 58, 81, 165–6
   police violence 191–2
   settler masculinity 13, 38, 190
   Texas Rangers 12–13, 173

slavery
  American Revolution 27
  Anderson County 58–9
  Congreso Revolucionario documents 160–2
  ideologies of manhood 5, 27–9, 34, 64, 91–92
  PLM discourse 45–8
  twentieth-century nostalgia 28, 60
  uprising 29–30, 34, 64–7
  U.S. discourses of Mexican Revolution 43–4
Slocum Massacre 58–61
  black self-defense 79–80
  Chicago *Defender* 78–9
  Colored Ministers Union 60
  constructions of "race war" 75–7
  descendants' fight for recognition 82 n.7
  public memory 80
  uprising conspiracy 56–7, 60–4
Smith, Lillian 136–7
Steward, Theophilus 31–3, 36, 42
Stoddard, Lothrop 30–9, 43
Stone, Alfred 72–3, 191

Texas Rangers 2, 16, 48, 76, 81
  1919 Texas Legislature hearings on misconduct 167–9, 170
  colonial narratives of violence 170–6
  "evaporations" 168
  nineteenth century 12–13
  Plan de San Diego uprising 151–2, 154–5, 156
  U.S. press 165–8
Tillman, Benjamin 30, 133, 174–5, 182 n.88
Twenty-Fourth Infantry 2, 6, 7, 11, 15, 18, 183
  commutation of death sentences 142
  execution 118
    Du Bois 118–19
    depictions in black press 119–20
  experiences in Houston 123–5
  mutiny 124–7
    invention of black casualties 127–8
  Pancho Villa 132
  patriotism 120
  reports of bearing in death 135–8, 139–41

Usher, Roland 96–7, 165, 167
U.S.–Mexico border 5
  construction of Mexican race 92–3
  "pacification" 12–13
  weaponized landscape 186

Vasconcelos, José 42, 93, 100–1

Watkins, Lucian B. 135
Watts Uprising 187–90, 191
Webb, Walter 12–13, 39–40, 169, 170, 175–6, 178 n.22, 190
Wells, Ida B. 35, 36, 62, 138–9, 148 n.69
White, Walter 11, 36, 88
white wrath 57, 75, 128, 190
Wilson, Woodrow 27–8, 43–4, 50, 54 n.71, 69, 128, 130, 132, 141–2, 173
World War I
  fears of German infiltration in black communities 121, 137
  surveillance of African Americans 121–2

Yanga 100, 107–8, 116 n.78

EU authorised representative for GPSR:
Easy Access System Europe, Mustamäe tee 50,
10621 Tallinn, Estonia
gpsr.requests@easproject.com